If you've ever loved a dog

Love stories from the front lines

If you've ever loved a dog

Love stories from the front lines

Vera Heidolph, DVM

This book is a collection of true stories as recalled by the author. The real names of people and animals were used except in cases where they are introduced in quotations, for example "Penelope."

Library of Congress Cataloging-in-Publication Data
Vera Heidolph, DVM
If you've ever loved a dog; Love stories from the front lines

ISBN 978-0-578-79336-8

1. Heidolph, Vera—2. Dogs – Love—3. Veterinary stories—4. Rescuing animals—5. Saving lives

Printed in the United States of America

https://www.amazon.com/dp/0578793369

Cover photograph is 10-year-old Dr. Heidolph enjoying the love of a dog in Wawa, Ontario.

Book design by Vera Heidolph, DVM, Claire Johnson-Hurry; cover design by Kane Scarlett

Acknowledgements

From childhood on, I've admired and been inspired by the many wonderful and varied species of animals that exist on the planet. I'm eternally grateful for my first family dog, Rex, my (male!) rabbit Lucybelle, all of the cats and kittens I would have liked to have, but couldn't because of my allergies, for the pony I always dreamed of but never got, each of my veterinary patients, and for my own dogs, Dallas, Dijon, Bosco, Coco and my god-dog, Sweet Pea.

I thank my mother for instilling in me a sense of wonder and a nurturing relationship with these animals. I thank my father for never letting me give up. High praise and many thanks to my East Coast Editor, Claire Johnson-Hurry for her 'Common Sense and Logic' approach to life, editing, and writing, and for her wonderful friendship of 40 years. Many thanks to Dr. Susan Krebsbach for always encouraging me as a vet student, a veterinarian, animal advocate, and more recently as an author. Her tireless efforts to act and speak up for animals are always an inspiration. Hats off to my sister, Karin Heidolph-Bremner, for being my accountability partner not just in completing this book but also in training for ½ marathons, 10Ks, and a marathon. We learned an important mantra at one race in Jamaica: Run the race within yourself! I want to thank the ECP for their support, humor, and decades of friendships, especially during the coronavirus pandemic.

Thanks to Drs. Tony de Carlo and Thomas Trotter at Red Bank Veterinary Hospital for their guidance through a rigorous small animal rotating internship. Kudos to Dr. Katherine Salmeri, whose compassion, surgical savvy, and gift as a veterinarian were all integral in my training and in healing many patients like Oscar, but also my dog, Dallas. Thanks to Dr. Kyle Mathews for his surgical finesse and kindness to an inquisitive vet student and her dog. To Dr. Dave Proulx, I have such respect for his talents as a radiation oncologist and for repeatedly being there to help treat the beast known as cancer with my own dogs and so many of my clients' dogs, too. Thanks to Dr. Fred Pike for reinforcing the mantra: "to cut is to cure" by skillfully curing my own dogs' and many of my patients' ailments. To Dr. Lara Rasmussen, thanks for demonstrating that a veterinary surgeon can also be an animal advocate, and for teaching me (on her own dime and her own time) how to perform spay and neuter surgeries in Pomona. A shoutout to the veterinarians and staff at Lodi Veterinary Hospital for their support and encouragement during my externship in Wisconsin. I have great admiration for the many technicians and technician-assistants who worked with all of these veterinarians and me to help so many animals. You rock, techs! Thanks to the many trustworthy and kind dog walkers and dog sitters who helped my dogs, enabling me to work and even leave home for a vacation. For all the dedicated animal shelter workers and rescue armies around the world, a huge hug and so many thanks for saving animals and spreading the word about rescuing, adopting, and spaying and neutering. I'm also grateful for the American Rescue Dog Show and the role it plays in educating people about rescuing dogs. Thanks as well to Scott Anderson of PETA for being a shoulder to cry on when I witnessed cruelty or injustices against animals and for encouraging me to keep up the fight as hearts are opened, people act, and laws change in favor of the voiceless.

Thanks also to Ben Edwards, MFT, whose guidance helped me navigate through crippling grief after losing Bosco. Praise to Pastor Darren Thomas, who also helped me through that very difficult time and who impels us to persist with courage in the face of fear. Academically, I'm so thankful for Professor Agarwal's patience in answering every one of my questions and bringing chemistry to life. I would like to acknowledge Mrs. June Thompson, my grade 1 teacher, who stirred up a love of reading and writing that opened so many doors. To Mrs. Lillian Thompson, posthumously, thanks for being such a strict English teacher and for bestowing upon me the English award in 1979. It gave me confidence to do something as bold as writing this book.

Finally, thank you to my niece, Alexandra Bremner, for asking me that simple question that sparked me to fulfill my dream of becoming a veterinarian, and for continuing to advocate for animals in her home and afar.

Contents

The verdict

I knew I was not supposed to call, but I also knew that I couldn't bear the suspense of waiting even one more minute to find out about my future. Would the greatest dream of my life come true or would my hopes be dashed? The statistics for successful admission to schools of veterinary medicine were not encouraging. I had remained undaunted and persevered, perhaps foolishly, in my quest, as I watched fellow science students being rejected by medical schools, pharmacy schools, and schools of veterinary medicine. Rumor had it that if I was not accepted into a school of veterinary medicine with my credentials, the odds were in my favor for acceptance into medical school. It seemed an implausible rumor, yet one that turned out to have some substance due to the relative scarcity of veterinary medicine schools. The statistics didn't warm my heart, because I had no interest in human medicine or anything else for that matter. All I had wanted, dreamed about, eaten, slept, and inhaled for the past two years of preparation was realizing my lifelong dream of becoming a veterinarian.

I was volunteering at a veterinary hospital and had stepped out to a nearby mall to make a private phone call out of ear shot of the veterinarians and technicians. As I walked in seemingly slow motion through a department store toward the service center where ladies were wrapping gifts, I realized I had stopped breathing. I gasped for air as I reached for the pay phone tucked in the corner. I dialed the memorized telephone number of the admissions committee and tapped in my credit card information to charge the long-distance call from New Jersey to Ontario.

Vera Heidolph, DVM

As the phone call connected and panic struck, I briefly contemplated hanging up to avoid the deadly stab of the curt "no" that I might encounter when I inquired about my status of admission. A recorded message directed me to the individual who would determine my fate. How could this individual possibly know how much this moment, this culmination of blood, sweat, and tears, meant to me and to the course of my life? She could dole out happiness or hell, depending on the answer. I would soon learn she didn't care much either way. I stated my name and my pitiful condition—the disease known as "can't wait-itis"—and mentioned that because I was in the United States and mail took a while to get from Canada to the United States, I wanted to make sure I had not missed receiving any news from Canada. Applicants had been instructed NOT to call. We were supposed to wait for "snail mail" to deliver the news. The greater her silence, the more I blathered on, fearing the absolute worst. She must be letting me run out of gas so she can tell me the bad news, I reasoned. If I kept talking, no bad news could be proffered. However, what if, just by some miracle, the answer was yes? I had called to hear "yes," but all I was thinking about was the tsunami of shame that would wash over me if I were rejected.

What flashed through my mind during this slow-motion air-holding episode was all of the effort and time I had invested over the past two years at Rutgers University, taking every possible science course I could for my veterinary school prerequisites. Every single day and a good part of each night had been exclusively dedicated to studying and preparing for exams. As I drove to each exam, my ritual was the same. A few minutes before parking my car at Rutgers University, I played the song "Reach" by Gloria Estefan, accompanying Gloria at the top of my lungs in the sound-proof safety of my car. The inspiration lasted through the exam and lifted me to do my best each

2

time. I strode, trance-like, humming the song across campus to the assigned classroom, reminded of my mission to reach higher, and not be intimidated by the hall filled with hundreds of competitors and equally eager science students with a comparable quest.

The pre-exam psyching out or psyching up was reminiscent of the warrior mentality we used in preparation for high school track and field races. Every hurdler lining up at the starting blocks puffed up her feathers by prancing, stretching, bouncing, deep-breathing, or just staring. Even though I was never the fastest runner and the other competitors scared me more than the race itself, that pre-race psyche-out taught me how to focus in the face of stiff competition. Our track coach, Bill Batty, never berated us for a suboptimal performance. Instead, he pushed each of us to put forth our absolute best effort at every practice and every race. I could safely say that I had no regrets about having given my best efforts toward this quest. But what if my best was not good enough this time, when "good try, but you didn't get in" meant the end? What would I do, having invested so much time and effort? Now that two years had elapsed since I had last been active as an investment banker, I had effectively relinquished my Series 7 privileges of being able to work in finance on Wall Street anymore without having to re-take that monster exam. It was neither a career I wished to revisit, nor an exam I cared to retake. Those notions swirled through my mind in a flash as I contemplated my future and the career risk I had taken.

My fear-filled daydream was rudely interrupted by someone on the other end of the phone saying, "Miss?" She jolted me back to the present moment, which included feeling the sweat pouring down my back through my scrub top. I responded with a meek, "Yes?" "I'm looking at your file and it says that you were supposed to wait for the letter in the mail," she rhymed off. Hadn't she heard any part of the initial conversation? I needed to know, regardless of good or bad, so I had to beg yet again to hear the verdict over the phone, out in public, where I might faint, vomit, or break down in a fit of tears. I summoned the last few ounces of courage I had and asked her to kindly inform me of my admission status. She reiterated brusquely that this was not the standard protocol. I pleaded my case yet again, hoping that this time she might realize that the quickest way to get me off the phone would be to tell me the news.

Another prolonged and seemingly eternal silence followed, punctuated by the distant sound of papers shuffling between an administrator's sighs and mumbling. I could feel the throbbing pulse in my neck increasing in speed as I awaited the verdict. She cleared her throat, as if the delivery she was about to make was rather hefty, and again the leaden weight of dread filled my legs and lungs. As she broke through my nightmarish daydream, I suddenly heard her pronounce flatly, "You've been accepted." As one of the highest points in my life, I would never forget the "where" or the "when" of that moment. I burst into a flurry of tears, sobbing uncontrollably, now attracting even more attention from the gift-wrapping ladies, who brought tissues to me at the pay phone. I apologized profusely for my emotional outburst to the woman on the other end of the phone, explaining how happy and overjoyed I was and how much this news meant to me. She responded blandly, "Yeah, I get that all the time."

Almost before the first phone call was disconnected, I had already dialed my family. I didn't even care if they weren't as excited as I was. I just needed to tell the whole world, at least one person at a time. My family and friends were quite happy for me, but no one could fully understand my utter euphoria at that moment. As I practically skipped out of the department store on my way back to the veterinary clinic, it dawned on me that now I could share this news with other veterinarians who had been through the exact same anguished phone call and protracted, painful process. Some, I would discover later, had experienced it *multiple* times before they were finally accepted into veterinary school. My head was bursting with thoughts about all of the animals I could help. I could travel all over the world and save animals in need, finally help injured animals on the roadside who needed a swift end to their misery, maybe start my own personal rescue, and educate the world about the plight of endangered species. Superlatives do not suffice when recounting the heady high of that day. The possibilities seemed unlimited! I returned to the veterinary clinic to share the bliss and revel in the moment.

Technicians and veterinarians alike were scrambling about taking care of all of the hospitalized patients at the clinic, so no one noticed my lunch break return initially. I could have been on fire and still remained unnoticed, it seemed, until I blurted out, "I got accepted into vet school at Guelph!" Everyone stopped what they were doing for a brief moment and looked my way, finally giving a brief, but hearty round of applause, almost in disbelief. I felt a camaraderie with the veterinarians that had not existed previously. I was now in the club! I felt that I had not let them down in their support of my application and would do everything to make them proud of me. The technicians may have felt some relief that there wasn't going to be a volunteer asking a million questions for the next five years, but then again, who would pick up all of the poop that only an overly eager vet wannabe would? I floated on air, elated, even while performing the dirtiest and most disgusting tasks that day. Nothing could bring me down or dampen the joy that I was experiencing. It was impossible to wipe the smile off my face.

The smile remained when I returned home that night to the rock star-like greetings of Dallas and Dijon, my Rottweiler and Boxer dogs, respectively. They had no inkling of my fortuitous news, of course, but it was their custom to greet me in this fashion, regardless of the events of the day or heroic achievements. On that day, I had so many reasons to give them extra hugs and kisses. They had, after all, been instrumental in my pursuit of a new career. As I pondered their role in my decision to become a veterinarian, they dutifully gave me the routine sniff-down to determine all of the events of the day that I couldn't explain as effectively in words. The more blood and guts I encountered in a day, the more interested they were. On that day they must have sensed my tremendous excitement, though, because their greetings outweighed their sniff-downs. I felt proud of my accomplishments in the sense of not letting the veterinarians down who had supported me, but I was also excited that I could be my own dogs' veterinarian. I had no idea, for better or worse, what an incredible journey that task would turn out to be, how my dogs would ultimately be my most valuable teachers, and how I would be their most humble student.

Inspirations

Decades before I met Dallas and Dijon, a succession of furry or feathered inspirations sparked my interest in animals and veterinary medicine. I grew up with animals around me, both indoors and outdoors in Wiarton, a small town in southern Ontario, Canada. We were surrounded by an abundance of nature year-round.

During winters, my fingers froze while prying open birdfeeders to fill them from heavy bags of seeds. Sometimes, a bold little chickadee would reward those efforts by hovering ever closer to me as I moved from one feeder to another. When I spoke quietly to the birds, they would occasionally fly onto my gloved hand to feed on seeds that I held out for them. I held my breath and remained still to avoid startling these tiny and trusting little creatures. These interactions gave me insight into birds' inquisitiveness, resourcefulness, and remarkable ability to communicate.

Every summer, we cheered on the efforts of the fledgling swallows, who had taken up residence beneath the rain gutter hanging over our living room's picture window. It was amazing to witness the progress from a newly hatched bird to those first tenuous, teetering flights, and finally to a free-flying swallow with graceful, exacting movements. Whether they were killdeers faking an injury to lure a predator away from the babies in their nest or woodpeckers tapping away furiously to bore out insects from a frozen tree trunk, these animals were at once quite different from us and yet similar. The care they gave their families rivaled that of many human families. The hardships they endured, especially during those long and cold Canadian winters made me respect them deeply. The longer I observed the birds, the greater the kinship I felt with them and all animals.

Inside my home, it was not an uncommon sight for birds to have their own little indoor "hospital ward," which was a cardboard box replete with grass, twigs, moss, water, and whatever food I thought they might eat, such as worms or seeds. The best part of those early rescues for me was the part that made my mother nervous: birds flying around the house and leaving random droppings along their flight path as they recovered from their ailments. I would practically squeal, albeit softly, so as not to frighten the birds, delighted by their recovery. Much to my mother's horror, the grand piano was their favorite place to perch and also relieve themselves. Thus, the perfect harmony of black and white piano keys was often artistically splattered with bird droppings. Even though my mother disapproved of my feathered patients' indoor potty habits, she still allowed me to bring them inside to nurse them back to health; a tacit message that she was also a softie at heart. One of my favorite pictures of my mom is her beaming face while cradling a tiny rescued hummingbird in her hands.

Ironically, many of the birds we helped had flown into our living room's large picture window. At that age, I was not yet sensitive to the roles that humans play in animals' misadventures. In reality, our home was a dangerous bird crash zone, as well as a bird hospital. Nevertheless, we enjoyed watching the birds in their natural habitat as they flitted about our yard from tree to tree and fed year-round from our feeders.

Although I did not realize it fully at the time, these experiences and observations were some of the first seeds of change in becoming an animal advocate. Small wild creatures were my idols, my heroes. They provided both entertainment and inspiration. Like a moth drawn to a flame, if there was an animal around, it would only be a matter of minutes before I was close by.

On occasion, my family took road trips across Canada, from Ontario to British Columbia. Along the way, animal sightings and encounters were the highlights for me. My parents fostered and encouraged my sense of wonder. If there were wild animals or particularly beautiful landscapes and I was reading, they would insist that I pay attention to the animals in their natural habitat. I marveled at the dexterity of mountain goats deftly ascending precipitously steep slopes and elk calmly crossing mountainous portions of the Trans-Canada Highway with a fresh dusting of snow, even though it was already June. As frightening as elk encounters were, the excitement evoked by these majestic animals staring us down like a gang of tough guys was so thrilling that I would wish for another meeting around the next corner. Once I was old enough to drive, I realized how fortunate we had been not to have had any run-ins. I developed a deeper respect for my father, who managed to keep both the wildlife on the roads and the family in the frog-green Suburban safe!

On one occasion, before we disembarked at a roadside rest area overlooking the forest-draped Rockies, my parents noticed a bear cub and its accompanying mother in the rest area. My sisters and I watched in awe and hid behind the safety of the car window, while I continually snapped photographs. I was like a puppy whose breath steams up a car window, panting at the close-up sight of those beautiful black bears ambling toward us. At the same moment, a monstrously large telephoto lens with a camera and a small man attached to it emerged from another car. The photographer kept edging closer and closer to both bears, especially the cub, who was positioned between Mama Bear and the photographer. Initially, the mother bear emitted a low growl. The photographer persisted. Her warnings escalated and when the photographer was within eight feet of the cub, Mama Bear had had enough and charged him. He tumbled backwards and crashed into our Suburban's rearview mirror on the passenger side. We waited, as he crouched on the ground, to see if Mama Bear was going to pummel him and his menacing equipment. But she seemed satisfied that he would finally leave her baby alone. He slunk away along the edge of our car and finally retreated to the safety of his car. The cub and his mom strode away. My parents did not need to explain the moral of that story. Leave bears alone!

This natural bear encounter and others that followed fascinated me. Large, lumbering grizzlies could suddenly sprint up a steep hill. Their massively long paws and claws could delicately pick small berries that we could barely see. One of my most entertaining and revealing experiences watching bears featured a mother bear who unsuccessfully tried to teach her cub some manners. The cub was acting like a naughty two-year-old, defying every utterance and perceived command that Mama Bear was barking at him or her. In a final act of defiance, the cub scrambled up a skinny pine tree, making soft squealing noises. Mama Bear, clearly displeased, grumbled from below. After several minutes of failed negotiations with Baby Bear, Mama Bear grabbed the trunk of the skinny pine tree in her powerful paws and shook it from side to side. Suddenly, Baby Bear was babbling like a brook, while hanging onto the skinny tip of the tree with its branches bending. Mama Bear stopped shaking the tree for a moment, possibly hoping her baby might capitulate and descend. But he did not. Mama Bear then shook the pine tree even more vigorously, until the tip of the tree snapped like a slingshot and catapulted Baby Bear into the air. He landed on the upper branches of a neighboring tree and eventually made his way down to the ground bumping and falling through layers of branches. Baby Bear spotted Mama Bear and humbly limped over to her, nudging her gently on arrival. Mama Bear coolly nudged Baby Bear back and off they toddled together into the forest. It was always amazing to witness the dynamics of animal relationships in their natural habitats, even if they were brief glimpses.

I didn't need video games or a mall because I had the entire animal kingdom with its year-round changing plot and scenery to observe. Nevertheless, the bears had made it clear that interactions with wild animals should be limited to admiring them from afar, unless there was some danger that I could avert or aid I could offer. I realized that I could observe domesticated animals more closely than their wilder relatives. In some cases, they even solicited interaction and affection. When it came to domestic animals, there were never enough hours in a day for me to spend time with them.

Rex, my family's German Shepherd dog, was one of my most memorable inspirations for becoming a veterinarian. He would not be considered a model companion animal by today's standards, but back in the 1970s, he was the typical family dog. He was not neutered and, as a result, he wandered our property and the vast neighborhoods, including the country road. My parents explained that previous German Shepherds had succumbed to vehicular trauma, so I always worried that he might share their fate. I had no idea at the time that the main factor affecting his flights of fancy was testosterone because he was not neutered. Although he would bite uninvited people if they wandered onto our property and his straying habits were undesirable, he loved all the kids in our family. Once my older sisters left to go away to school and I was the only child at home, Rex became my new best friend. He was as loyal as his species would imply, and always game to accompany me on any adventure I concocted. We hung out in the surrounding forest and along the shores of the bay, exploring nature together and providing companionship to each other. As I grew up with him and felt the strength of his protection, it never occurred to me that someday he would need mine.

Gazing out of my bedroom window one summer afternoon when I was nine years old, I heard a car rapidly approaching our house from the main road followed by the sound of Rex barking with agitation. The driveway was long and only a small stretch was visible from my window, so it was a miracle that I witnessed the fateful events that unfolded. A speeding Volkswagen Beetle came careening down our driveway. Rex rushed at its tires, barking furiously, attempting to chase the car away. In a flash, Rex was run over by the front tire and lay motionless on the pavement. I raced out of my room screaming at the top of my lungs, perhaps at the car, and certainly in despair for Rex. Before I could reach him, he hobbled off into the surrounding woods and disappeared. It still amazes me that even with severe injuries sustained from a moving vehicle, he mustered the courage and adrenaline to hide in the woods. While his disappearance was terrifying for my family and me, it was another example of why dogs are champions and why we love and admire them so much.

We searched and searched, but for the next 24 hours, Rex could not be found anywhere. My parents assured me that his behavior was not uncommon for injured animals and that he would return when he was ready. How frustrating it was to want to protect him, but to feel totally helpless. He had always been there for me and now I could not do a thing for him. Many tears of sorrow and frustration were shed during that 24-hour period. My parents were effective at helping kids forget their woes, which usually involved assigning work. It was no different this time. The next day, we were all together in the garden picking red currants, when we heard a rustling in the woods that encircled the garden. Everyone turned toward the noise and remained very still. The silhouette drew closer and I saw the outline of a familiar black and tan face. I raced over to a limping Rex, exercising great restraint by not squealing with glee at his return. He immediately flopped down, clearly exhausted from his journey. His front right leg looked so painful that I did not dare touch it. Now, he needed my help and was finally ready to accept it.

Fear was coupled with excitement as I debated what to do and how to help him. It might not have been my parents' first thought, but all I could think of was how to fix what appeared to be a broken leg. I knew there were better medical options than the remedies we had employed with little birds. I begged my parents to let us take Rex to a veterinarian to fix his leg and, thankfully, they agreed to drive him to The Veterinary Teaching Hospital at the Ontario Veterinary College (OVC) in Guelph, Ontario. Guelph is located about an hour west of Toronto and two-and-a-half hours from my parents' house by car. My job during this car ride was to manage Rex, the patient. I did the best I could with no pain medications or splint for temporary stabilization. All I could offer Rex on that first trip to the veterinary hospital was comfort and companionship, which he had given me so often.

We arrived at what I perceived to be The Land of Miracles. We entered OVC's Veterinary Teaching Hospital. Everyone wanted to help Rex right away. They administered pain medications, took X-rays, and conceived a plan to repair his front leg. I don't recall the details of the surgical plan, but I remember thinking that the plan, execution, and final outcome were nothing short of medical magic. Rex had to wear some sort of cast or splint for support after the surgical repair was completed. Over the next several weeks, while returning Rex to good health, we bonded even more. My mission was to help him, which was not a coincidence or a one-time event. One day, this mission would become my vocation. I had caught the bug of needing to fix living beings, preferably animals. My vision did not manifest for a few decades after my initial visit to OVC, but I remember thinking that if I worked really, really hard, I, too, could perform seemingly magical medical and surgical feats. Eventually, my optimistic childhood dream would become my reality. Rex would be my first companion animal inspiration, followed by Dallas, Dijon, Bosco, and Coco, and interspersed with thousands of animals I would meet and treat as patients.

Angel for a night

After graduating from the five-year veterinary medicine program at the University of Guelph's Ontario Veterinary College, I was accepted into a small animal medicine and surgery internship at Red Bank Veterinary Hospital (RBVH) in New Jersey. I felt incredibly lucky to have been admitted into the intern class because small animal internships in veterinary medicine are highly sought-after positions. RBVH was one of the largest privately-owned veterinary hospitals in North America at the time, so we would see more patients in a year than many veterinary schools. We were assured that this large caseload was a good thing because we would learn a lot from so many patients. The downside was that we would be working a marathon schedule to treat thousands of patients. Sleep became a rare luxury due to the grueling schedule. If we had earned more money, I would have paid someone to stand in for me just for a few hours so I could get some shut-eye. At an annual salary of $18,000, plus some compensation for each emergency we saw, interns didn't even earn minimum wage if their hours—in my case, 80 to 120 hours per week—were taken into consideration. The bulk of our remuneration was in the form of the teaching and guidance that we received from the specialists and general practitioners. Fortunately, most of them liked teaching, so we could learn a tremendous amount between tending to our patients and completing the accompanying grunt work. In that year of repeated questioning about each decision, interpretation, and medical plan, we would become methodical in how we practiced medicine and develop a gut feeling that would guide us whenever medical facts alone did not suffice or make sense.

Vera Heidolph, DVM

My methodical medical training and gut instincts were put to the test at ten to six one evening. I was nearing the homestretch, which would have been a very early six p.m., after a day in the cardiology department, and felt that if I could just finish my paperwork without another emergency arriving, I would be free to rest for a few hours and go out with one of my housemates, who was a visiting veterinarian from Italy. Hearing "Dr. Heidolph, you've got to see an emergency right now!" sank my spirits like a lead balloon. There was no time to lament over lost free time. Technicians were not shy about putting a patient directly into a veterinarian's arms if they required urgent attention. Oscar was a middle-aged Sheltie dog, whose tear-filled guardians accompanied him as he was wheeled into the treatment area on a gurney. Everyone spoke simultaneously. The most commonly asked question was posed before I had a chance to examine poor Oscar: "Doc, what's wrong with him?" Sometimes, it's hard to explain that I have no clue as to the problem because I haven't performed a physical exam or any diagnostics yet. As the dog's dire situation became clearer, I focused on him and didn't notice my Italian veterinarian housemate leaving the building and waving goodbye for the night. I had no idea how long that night would be at ten to six or what the outcome would be, but it would be a night to remember.

Oscar was a beautiful white, black, and tan colored dog, who looked like he had been metaphorically run over by a truck. He was weak, in pain, in shock, and just plain miserable. My heart went out to him immediately. Too tired to lift his head, he stared at me intently with only his eyes following me, as if begging for help. I commented to his family that he had beautiful green eyes. This comment, however, upset the family even more as they remarked that he actually had *blue* eyes. While I finished examining Oscar, the highly trained technicians were placing the intravenous (IV) catheter that I had requested and were obtaining his vital signs. They took some blood to get a baseline of his metabolic status. They attempted to get his blood pressure, but the machine did not register. Oscar's blood pressure was so precariously low that it required immediate intervention. I checked his pulses on the insides of his back legs and could barely feel anything. I ordered an IV fluid shock dose bolus, which is a rapid infusion of a large volume of fluids, to help increase his blood pressure and general circulation. Like a precise and proficient pit crew at a Formula 1 race, this amazing team of veterinary technicians took care of business so efficiently that all of the most critical things that needed to be done were completed almost before I finished asking for them.

His blood work showed that he had an extremely high white blood cell (WBC) count and liver enzymes, suggesting an infection and liver abnormality, respectively. His albumin (one of the body's proteins) was extremely low, so he was leaking proteins somewhere. Those proteins normally help keep fluids like blood inside the veins and arteries, which maintains normal blood pressure, so with minimal albumin, it would be hard to get his blood pressure back to normal. The sky-high liver values explained why Oscar's normally blue eyes were green. Liver failure can cause jaundice or a yellowing of certain tissues like the skin or eyes. It was the first time that I literally saw the yellow coloring of jaundice, or icterus, through a dog's eyes. I had only seen the white part of the eye, the sclera, turn yellow, but never an actual color change of the iris. The notion of looking at an animal and the truth being revealed through his eyes, as the ophthalmologists had taught us, took on new meaning. I decided that Oscar was a pretty keen canine, even in his shocky state. If I was going to help him, I would need to pay attention not just to the facts and figures of his lab work and vitals, but also to his eyes and body language. No textbook or professor in vet school had ever mentioned anything like that before.

I could see from his eyes and body posture that his belly was very painful. I had given him hydromorphone—a very potent pain medication—shortly after his arrival, but he still seemed uncomfortable. X-rays of his abdomen suggested that there was fluid in his belly. When we tried to obtain a sample of the fluid through a needle, there was only a small amount, but not enough to drain his abdomen at that point. We saw that the fluid was not blood, but where it was coming from remained an unsolved mystery. An intestinal perforation can cause abdominal fluid and create the loss of detail we had seen on the X-rays, but it wouldn't necessarily cause all of the liver enzymes to be off the charts. Dogs in liver failure can have all of the symptoms Oscar had, but the question I needed to answer was: Why would a relatively young, otherwise healthy dog have such an acute bout of hepatitis? Toxins are often the culprits of acute liver damage, but Oscar hadn't gotten into any toxins. Although he had vomited earlier that evening before his family brought him to us, he had no other gastrointestinal (GI) signs before that, which made the possibility of some bacterial disease like salmonella or something similar less likely. He was also up to date on his vaccines, so the possibly fatal parvovirus, distemper, or infectious hepatitis virus were ruled out as well.

I was trying to sort out all of the facts surrounding Oscar's case and decide how to help him. Pain meds, fluids, antibiotics, and stomach protectants can often make patients with milder cases of acute onset hepatitis feel much better or at least make a dent in their discomfort in a relatively short period of time. As I watched his eyes, even in his drug-induced state, I knew there was more to Oscar's case. A few other veterinarians peeked in on the case and seemed to feel I had it under control and that all of the usual tests and medications were heading in the right direction. Theoretically, his blood pressure should have improved with IV fluids, but it didn't. As the day drew to a close and fewer two-legged bodies remained in the hospital, I felt a distinct discomfort about this case. Oscar still seemed to be in great pain, despite the pain meds and every other type of medication. I stayed with him, adjusted his meds, re-examined him, and tried to figure out what I was missing. The night crew had long since taken over the daytime cases and did not seem quite as worried about Oscar as I was, which concerned me even more. I couldn't just take it easy and let someone take over who didn't have the same level of neurotic worry about him that I had. There were dozens of other patients in the hospital who also needed attention and were being attended to by the overnight veterinarians and technicians, but this dog needed extra special care and was trying every way he could to express that need.

The beauty of an internship is that when an intern is truly overwhelmed, it is acceptable to call a lifeline. That night, the lifeline was Dr. Kathy Salmeri, my favorite surgeon, who had been one of my greatest inspirations for becoming a veterinarian. She had performed two knee surgeries on my own dog, Dallas, and allowed me to scrub in on both. I had seen her in action hundreds of times and knew that if there was a surgical case that had a glimmer of hope of surviving with the intervention of surgery, she could save it. She was confident, calm, and cool, yet one of the most compassionate surgeons I have ever met. I apologized for calling her after hours, knowing it would deprive her of much needed sleep. I respected her need to rest, so I would never call her with a frivolous problem. However, Oscar's predicament was anything but frivolous. I explained the facts and expressed my concern about his painful abdomen in conjunction with the elevated WBC and liver enzymes and his low blood pressure. I suspected, more in my gut than anywhere else, that this dog needed abdominal surgery to evaluate what was wrong sooner rather than later.

Dr. Salmeri and I discussed Oscar's situation in detail and created a plan. I would make some minor adjustments to his current therapy, monitor his response, and get back to her with an update. Part of the plan was to try to scan his abdomen with an ultrasound. This task proved very challenging not just because my ultrasound skills were limited and the specialist who would normally perform an ultrasound had left for the day, but also because Oscar still had a painful belly, so any pressure applied to his abdomen worsened the pain. Even with the help of the overnight emergency veterinarian, who had better command of an ultrasound, the only new piece of information we acquired was that there was more haziness in the upper part of Oscar's abdomen, namely around his liver. With this sliver of information, I contemplated whether or not there was a mass in his abdomen, a horrendous infection, or something blocking his bile duct, which empties out the gall bladder. The therapies that we had modified did not seem to be helping him much. I called Dr. Salmeri back with an update. I begged her to come back to the hospital and look at him.

When she arrived, Dr. Salmeri's facial expression hinted that I might be an over-reactive intern, who panics and thinks everything needs surgery. After all, to cut is to cure, right? However, as soon as she examined Oscar and reviewed his lab work, we reevaluated the plan. She agreed wholeheartedly that he needed surgery, but his blood pressure was still so low that he would probably die on the table if we took him to surgery at that moment. As she verbalized my worst fears, my heart sank. How could we ever save this poor dog if we could not perform surgery and figure out what was making him so sick? The fluid in his abdomen was accumulating and he was tanking. We decided to start by flushing his abdomen, which is a procedure known as peritoneal lavage. A small tube is inserted into the abdomen after using a local nerve block on the skin and muscle layers on top of the abdomen, instead of general anesthesia required for surgery. One of the risks or side effects of general anesthesia with healthy animals and humans is hypotension (low blood pressure), which is why Oscar, with his blood pressure already perilously low, was such a poor candidate for surgery and anesthesia at that point. Peritoneal lavage involves suctioning existing fluid out of the abdomen and flushing sterile saline back into it. Lavage means to bathe or cleanse, so we were literally bathing and diluting the fluid in his abdomen or the peritoneum, which is the lining of the abdomen. This procedure helps minimize bacterial contamination if there is septic peritonitis and in cases of severe pancreatitis, it can help normalize severely low blood pressure when IV fluids and meds alone are insufficient. The procedure itself is not without risks. If done incorrectly, organs can be penetrated or perforated by the large bore needle inserted into the abdomen, causing even more damage. Sometimes, the change of pressure causes a patient who is hanging on by a thread to bottom out completely because their body has temporarily adapted to their diminished condition and a sudden change in pressure, even if it should be in the right direction, can push them over the edge and kill them.

With this knowledge in mind, I breathed cautiously and haltingly as we prepared a sterile field on Oscar's tender belly for Dr. Salmeri to start the peritoneal lavage. It was uncomfortable for Oscar to lie on his back, probably because of whatever it was around his liver that was compressing his organs. We would have to move quickly to minimize his discomfort. We were limited in upgrading his pain meds or even anesthetizing him, as we sometimes do for extreme pain, by his frail vital signs. I assisted Dr. Salmeri with the peritoneal lavage for what seemed like hours, pulling off only incremental drops of fluid and flushing back pre-warmed sterile saline to dilute and cleanse Oscar's contaminated abdomen. Impatiently, I expected his pressures to improve during this procedure and was so disappointed when that miracle didn't materialize. I started losing both faith and hope, and felt a wave of despair washing over me, even with the best possible expert helping Oscar. We left the tube in his abdomen in place for subsequent lavage, and declared the procedure finished for the time being. By now, it was way after midnight and even my idol, Dr. Salmeri, looked beat.

The plan was to continue monitoring Oscar's vitals, adjust his meds accordingly, pray like mad for a miracle, and call Dr. Salmeri with updates. She had suggested that I go home to get some sleep, but I couldn't leave him while he still needed me. Those green eyes still watched my every move, even as lethargic as he was. He was watching me, so I had to watch out for him. My fingers tapped anxiously as I wrote up his records and kept checking on his vitals to see if our therapy was having any positive effect. The overnight veterinarians and technicians told me to go home and get some sleep, but I insisted on staying there for Oscar. Even though they were excellent veterinarians, I knew in my heart that no one else had that connection that we had shared through his penetrating green-eyed gaze. I remembered the utter humility and helplessness of being hospitalized after my own back surgery and knew what it was like to desperately need someone's help, but not always be able to voice that need. I would stay with him until he was safe or until he could not go on any longer.

Within two hours of the peritoneal lavage, his vitals started improving. We got his blood pressure from barely reading up to 60 mm Hg, which is still very low, but it was a tremendous sign of hope for foolish optimists. I had been in regular contact with Oscar's family since his arrival at the hospital and could finally give them an update that had a faint ray of hope in it. I cautioned that we couldn't be too optimistic, but that there was mild improvement and we may be getting close to taking him to surgery. More tears on the other end of the phone. There is a delicate balance involved in delivering bad news or possibly a slight turn of events. It's hard not to let one's own hope paint too rosy a picture for a dog's family when the situation is so desperate. However, sometimes hope is all people want, even if those hopes might be dashed. I let Oscar's family know that as soon as he was able to go to surgery, Dr. Salmeri would perform the abdominal exploratory surgery (laparotomy), and do whatever needed to be done to help him. A sigh of relief resounded over the telephone. Oscar's family thanked me profusely. I felt undeserving of being thanked because we were far from saving him, and the chance of him dying that night was still very high. The pressure mounted as I awoke Dr. Salmeri from her sleep to let her know Oscar was ready for surgery if he got her blessing.

A weary Dr. Salmeri arrived soon after our conversation. She evaluated Oscar's vitals and we discussed the plan for anesthesia, which I had already prepared. With her unique brand of kindness, she reminded me of the great surgical risk that he presented to us and of the significant chance that he might die on the table despite our best efforts. I acknowledged her admonitions with a nod, choking back tears of fear and hope.

We prepared the surgical suite swiftly and soberly with the multitude of instruments that would be needed, such as suction to drain fluids intra-operatively, cautery for any bleeders, and cavity spreaders to hold open his abdomen and place hands and instruments inside. Dozens of clamps and hemostats (used to stop bleeding) were available should they be needed. I clung to every moment of preparation, knowing that in those moments before we embarked on his surgery Oscar was still with us and still had a chance. Once we started surgery, there was no turning back. This decision-making process was no place for cowards. The leap of faith that is made by patients who place their trust in the surgeon must also be made by the surgeon and her team, knowing that the patient may die in her hands despite her best efforts. Oscar was induced (given injections to make him unconscious), intubated (a tube placed through his mouth into his trachea to allow oxygen and anesthetic gas to flow into his lungs), and gas anesthesia started. I monitored his vitals and ensured that his anesthesia was well regulated, while his abdomen was shaved and prepped.

I had planned on scrubbing in on the surgery with Dr. Salmeri and was therefore surprised to be re-directed to go home and get ready for work. It's easy to lose track of time when you are intently focused on your job and love what you are doing. I didn't realize it was already four-thirty a.m. and I had been at work since six a.m. the previous day. In one-and-a-half hours, a new day of internship would begin with early morning patient assessments, performing rounds, taking care of incoming cases with the respective specialists, calling patients' families with updates, seeing emergencies, and so forth. Until she sent me home, I hadn't realized just how tired I was or how this night had flown by so quickly. I hesitated briefly, not out of disrespect to or defiance of Dr. Salmeri, but out of indecision as to whether I should leave Oscar. His eyes were closed, he was finally entirely pain-free as he lay unconscious on the surgical table, he was breathing well on his own under anesthesia, his pressures were still very low, but he was hanging in there. Most importantly, I looked into Dr. Salmeri's eyes and knew Oscar was in the best possible care for this part of his treatment. For the first time since ten to six the previous night, I felt a mild sense of relief. Although I would have loved to scrub in on the surgery to assist and see what was going on inside Oscar, I followed Dr. Salmeri's sensible orders and drove the one mile home to the intern house.

I almost fell asleep in the shower, but kept getting jolted back into reality by thinking of Oscar and wondering how he was doing. The timing of the touch-and-go landing and take-off at home was enough to get cleaned up, take the dogs out, get coffee, grab a frozen lunch, eat a quick breakfast, and embark on another day as an intern. The suspense of Oscar's surgery was unbearable. I wanted to call the hospital, but knew that such a call would only be an annoyance that no one needed. I kissed my dogs goodbye and thanked the heavens for diligent dog walkers. Every time I saw animals in such bad shape, it always made me appreciate my own dogs even more. I thanked them for being healthy and sped back to work.

My first stop was the surgical suite. I peered inside, but Dr. Salmeri was no longer there. My heart sank, figuring that her absence meant she had aborted the surgery and Oscar had died. I bit my lip and tried to imagine a more uplifting outcome. Suddenly, I heard her voice. She had just come out of surgery and Oscar was alive and recovering well. His pressures were getting close to normal. Those numbers rang like a beautiful symphony in my ears! My curiosity could no longer be contained. I had to know what on earth Dr. Salmeri had found inside Oscar's abdomen. Like a trophy, she held up a surgical bowl that was filled with bloody fluid and a rock-like, yellowish, oval-shaped object that was about three inches long and two inches wide. I grabbed gloves to examine this odd-looking object. As soon as I palpated it, I realized what it was, although I had never seen one before: a cholecystolith (a massive gallbladder stone). Oscar's gallbladder had been bursting because of the gallbladder stone, which explained everything else.

Although Dr. Salmeri had performed the most important, life-saving portion of Oscar's treatment, namely surgically removing the cholecystolith and repairing the ruptured gall bladder, she let me present his case in rounds. I passed the bowl around and its contents truly turned heads, which took a lot in that crowd of seasoned specialists. This kind of show and tell really excites veterinarians, even as they are munching on their morning bagels. We have strong stomachs for this kind of assault to the senses. It was actually a beautiful thing to see, especially because it was no longer in Oscar's gallbladder. I had the utmost respect not only for Dr. Salmeri's amazing surgical skills, but for her ability to get Oscar to surgery safely. She not only knows how to cut, but also when not to cut and how to get a critical patient stable enough for surgery. She was my hero and without her Oscar would undoubtedly have died.

I could not have been happier to call his family to let them know the good news. Even though he was not completely out of the woods, he was well on his way to recovery and had a much better chance of surviving. Over the next two days, I checked on Oscar frequently and communicated numerous times each day with his family. Two days post-op he was ready to eat food again, which is one of the factors determining whether or not a patient can be sent home. He was still somewhat hesitant when he moved and tender from his large abdominal incision, but he always cheered up when I visited. To give him something special for those times when I couldn't be near him, I ran to the store across the street and bought him a large red squeaky toy, which I made sure was large enough so he could not swallow it. He perked up considerably as he rested his head on his new red plush toy, which had become his pillow. He was finally homeward bound.

A few weeks later, I was paged to see Dr. Salmeri in an exam room. Oscar's beaming family and a newly energized Oscar were in for a post-op re- check, replete with unexpected trinkets of gratitude. His mom had crafted a handmade quilt for Dr. Salmeri and presented me with a glass statue that had an angel etched within it. She also produced a picture of Oscar with his new favorite toy—the red plush squeaky toy. It was delightful to see the contrast of his beautiful, serene *blue* eyes against the red toy. It was a moment of joy that I will never forget. By some miracle and with a lot of hard work, we really had pulled off a seemingly hopeless medical and surgical feat. As we hugged each other, Oscar's mom whispered to me, "Thank you so much for being Oscar's angel that night." What an honor to be a veterinarian! I had just done my job, but in the eyes of one family, I was their dog Oscar's angel for a night.

Vera Heidolph, DVM

Dallas in New York

Although I had a natural affinity to all animals as a kid, as I grew up, I looked forward to the day when I could be a guardian and caregiver for a dog as my companion. The only maternal instincts I ever had involved four-legged beings, especially dogs. I couldn't pass a dog on the street without asking to say hello and "get my dog fix." It is difficult to suppress those instincts for an extended length of time, even for logical reasons, such as scarcity of time, work, or space. I longed for a companion like my childhood dog, Rex, who always protected us, played with us, and made exploring the surrounding woods and waters safer and more inviting. Anyone who knew me knew that it was my heart's desire to have a dog to love and to spoil. It would be difficult to conceive that anyone would want to come between me and my dream of being a dog mom. Yet, it happened. My husband at the time tried to thwart my every attempt to realize my dream of expanding our family by four legs. I was backed into a corner and forced to make an ultimatum, even though decisions that start with an ultimatum might result in disaster or at least a suboptimal outcome. My first adult-owned dog, however, was the happy product of such an unfortunate ultimatum.

I was working in New York City and had waited and planned for years with great anticipation for the day I could have a dog. Having had my dog Rex as a child, I was aware of the work and time required to care for a dog. I was also very serious about my ultimatum. The "con" side—the spouse—of the dog argument always concocted some reason why I couldn't have the dog I had dreamt about, and I was tired of not having the one thing that I knew I really longed for. The impetus for making an ultimatum was watching *Home*

Again, a heart-wrenching movie about a dog who becomes lost and desperately tries to find his way home. I cried so hard as I watched the movie, knowing I wanted to be a dog's guardian and experience that wonderful canine-human bond that I had enjoyed with Rex once again.

I re-stated my case to the "con" side of the dog argument, but was only met with lame excuses. When we lived in Germany, the claim was that our yard wasn't big enough, although it now seems huge by comparison to my own yard and would have easily accommodated a dog in a very dog-friendly country. Upon moving to New York City, there was no yard, so it was argued that we shouldn't have a dog. But lots of people had dogs in the city. We were both working full-time and wouldn't have time to walk the dog was the next argument. But many dogs in the city have dog walkers and the rest of the walks and outings I could handle. The only reasoning tool I had not used to illustrate the strength of my conviction was an ultimatum. It was not an ultimatum I made lightly. I wanted a dog (plan A), or I was going to ask for a divorce (plan B). I was fully prepared to follow through with plan B if plan A didn't materialize. I had never made an ultimatum during my marriage, so it was not a case of crying wolf. It definitely caught the attention of the intended party. I was still trying to do the right thing and run big decisions by the spouse. In retrospect, that might have been a mistake. Instead of saying I could definitely have a dog, which he knew was my dream, I was treated like a child who had to earn points toward getting a bicycle. The counter on my ultimatum was that he would "allow" me to get a dog only if and when I passed my Series 7 test, which is required to trade securities on the New York Stock Exchange. I had just transferred to the New York Salomon Brothers finance desk from Salomon Brothers in Frankfurt, Germany, so I needed to pass the test anyway, in order to be able to work there. I was already working 12-hour days, followed by evening courses in preparation for the Series 7 test. I had no intention of NOT passing the test! If the ultimatum counter was a challenge, it worked on multiple levels. It reminded me that I was not free to make decisions that were very important to me, and that I could rise to the occasion if I set my mind to it, in spite of control tactics.

The moment I passed the Series 7 test, I was searching for a dog. I didn't care if he or she was blind, had three legs, or was deaf. I just wanted a dog. I was thinking of a black Labrador Retriever as a dog that might do well in a busy city like New York. I knew I would need to make time to walk this new dog and train him or her, too. I could not wait! I had found information about breed rescues and felt confident that the details of "my" dog would by "my" decision. Yet, they weren't. Months had elapsed since I had passed my Series 7 test. Unwilling to wait much longer and growing weary of fighting over every detail about this dog, I succumbed to the overpowering veto rights of the spouse. He wanted a dog from a pet store, of all places! I was mortified. I didn't know everything I know now about pet stores sourcing their dogs from puppy mills, but I knew you shouldn't buy dogs, but rather you should rescue them. There was an over-population problem that was being exacerbated by pet stores and breeders selling cats and dogs, and I didn't want to contribute to it. I was being stonewalled at every turn, however, and wanted so desperately to have a dog.

On a Saturday in the middle of winter, I was instructed to come to the pet store to look at a puppy with the spouse. The puppy was not a Labrador Retriever. She was not a rescue dog. She was an older puppy at four months old and was a Rottweiler, which probably meant that the pet store couldn't sell her and was anxious to unload inventory. Reluctantly, I approached the puppy, still seething about having every single one of my requests for a dog denied.

Anyone with a heart for cold noses can imagine how the meeting went. Girl meets puppy, girl falls in love with puppy, and the rest is history.

In contrast to other puppies whose attention quickly darted to the next moving or shiny object, this little Rottweiler focused her beautiful eyes on me steadfastly, drawing me in immediately, and just wanted to snuggle. I held her in my arms, feeling that wonderful, rapid heartbeat against my chest and her soft, fuzzy fur on my face and arms. I had to catch my breath as the exhilaration nearly lifted me off the ground. All of my anger about the disagreements leading to her discovery vanished in that moment. She clung to me with all four limbs, attached like a newly formed appendage that would not detach, unaware of the turmoil her arrival had caused in one household. I only cared about what was best for this little darling. She was so loving and affectionate. We connected immediately. There was no way I was leaving that store without her, legally or otherwise! She needed a home and I was going to burst out of my skin if I couldn't have a dog to care for soon.

After purchasing all of the possible dog accoutrements necessary, the only thing she needed was a name. I didn't realize that even though she was supposed to be my dog, I would have very little say in most of the decisions involving her. I had several suitable names, but all were summarily shot down. I was informed that she would be named Dallas because of my husband's football interest. I didn't care for the name, but conceded because I was just happy to have my dog and didn't have the energy to argue anymore. It may not come as a surprise that I followed through on my ultimatum and divorced the husband anyway a few years later. My advice to anyone getting into a relationship in which animals might be involved is to set the guidelines and discuss all the details for expanding the four-legged family BEFORE settling down together! Discovering fundamental differences after the fact can be very disturbing and, ultimately, a deal-breaker. The list of questions should include things like, "who will decide on where to rescue or adopt our dog?", "does age, ability, color, length of hair, or tail matter?", and "who will have custody of this dog if the relationship unravels?" As humans, we will survive a breakup or even a divorce, but sometimes animals suffer as a consequence and may even be relinquished.

Dallas was officially my first "child," so my best friend, Claire, and her husband, Doug, came to my apartment to celebrate the momentous occasion with me that night. They brought all kinds of snacks for Dallas, which she munched on readily. We wouldn't know until later that night how sensitive a dog's digestive tract is to an entire bag of Snausages! Diarrhea aside, it was so much fun to shower Dallas with love and affection, some toys and treats, and to introduce her to her godparents. At the end of the dog party, Dallas fell asleep on my lap and I felt like I had just won the lottery. I couldn't have been happier welcoming this bundle of love and sweetness into my home.

Now it was time to get better acquainted. I could see she was very curious and less sure of herself than I might anticipate a puppy to be, probably because she was already four months old and not the standard two months old when people usually obtain a puppy. Due to her unfortunate start in a pet store, there were things she had never experienced, so she needed an introduction to the world, specifically New York City. First, she had to get out of the apartment building. There was an elevator to overcome. It must be an unsettling feeling to experience the floor falling out from under your feet if no one has explained that it will happen, and that you will still be safe. Her eyes widened in a panic as this new and scary ride descended. I held her in my arms for the first few rides. Over time, this method of transport had to be revised because she was 40 pounds and growing rapidly, becoming a heavy load very quickly. Once she stood in the elevator, her fear was visible. She peed on the carpet the first few times. I couldn't reprimand her for something that had literally scared the pee out of her! We used the stairs intermittently because it dawned on me that she might never have experienced them before. She had no idea how to navigate something that seemed so much taller than she was, and was something that also seemed to terrify her. I had to help her up with her front legs first, and then coax her back legs. She stood, frozen, unwilling to move on those treacherous steps. Perhaps she awaited that feeling of the floor dropping like the elevator. At this point, I learned how important it is to tap into what motivates a dog. In Dallas' case, it was food or snacks, so with some freeze-dried liver treats we tried the steps again with much more success and confidence. We had to work on the steps a few times a week for a month or more before I could persuade her that they weren't going to envelop her.

Outside, a bitter cold New York City winter prevailed. I wanted to protect my little girl from the elements and keep her feet and little body from freezing, so I found dog booties to prevent the salt on the sidewalk from burning her soft little foot pads. The denim and fake fleece-lined jacket would keep the rest of her black and tan body warm. Little did I know that dressing her up in her protective gear would not go over well. She didn't fight the fitting of booties or jacket, but once in place, she lay flat on the ground and refused to move. I had to carry her from the doorway of the apartment to the elevator, pray she wouldn't pee in the elevator out of fear, and then carry her from the elevator to the street, hoping I could compel her to walk and do her business once outside. On our first try, she lay flat on the icy sidewalk and I thought it might be a hopeless cause keeping her feet dry and her body warm. I lifted and propped her up onto her booty-clad feet. She acted like she had four broken legs. It must be another very odd sensation for a dog to have her sensitive foot pads covered with an unfamiliar texture. She gradually became accustomed to the new sensation and accepted the booties. I was relieved because I saw the damage the salt was doing to my own winter boots and couldn't imagine how badly that would burn her tender little feet. I remember being awoken around four a.m. one night by some whimpering. I quickly threw on some clothes, grabbed her booties and jacket, and ran to the elevator, where I finished dressing her in her protective winter armor. As we exited the building and felt the hail and ice rain firing down on us, Dallas attempted to spin around and run back into the apartment building. She hated rain! There was no way we were going back in now that we had geared up for this late-night adventure. I knew there would still be a full puppy bladder that would need relief if we turned back now. Tough love dictated that we stay outside and brave the nasty weather a few more moments until Dallas had done her business.

Dallas and I explored as much of New York City as we could reasonably do on foot. She enjoyed the parks, passersby on the street, and the other dogs she encountered. As soon as we ventured out for walks, I noticed people commenting about her breed. Mothers with children often pointed to her and said she was a bad dog, before even meeting her or having any contact with her. At first, I did a double-take, thinking they had mistaken my sweet puppy, Dallas, for another dog who had done bad deeds and had earned a bad rap. I envisioned a poster at the local post office with her picture and a caption, "Wanted for Armed Robbery." Then I realized she was being judged because she was a Rottweiler, even though she was still a puppy and hadn't hurt a fly. For anyone who had a minute to listen, I reminded them that the children's book *Carl* depicted a gentle, kindly Rottweiler named Carl, who often acted as the children's babysitter.

At the dog park, she was keenly interested in other dogs and loved to play and interact. Some of the more neurotic small dog guardians would get very nervous if Dallas even approached their dogs. They started yelling at me or Dallas in anticipation of bad things happening. One Shiba Inu barked repeatedly at Dallas, who just stood there and listened and didn't respond. The Shiba Inu became more vocal and kept taunting Dallas. Finally, Dallas responded, without moving, with a single bark. The Shiba Inu melted instantly at this single bark and lay submissively on his side directly beneath Dallas, who was still just standing above the other dog. Like an automatic assault weapon, the Shiba Inu's owner unleashed a rapid fire of insults and threats at Dallas and me for purported crimes that neither one of us had perpetrated. I looked at her quizzically and quietly, in utter disbelief that someone would verbally attack a stranger and her motionless dog for no good reason. It would not be an isolated incident. As little dogs sometimes humped her back legs, Dallas would ignore them and continue trotting through the park, unfazed, intermittently sniffing flowers and searching for crumbs on the ground, while the little dog clung to her back leg.

There were lots of new sights and sounds like traffic, horns, throngs of people, and subway vents to get used to. Unless there is a park nearby, New York City dogs have to learn to do their business on either plain cement sidewalks or streets, with a poop bag at the ready, or against the scarce, skinny little trees. It is slim pickings, so I was grateful that Dallas had no issue with her limited choices. I tried to protect her from the dirt and grime by washing off her paws, once the booty season was over, with baby wipes after each outing. When you see the green vehicular fluids left behind on the streets, it is frightening to imagine what gets tracked into apartments on your poor poochie's feet. I especially didn't want her to lick her feet and ingest whatever filth and bacteria she might have encountered. She was relatively brave for living in a city with so much commotion and activity. However, one of her biggest fears was the steam that arose from manhole covers. Another thing Dallas feared was the horses ridden by the New York Police Department's mounted division. At first, she was curious when she spotted them from afar, but as we neared the horse and rider and they became progressively larger, she pressed her body closer and closer to the ground and then refused to move. The horses we met were always quite gracious with her and a bit curious. I tried to encourage her to interact with them by approaching them and letting them sniff her, while getting a treat. She never seemed to develop any real confidence that these large beasts weren't going to devour her, but when given treats, she would at least slink by horses and manholes safely.

I had become accustomed to being Dallas' eyes and ears on our walks and knew which things to avoid and how to quickly move her out of harm's way. During one of our walks near our apartment building, she suddenly tugged on her leash with great zeal and force, almost pulling me down. I held on and nearly lost hold of her leash as I saw her sniffing intently and pulling toward an object she had not encountered before. I gasped. A used condom on the sidewalk near my apartment! I nearly vomited. I pulled her away just before she reached the source of maximum smell. How could we live in a place that had this kind of rubbish on the sidewalk right by my apartment? Had we lived closer to one of the city's parks, this dilemma might not have been so serious. In addition to the scarcity of nearby parks for her to play, I now had to worry about the condom conundrum. It was time to find a place outside the city, at least as an escape on the weekends where she could sniff and play more safely.

Who knew that the very exit out of the city would elicit nausea in Dallas? It was not evident until we drove to New Jersey in a rental car and she projectile vomited from one end of the back seat to the other. Her sad little face broke my heart as her stomach contracted forcefully and she heaved repeatedly. How would I get this poor little girl back to New York? She loved house hunting in New Jersey, especially at the beach, but had more episodes of vomiting on the return trip. Once we found a permanent weekend getaway, the trips resulted in fewer vomiting episodes, especially after I removed food from the equation on the morning of the drive. It took a while, but her condition improved with time. Despite nausea, Dallas loved outings in the car. She was game to go wherever I wanted to go. Gas stations were one of her favorite stops, most likely because one New Jersey gas station attendant frequently offered her dog treats and head rubs when we fueled up. Every time we pulled into a gas station, she perked up, looking all around for someone who might deliver her beloved dog treats. From Dallas' perspective, anyone approaching the car was a possible dog treat dispenser, so she would greet them enthusiastically. A benefit of having raised her in New York City and having to relieve herself in suboptimal dog conditions was that she would do so on command. Her cue phrase was, "Hurry up." Within seconds of hearing this command if we were at a rest stop, she would squat to do her thing. People often marveled at her conditioning. It was beneficial not to have to wait for her to find the right bush, tree, grass, or angle of hill like some dogs require for their daily constitutional.

Because of her love of travel and adventure, and her improved response to being in a moving vehicle, we embarked on many road trips together, both up and down the east coast of the United States and to Canada, and across the United States from New York to California. She was the perfect companion, never fussing over directions or asking if we were there yet. She also served as a security guard if anyone acted strangely or menacingly. We had a secret word that would modify her demeanor from friendly to protective within a second. No one ever challenged her without being barked at. Both in New York and across the country, being with Dallas enabled me to see things and encounter people I might not have otherwise.

I first realized just how much I enjoyed her company and considered her an integral part of the family when I was sent to London for a business trip. The trip was only two weeks long, but by the second day, I was already missing her presence and our routines and rituals. I was actually grateful for the long days at the London Salomon Brothers office, which kept me from spending too much time thinking about how much I missed my little girl. At this point, Dallas was already seven or eight months old, but she was still a baby in my eyes. Upon my return, I was surprised by how much she had grown in those two weeks and was looking more and more like a large adult dog. I felt like a part of me was missing when we were apart, in a way I never felt with family members. I had traveled a lot and said many goodbyes to my family and loved ones from a young age, so I had become accustomed to being independent and handling those separations well. It was an entirely different story with Dallas, though, because she relied on me for everything—food, the ability to relieve herself, warmth, shelter, love, and affection. When my boss in New York offered to send me to Hong Kong for a few months at a time on another project, I declined because I didn't want to spend extended periods of time away from Dallas. While I didn't expect the boss to be entirely understanding, I also didn't think she would express her utter disdain and condescension so overtly. She rolled her eyes, laughed at me, and thought I was crazy. Interestingly, no other employees who declined to leave their human families for extended periods of time were questioned for refusing the Hong Kong assignment. I remained steadfast in my commitment to being with Dallas and have no regrets about how that choice affected my career. If you've ever loved a dog, you've made sacrifices for him or her without worrying about the what-ifs of that choice. One Christmas season, when many of my colleagues on the Salomon Brothers finance desk had baskets of sweets from clients adorning their desks, one of my colleagues, Schmitty, who was also a dog lover, gave me a basket of dog treats made out of red and green colored rawhides for Dallas. His note read "From Duchess (his Dalmatian) to Dallas." It was so touching and thoughtful. When my boss marched by and inspected the basket, she rolled her eyes and exclaimed, "That's the most pathetic thing I've ever seen!" Experiences like those in investment banking made me realize I was not working in a profession of my true calling with colleagues who shared my values.

Although I worked diligently at my job, my heart wasn't in it. I derived more satisfaction from hanging out with my own dog and donating the remaining dollars from my paycheck to animal causes both locally and internationally. In my free time, I read more and more about the plight of animals and felt something drawing me in viscerally. I couldn't define it at the time and didn't understand the significance of this pull, but would soon realize the path that was beckoning. Sometimes, I felt overwhelmed by the many animal causes that existed for many species around the world. It was hard to hear people at work complaining about their perceived lack of material toys when I knew that there was so much suffering for helpless animals. At times, I just thought I would work hard, try to retire early, and then do something to work with animals. However, at the age of 30, my breakthrough presented itself.

Shifting gears

While pondering the future of my career and how I could help animals in more ways, I returned to Canada for a family visit. I was talking to my niece, Alexandra, who was eight-years-old at the time, when the penny dropped. Alexandra had always wanted to be a veterinarian and loved animals dearly. As a young girl does, she showed me every stuffed animal in her room, every horse statue, and every picture of herself with animals, talking incessantly about how much she loved each and every one of the animals she encountered. Caught up in her reverie, I absent-mindedly conceded that I, too, had wanted to be a veterinarian. Without missing a beat, she looked at me with big inquisitive eyes and asked, as only an eight-year-old could, "Why aren't you?" I couldn't muster a rebuttal simple or sound enough for an eight-year-old. It hit me like a ton of bricks.

Within three days of this eye-opening conversation, I had decided to prepare for the Graduate Record Examination (GRE), which is the standardized test required for admission into most veterinary schools, enroll in pre-vet studies at Rutgers University in New Brunswick, New Jersey, and gear up to apply for schools of veterinary medicine. I was not at all keen on spending more time in school. I had already spent six years in university after high school; four years of undergraduate school for an Honors Bachelor of Arts in languages, and two years getting a Master of International Management. The last time I had taken a science course was sixteen years earlier in high school. I would need to take all of my science prerequisites, which would take about two years, before I could even apply to vet school. Fortunately, a wise advisor at Rutgers University explained that time would pass at the same pace, regardless of whether or not I was pursuing my dream. The only difference would be that at the end of that time, I could realize my dream if I invested in my future by studying. I was looking at another six to seven years of studying with no paycheck during that time. What a change of reality! As soon as I set my mind to execute my new plan, I looked for veterinary clinics where I could volunteer to gain experience in the field. It is definitely a sign of finding your vocation when you don't mind spending 1,000 hours volunteering in pursuit of your dream. I couldn't have imagined working for even one hour without pay in investment banking, so this newfound excitement over something that didn't involve material rewards was proof-positive that my heart was fully invested in my new career path.

As I set forth in this new direction, it dawned on me that it was meant to be because I'd had a revelation a few years earlier while undergoing back surgery for a herniated disc. Initially, doctors had difficulty accepting that a 26-year-old woman could truly be in such agonizing pain that she might require more intervention than some pain pills. It took six doctors on two continents until I found the right one to diagnose and treat me. One orthopedist had the nerve to say, in a most patronizing fashion, that all pain starts here, as he pointed to his head, mere minutes after giving me an excruciatingly painful steroid injection into my spine. I would have tried to kick him in his head for such an affront, but I could barely walk, much less lift my leg to kick him. Another doctor, this time a neurologist, suggested I lie down for six months and rest. That was all he suggested! No physical therapy, no further diagnostics. He proffered this nonchalant recommendation with his feet up on his desk and his iced Slurpee drink sweating onto my $1,000 magnetic resonance imaging (MRI) scans. When I asked what I should do if my back was not better after those six months, he casually suggested I lie down for another six months. This bout of excruciating pain devoid of medical compassion was a revelation. I made a mental note to myself that if the investment banking profession didn't work out, I would get into medicine so that there could be some compassionate care for patients. I didn't think about this line of thought much further as I recovered from back surgery, but my experience as a patient was priceless in appreciating the helpless condition of many patients, especially those in pain. Most human patients can ring a buzzer for pain meds, let nurses know that they need to use the restroom, etc. To be a voice for the voiceless would truly be a challenge, but even more rewarding considering their dire need for an advocate. Now I just had to find a clinic to gain some experience working with animals.

Although there were many veterinary clinics in New Jersey, most of them were not set up for volunteers. I volunteered at two clinics: one was an equine practice that mostly performed orthopedic surgeries, and the other was a small animal specialty practice. The years of volunteering and studying were quite humbling because there was so much knowledge and experience to obtain and retain. Sometimes, the dose of humble pie was doubled because of the inherent hierarchy in veterinary medicine, as in many other professions. I was starting from the bottom, so I had to earn my stripes at every level, be it picking up or shoveling poop or holding animals for exams and small procedures. I sought out technicians, veterinarians, and receptionists, who were supportive and knowledgeable and tried to learn as much as possible from them. Sometimes, I was asked not to pose so many questions, which was a natural instinct that was difficult for me to suppress. I understand now how it can be distracting for a veterinarian to do their job while being peppered with questions. When you are starving for knowledge, though, and eager to sop up every drop of information possible, it's hard to rein in that enthusiasm. I didn't mind cleaning stalls or cages, sitting with animals for hours after they recovered from surgery, or holding foals during foal watch season and nursing them from weak, frail beings to feisty little bucking broncos that used me for target practice, while perfecting their kicking skills. I loved them all. It was a far cry from being chauffeured to the airport and flown first class overseas for work, while flight attendants baked chocolate chip cookies and catered to every need. Instead, the long work days often involved a lot of mess and physical exertion, and I would be bone tired by day's end. But the volunteering was one of the happiest and most exciting times of my professional life.

I still remember my first day volunteering at the small animal specialty hospital, Red Bank Veterinary Hospital (RBVH) in Red Bank, New Jersey. After helping take care of some in-hospital patients and being given a tour, I was somehow miraculously allowed to enter the surgery suite to observe a surgery. Unbelievable! My heart was beating so fast I had to slow down my breathing through the surgical mask so I wouldn't pass out from excitement! I wondered how it would be to watch a real-life surgery on a patient. I didn't want to faint or vomit or do anything stupid that might get me evicted from this sacred space. I had met the little dark brown Dachshund who was about to undergo surgery while she was still awake and hobbling about slowly, both hind limbs dragging limply behind her. Her hind legs were paralyzed and she was in tremendous pain because her intervertebral disc had herniated into her spinal cord, just like mine had a few years before, but much worse. Now, she was going to have back surgery to remove the portion of disc that was herniated, just like I had. Unsure of my tolerance for gore, I averted my eyes while the surgeon made her initial incision over the anesthetized dog's back. Psychologically, it helped that the remainder of the Dachshund was covered up by blue sterile surgical drapes, so all that was visible was a six-inch narrow sliver of her sterilely prepped and shaved gray-white skin over her back. I was apprehensive about having a bad reaction to the cutting portion of the surgery, so I forced myself to look away in order to remain professional.

Once the initial incision was made, I couldn't look away any longer. Instead, I stared intently, barely blinking, for the remainder of the surgery as the surgeon cut through various layers of skin, subcutaneous tissue, fat, and muscles, and then drilled through vertebral bone to access the spinal cord and the offending diseased and herniated disc. I was so mesmerized that I don't even remember inhaling or exhaling during the entire surgery. If surgery was a drug, I was hooked! If anything, it was beautiful. Precise movements of the blade opened up a clear-cut path to the source of pain and subsequent movements facilitated removal of the disc. Any miniscule untoward movement could cause paralysis or hemorrhage. It was art, it was science, it was beauty, and it was brilliance. As the surgeon proceeded, her manual maneuvers were like a well-rehearsed theater performance, where each scalpel blade motion parted the curtains for the next act, revealing a new, mysteriously enticing scene with a progressively more intricate set as she approached the spinal cord. At that moment, I understood why the term "to cut is to cure" existed. Although I enjoyed all aspects of volunteering at the two vet clinics, observing and eventually being allowed to scrub in to assist on surgeries was the highlight of any day.

The excitement of being able to actually help animals and make a difference in an individual's life motivated me to get out of bed each day to volunteer again. During this time, I started my pre-vet courses at Rutgers University, which was about an hour's drive from my home in Bay Head, New Jersey. I tape recorded some of my lectures so I could listen to them on the drive to the university or back home to maximize studying time. Many students in my courses, which consisted of jam-packed lecture halls of 300 to 600 students, would confidently state that they were headed to med school or vet school. I wasn't sure what made them so confident, considering the statistics. I knew the statistics for vet school admission were even worse, because there were only four vet schools in Canada and twenty-seven in the United States at that time. All I could do was study as much as possible, focus, and volunteer every possible day; at that pace, the time flew by in a flash. I saw a lot of pre-med students drop out as their lofty aspirations were dashed by grades that would not support their dreams. This high attrition rate was a constant reminder to not give up and to excel. The more I studied, the more I started seeing the medical connections between what I was learning in those endless lectures and what was happening at the veterinary clinics. It was as if the lights were turning on, and the symphony was beginning. Instead of intimidating me, the more I learned, the more excited I became about where I was going. I could see the finish line and just had to keep running the race.

Vera Heidolph, DVM

Dallas as inspiration

During my pre-vet studies at Rutgers University, Dallas became more and more of an inspiration for pursuing a career as a veterinarian as she became a frequent flyer at the vet hospital. One Saturday, while running around and playing in the back yard, Dallas suddenly emitted a high-pitched yelp and fell to the ground. It was so shocking to see my own dog, only four years old, who was normally so tough lying helplessly on the grass looking to me for comfort. Red Bank Veterinary Hospital (RBVH) was open 24/7, so I knew where to take her. The same surgeon I had grown to admire and respect, Dr. Salmeri, who had allowed me to observe many of her surgeries, was the veterinarian who saw her. In my mind, it was life and death. Because Dallas was my own dog, I was thinking more like an emotional dog guardian than a veterinarian-in-training. Dr. Salmeri assured me that Dallas was fine except for the left anterior cruciate ligament (ACL) in her knee, which she had just torn. A torn or ruptured ACL is a common injury in athletes, as well as larger dogs. However common it might be, it was a struggle to see my brave dog suffering and not be able to alleviate her pain immediately.

Although it seemed like a life and death emergency to me, Dr. Salmeri explained that Dallas could wait until Monday for her surgery and would have pain medication until then to keep her comfortable. Torn ACLs are a common condition in Rottweilers, so Dallas would most likely require surgery on her other knee within a year. I felt so bad for my poor girl. I packed her up in the car, lifting her 90-pound body into the back seat, praying my own back would hold up, and drove her home to rest and wait for surgery. This surgery would be one of nine non-elective surgeries that Dallas needed throughout her life.

Fortunately for her, she was an excellent patient and loved going to the vet clinic. She always had hope that a kind technician or veterinarian would offer some cookies or a back rub to make the trip worthwhile. The major objection that Dallas had the morning of her surgery was the lack of breakfast or treats. Ever the optimist, she "talked" (sort of like Scooby Doo) to anyone who was near her. Even without the use of her left back leg, she managed to lean against the surgery technicians and look up at them with her sweet brown eyes to make one last pre-op plea for a cookie or a back rub.

Her surgery was successful and uneventful, the way I always hope airplane rides and surgeries to be. I scrubbed in with Dr. Salmeri and witnessed her opening up Dallas' knee joint, cleaning out any extraneous tissues, and placing a figure-eight suture to mimic the stabilizing characteristics of the ACL. Since the time of Dallas' surgery, other methods of knee surgery have been developed that are considered superior, but at the time, it was the treatment of choice and is still used by some surgeons today. Recovery would be long, but the hardest part would be keeping her still and convincing her to rest. A testament to Dallas' tenacity in the face of pain was her ability to mobilize despite immobilizing discomfort. The postman coming to the door was a trigger for this type of behavior. I didn't realize that Dallas would defy her "good patient" reputation that involved being lifted up onto a bed to rest and remaining there until it was time to be lifted down again to go outside for a bathroom break. After a brief rattling of the mailbox outside the front door, I heard loud barking followed by scrambling toenails on the wood floors rushing to the front door. I couldn't believe that she was so naughty, or so protective of her house, that she still carried out guard duties. It became evident that I would have to act as her brains because she would be more heart than brains during her recovery period.

As predicted by Dr. Salmeri, Dallas' right knee would soon follow her left knee in requiring surgical repair for a second torn ACL. Again, Dr. Salmeri allowed me to scrub in and assist on the second knee surgery. Much to my astonishment and dismay, the surface of Dallas' exposed knee joint felt like moguls on a black diamond ski slope. Seeing Dallas suffer through orthopedic injuries that were the side effects of bad breeding broke my heart for my innocent dog. Even with arthritic joints and a big surgery behind her, Dallas recovered stoically from her second knee operation. Now, as a veteran patient nurse, I was better able to manage Dallas' comfort and pain after the second surgery, and also became more confident about my bedside care with other patients. Although it was emotionally straining to see my dog in pain, the reward of helping her heal motivated me further to become a veterinarian.

At that point during Dallas' recovery, I was completing my final pre-vet courses at Rutgers University, volunteering at RBVH and New Jersey Equine Clinic, and awaiting the verdict about my admission into veterinary school. Just as I thought we had overcome one hurdle regarding Dallas' well-being, there would soon be more unexpected and unwelcome surprises.

As soon as I was accepted into the Ontario Veterinary College (OVC), I began planning my move with the dogs from New Jersey to Ontario. Dallas and Dijon, my Boxer, would be my canine companions, my ongoing daily inspirations, and reminders of my goal to become a veterinarian—or so I thought. I was so focused on my plan of becoming a veterinarian while taking care of my dogs that it never dawned on me that there might be further nefarious dealings in the name of divorce. However, I realized the gauntlet had been thrown down when I received an emergent court order seeking custody of my dogs just three days before I was scheduled to move. On that fateful Friday, the threat was launched that if the ex did not win full custody of my dogs, he would personally open up every box on the moving truck. How cruel and absurd! Even my hardened divorce lawyer was stunned by this malevolent move, especially when I explained to him that the ex had already bought another Boxer by that time. The loaded moving truck could not leave without me. Instead, I was charged $500 per day by the moving company to wait because I had to stay in town to fight for custody of my dogs. All of my friends and family were certain that I would win this case because I was the one dedicating my life to helping animals and the one who had done the lion's share of caring for the dogs. For a moment in court, however, the judge questioned my ability to find time to care for my dogs while I was studying to become a veterinarian. Only because my lawyer squeezed my hand did I not scream out in protest at such a blasphemous suggestion. It was also proposed by the ex that I would only be "allowed" to keep the dogs if I gave him the house. This proceeding would be the beginning of many contentious court appearances I was forced to make over the next few years. Ultimately, the judge ruled in my favor, and the dogs and I could proceed with our planned move without any further hindrances for the time being. Just as children are often manipulated as pawns in divorces, my most beloved companions were very nearly ripped away from me. Although I couldn't imagine loving them more, I became even more protective of them, realizing that I was their only gatekeeper now.

As part of this protective nature and because of the bitter battle for custody, once we arrived in Guelph, Ontario, I was on the lookout for any signs of being watched or followed. Even though we were more than 1,000 miles away from New York and New Jersey, my radar was set off by my dogs' nervous sniffing, barking, and bristling on several occasions at night and even during the daytime. I was grateful for their protection and alerts, especially when my suspicions of being watched were confirmed months later when I was dragged back into divorce court hearings in New Jersey and was shown pictures by my ex's attorney of my residence in Ontario taken at close range. I was sickened at the thought of being followed, watched, and photographed, even though the lawyer insisted it was a private investigator who had taken the photographs and not my ex. I felt terrorized as I realized I was being watched directly or indirectly by the same party who had tried to inflict the maximum pain on me by stealing away the most precious beings in my life. Subsequently, I worried more that my dogs would be stolen and often dreaded leaving the house to attend lectures each day, for fear of finding them missing upon my return.

When I wasn't fighting legal battles during that first year of veterinary school, my schedule consisted of studying, lectures, and dog fun. For the next five years, that schedule repeated itself. Sometimes, we wouldn't go for our long walk until late at night. During the winter, those were chilly but wonderful memories, because the town was so quiet and we could enjoy the peace and beauty of a Canadian winter's evening walk. The dogs didn't mind the cold once they had their fleece jackets on. They enjoyed playing in the snow, shoveling it with their muzzles, and tossing it up in the air to catch and eat it like a snow cone. What they really loved were visits to my parents' house, which was a two-and-a-half-hour drive from Guelph. The prospect of off-leash access to forests, streams, and a bay were very inviting to two inquisitive and energetic dogs. Dallas also loved unearthing things that should not have been unearthed, such as my mother's compost pile. The only way to get her to stop foraging in the pile and return to the house was to shout "carrots!" This prompted her to lope back to the house, eagerly demanding the promised carrots, her muzzle speckled with dirt and debris. Miraculously, neither dog was ever sprayed by a skunk or quilled by a porcupine, both of which are common nature run-ins in Ontario.

Although Dallas had initially recovered from her second knee surgery, she had a flare-up of some pain and swelling several months later, so I made an appointment for evaluation with one of OVC's surgeons. I had started working for this surgeon to help with dogs who were in a study that he was conducting. I was very new to academics in veterinary medicine and research. My understanding was that the dogs I was walking needed hip surgery, so I would act as their walker after their surgery to provide bathroom breaks and a bit of gentle exercise. I would later discover that the research entailed something quite different. My misgivings about the merits or the basis of the research started the day the surgeon, Dr. B., examined Dallas. I would soon learn about the biases that not just the public, but even some veterinarians have against certain breeds like Rottweilers, and that not all veterinary surgeons were like Dr. Salmeri. While Dallas was lying on her left side with Dr. B. manipulating her back leg, I held her head with one arm around her neck to comfort and control her, just as a technician would. Dallas tensed and retracted her right hind leg with certain manipulations, but remained silent at first. I talked to her and reassured her, but then something rather unexpected happened. As Dr. B. manipulated her painful leg repeatedly and more forcefully, Dallas tensed again and emitted a very soft, low growl. Dr. B. promptly smacked her on her head, narrowly missing me as I was holding her closely to my own head and neck. I couldn't believe the nerve or callousness. He seemed nonplussed, but I was fit to be tied. The exam was over in my mind. When I said something like, "hey," he merely grunted that he didn't trust Rottweilers. Well, I no longer trusted *him*, in spite of his status and position. That feeling would only grow in stark contrast to my reverence for Dallas' main surgeon, whose specialty I found particularly admirable. I would never subject Dallas to any further interactions with Dr. B. I promptly extricated myself from working with his hip surgery dogs once I discovered what was really happening to them and why I was reprimanded for offering to spend more time with them off the clock to prevent them from soiling their runs. It was one of the first of many times I would have to stand up for my dog's wellbeing at the risk of my academic or professional career. No one should feel forced to stay with a veterinarian who doesn't respect their dog.

There were other clinicians at OVC who were also intent on reinforcing their position in the hierarchy when I brought Dallas to them as a patient. Call it veterinary school indoctrination by insult and beating down. One morning a couple of years into vet school, Dallas was noticeably absent from breakfast, which was a huge deal for her. She normally had bionic ears that could detect the sound of a mere crumb falling into her bowl and would race to the kitchen to investigate. As a puppy, I had once discovered her hind limbs and butt sticking out of a bag of dog food that she was actively devouring. I quickly checked the bedroom to see if she was still sleeping on my bed and, if so, why? She barely moved from her sleeping position, even when I brought her a few pieces of kibble. How could she have such a quick transformation from being fine the night before to looking like a train hit her the next morning? I could barely coax her into my car to drive her to school with me. Although I clearly explained her symptoms and how unusual they were for her, the fact that she had brightened a bit in the hospital made me look like a nervous veterinary student to some of the skeptical interns. To me, she seemed to feel lousy all over, including her bones and joints, so I offered the possibility of her having a disease called Ehrlichiosis, which is a tick-borne disease that I had seen in dogs while volunteering in New Jersey. Even though I mentioned that I spent summers and all of my time off in the United States, where there was a greater chance of Dallas getting Ehrlichiosis than in Ontario, the intern also shot this idea down, as if it was pretty far out. When I asked if we could just run the Ehrlichia test to be safe, she stated rather coolly that it was an expensive test and that, as a vet student, I probably wouldn't be able to afford it. I assured her that cost was not a concern for my Dallas, but thanked her for considering my finances. Dallas was treated symptomatically at first because we wouldn't get her results back for a few days. Once they were in, it was a relief to know that she *did* in fact have a treatable disease, and that I was not losing my mind by thinking of diseases she might contract from ticks in various states on her travels. With antibiotic treatment, Dallas recovered well from Ehrlichiosis, but I was becoming progressively less enamored of the suboptimal treatment given to veterinary students and their animals by my superiors. This suboptimal encounter with future colleagues who really should be collaborating to solve patient concerns was a reminder of the competitive nature of the profession, especially within the veterinary school. It was comforting to find a local veterinarian in Guelph who was much kinder to my dog and to me than the interns, senior students, or specialists at OVC. When Dallas needed a large, benign, fatty mass (a lipoma) removed from her chest, I was allowed to scrub in on her surgery with the local veterinarian and got to witness the "peeling of an onion" effect of shelling out a lipoma that expands before your eyes as it's removed.

Dallas would require many subsequent vet visits and surgeries throughout her life. As a pet store puppy, which equates to a puppy from a puppy mill, it was not surprising that her health problems were mounting. Having American Kennel Club (AKC) papers attesting to her alleged lineage, proved worthless, except to the AKC, who collected $30 to $40 per dog, sight unseen. A dog with one eye and three legs could still get AKC papers as long as the dam and the sire had AKC papers as well. She had already had two knee surgeries that were caused by irresponsible breeding. I had no idea that this profit-driven breeding with a focus on external aesthetics would cause so much physical pain and heartache for my dog and me, respectively, over the course of her life. Each of the nine surgeries she required was living proof of poor health being genetically propagated for profit.

It would become my mission throughout the course of her life to try to fix all of her parts that broke down and to overcome the medical problems to which she was predisposed. Although she became my inspiration for surgery being the cure, she also became one of the worst examples of breeding for aesthetics instead of health. She often had ear infections in her left ear, for example. They would arise rather quickly and would cause her discomfort, as evidenced by her shaking her head or rubbing her ear on the carpet or furniture. I would treat the infections, but they seemed to occur more than I would have anticipated for a dog, especially in just one ear. I had always maintained from the first day that I met her that Dallas had a "wonky" left ear. Wonky isn't a medical term, but everyone gets the idea. It's a bit different or weird. The pinna (ear flap) was raised a bit more on the left side than on the right, although some people argued that it just looked that way because she often tilted her head to the right as she listened to you. I didn't know what was going on inside her ear until the solution to one problem became the discovery of another one.

After surgically removing a small growth on Dallas' forehead, the histopathology report came back as a hemangiopericytoma, which is a malignant tumor. Again, Dallas hadn't exactly read the textbook because these types of tumors are supposed to be found on limbs or extremities. Regrettably, the report also noted that her tumor was not completely excised (removed)

54

because there were still some cancer cells present beyond the margins of what had been removed. Hemangiopericytomas are tumors that are locally aggressive, but do not tend to metastasize or spread to other parts of the body. The mass was above her right eye and had already been carved down to her muscle and bone, so I was concerned about the tumor spreading in this area and the inability to remove the remaining cancer cells surgically. I consulted with some veterinarians on the matter and received conflicting opinions. Dallas had her surgery just before we headed to the NC State Veterinary Hospital in Raleigh, North Carolina, to do some clinical research for veterinary cardiologist Dr. Clarke Atkins for the summer. Once I arrived in Raleigh, I received the histopathology report. Fortunately for Dallas, she was in good hands at NC State, and none of the veterinarians she met there had any issues with Rottweilers. The first specialist she needed to see was an oncologist, because I was leaning toward radiation therapy. Dr. David Proulx, who reminded me of a much younger version of Paul Simon, but more importantly was double-board certified in both radiation and oncology, became her oncologist. He set up a computed tomography (CT) scan to determine the extent of the remaining mass on her forehead and to plan the radiation therapy that would follow. In addition to finding a bit of remaining abnormal tissue over her right eye, Dallas' CT scan revealed an abnormality at the bottom of her left ear canal. It could not be definitively determined by just the scan, but it showed a narrowing of the tip of the ear canal that led to the eardrum. The second oncologist offered flatly that it was most likely a tumor, in spite of my suggestion that it might be a wonky ear that Dallas had since birth.

The plan was to remove the entire ear canal surgically, a procedure known as a Total Ear Canal Ablation (TECA). We suspected there was fluid in the inner ear, so the circular hollow bone (the bulla) would be drilled open to flush out the inner ear, a procedure called a bulla osteotomy (BO). Dr. Kyle Mathews, Dallas' surgeon for this procedure, allowed me to scrub in on her surgery. I wanted to make sure that the anesthesiologist knew about Dallas' breathing issues when anesthetized. She had stopped breathing during anesthesia for her last few surgeries and would most likely need help breathing during the entire procedure. Some dogs have this reaction to certain drugs or just general anesthesia. As a teaching hospital, NC State had a ventilator, which I thought would simplify any breathing concern, so I was optimistic that Dallas would have an uneventful surgery. She refused to breathe on her own once anesthetized, so the anesthesia team tried breathing for her for a while until they realized I was telling the truth and that Dallas would need the ventilator to help her breathe for the entire procedure. While standing on a stool for the best possible view beside a tall surgeon, I was allowed to assist Dr. Mathews as he masterfully and delicately teased away the ear canal, which is essentially a firm, cartilaginous tube that's very well adhered to the surrounding tissues, including their blood vessels and nerves. One of the common complications from this procedure is Horner's syndrome, a one-sided facial droop, which results from damage to the facial nerve. Fortunately, Dallas did not experience any such complication. Because her head was rather large and block-like, the second part of the surgery—accessing and incising the bulla—would have to be done from a different angle. We turned Dallas over from her side to her back and proceeded to shave her neck area, through which Dr. Mathews would be approaching this part of the surgery to access the bulla on the inside of the ear. From my vantage point beside him, it looked like he was going to cut all the way through her brain, so this was a bit of a scary ride as a passenger, but everything went exactly as planned and the excess fluid in her bulla was safely drained. My mother inquired how Dallas would be able to eat after having surgery on her neck and throat. She worried that Dallas might go hungry for a few days as she recovered. Between a pre-op fentanyl patch that was applied to her skin for pain relief and her dogged determination to eat, no meal was missed, and her appetite never waned. She healed quickly and the histopathology report determined that there was no cancer in her ear. She just had a congenital wonky ear canal that narrowed excessively, causing chronic ear infections. It was another successful surgical repair, even though she looked a bit like Frankenstein post-op with most of her hair missing and many inches of incisions on her head and neck. Dallas was on her way to becoming bionic.

That summer, she still had radiation therapy ahead of her, which she managed with flying colors. Technicians placed a jugular catheter in her neck so that they wouldn't have to poke her veins repeatedly each day to anesthetize her for radiation therapy, which consisted of five daily treatments each week for four weeks. At home, I had to flush the catheter in her neck with saline a few times a day to keep it from clogging. Dallas didn't love the sensation of saline going into her jugular vein, so I enticed her with a cookie to distract from the flushing part of the process. I would beckon her by calling out "cookie needle," which brought her running to me and helped me keep her catheter in top shape. The end result of her radiation therapy was the complete destruction of any cancer cells and a rectangular-shaped white patch of fur, once the sunburned skin healed and her hair grew back. This snowflake appearance on her head invited much speculation and curiosity, and even brought into question her Rottweiler status at times. I was relieved to have the surgeries and radiation from that spring and summer behind us as we returned to Guelph for the next semester of vet school.

Although Dallas had always been very keen about her food, it wasn't until she started defending it that it became a problem. Over time, she began resource guarding, which sometimes manifested as her going after another dog if she perceived that they were a threat to her "resources," be they food, prized toys, rawhide chew toys, etc. It was odd to me that this behavior had developed over time because she had peacefully cohabitated and co-dined with her housemate, Dijon, for many years and was very cordial with any dog she met on the street or in the dog park. Fortunately, there was a veterinary behaviorist at OVC who could help me understand how to deal with her resource guarding or resource aggression. The key to dealing with any kind of aggression, she explained, was not countering it with any aggression on the human side, such as force, pain, shouting, shock collars, or any of the things that might cause more fear or discomfort. Such action would only escalate any fearful or aggressive outbursts. We learned how to avoid situations where resources might become an issue by putting prized toys out of reach or sight when canine visitors dropped by, and feeding the dogs separately for quite a while. Dijon was puzzled by this experience because she cared relatively little about eating at that point in her life. I had to leash both dogs during meal times until I could convince Dallas that no dog was going to compete with her for her food. It took some time and training, but was successful. Just because we've had dogs all of our lives or are in the veterinary profession doesn't mean we are adequately equipped with tools or knowledge about every aspect of our pets' physical or emotional wellbeing. It was a breath of fresh air to know that there are such useful resources as veterinary behaviorists to help understand what we couldn't perceive was happening and to offer a solution for our pets.

It is important to note that behavior problems, whether they are aggression, excess shyness, or inappropriate urination, are the number one reason pet guardians relinquish dogs and cats to shelters. Most behavior problems that are not caused by underlying medical conditions have solutions, which can be obtained from a behaviorist or perhaps from a veterinarian if they are basic behavioral problems. Again, Dallas taught me more about resource aggression than I could have learned from a book, although I would have preferred to learn that lesson from a book. As perfect as I wished my little angel were, she not only had surgical scars to show from her many malformations, but she had behavioral imperfections that I would need to manage for the rest of her life. Fortunately, they became easier to manage over time with behavioral therapy and training.

As I focused on helping Dallas overcome her resource guarding issues, another year of vet school raced by with lectures, labs, studying, and dog walking. Dallas and Dijon were my sacred place and time to enjoy at the end of each day. They recharged my battery, which was sometimes just low from lack of sleep and the volumes of information compressed into my brain. They inspired me to study hard and learn as much as I could to help as many animals as possible. By the end of the next school year, we were ready for another summer on the road. This time, it would be a cross-country trip to California. Along the way, we had time to explore some of Colorado's breathtaking national parks. Dallas and Dijon were the perfect car and trail companions. They slept as I drove and didn't fuss about directions or destinations. When there was trouble, Dallas gave a warning bark that would keep away anyone with questionable motives. Dijon kept up the comedic part of the team with her goofy antics. We spent a few weeks in Pomona, California, where I learned how to perform spays and neuters with board-certified veterinary surgeon Dr. Lara Rasmussen, who was teaching surgery at Western University's College of Veterinary Medicine. Getting involved in this hands-on activity was an eye-opener, almost as much as Pomona's Inland Valley Humane Society & S.P.C.A. I witnessed several cases of abused and neglected dogs, ranging from Saint Bernards to Boxers and Pit Bulls, as well as many stray and dumped animals at the shelter. The statistics were not favorable for most of those dogs. There is nothing so shocking or traumatic as seeing a waist-high empty oil barrel filled with dead bodies of cats and dogs that have been euthanized only due to over-population. My heart broke over this unfathomably cruel scene. I questioned the term "shelter" for what we are doing in North America. How is it possible that we are killing healthy cats and dogs just because there are too many animals and not enough homes? I cry every time I think about this situation and have had to turn my tears into action or what some might call proselytizing about spaying, neutering, and adopting instead of shopping for pets. It is literally a life and death situation that each individual can change by making a choice to save a life, instead of contributing to the millions of animals killed each year. If I hadn't already had two dogs with me on that trip, I would have adopted some of those dogs. The Saint Bernards were so emaciated and fearful, it was disgusting to see what humans had done to these beautiful creatures. Within a couple of weeks of patient and kind care, they were gaining weight and allowing technicians to bathe and pet them. All they needed was love. It made me love on my dogs even more. In some of the neighborhoods where I walked Dallas and Dijon, we saw Pit Bulls in the yards with home-cut ears, some of which were still bleeding. It was a far cry from some of the animals I encountered while volunteering at a surgical hospital in Los Angeles. Most of the pets there were very well maintained, while some were animals that should never be pets, like a monkey from the Playboy Mansion.

Armed with a dog-friendly resource book, I found places where four-legged family members were often not just welcome, but honored, like the

Cypress Inn in Carmel-by-the-Sea, California, owned by animal lover Doris Day. Next, we visited the delightful town of Mendocino, which is northwest of San Francisco. As we explored its quaint and welcoming streets, I was thrilled to learn that this was the town used to film *Murder, She Wrote*. Once we passed the northern coastline of California and ventured into Oregon, there were even more open spaces and lots of enticing long stretches of empty beaches where Dallas and Dijon could run free. With both dogs in tow, I visited areas that I would never have explored alone. It was wonderful that they opened up my world at a time when I had a very narrow focus on my studies and volunteer activities. I had some time to recover from the shock of shelter life and mass euthanasias for over-population as I soaked in the natural beauty of nature and my dogs. Finally, we had to head east for the next leg of our summer adventure in Chicago.

I was scheduled to spend three weeks at Chicago Animal Care and Control volunteering to perform spays and neuters at their shelter. It was scenes of the Pomona shelter all over again, except on a larger scale. Within the first hour of my arrival, I witnessed two dogs being taken in and euthanized soon thereafter; one from bullet wounds, and the other from a horrific dog fight. As I watched their lifeless bodies being taken away, I knew I would never be the same again. In the same breath as we talked about what had happened to those poor dogs, I was instructed how to handle the removal of bullets from a dog who has been shot in order to preserve it for further forensic investigations. It felt more like a war zone than a place where we could help animals. They were overcrowded by about 200% (space intended for 300 animals now housing 600+). Decisions to euthanize were made very quickly due to the high volume of animals brought in each day. I saw a degree of fear in many dogs' eyes and bodies that I had never seen before. It was beyond haunting and chilling. Every time I walked through the rows of runs and cages, I cried at the sight of so many trembling, terrified dogs. What had people done to these helpless beings to cause such panic and deathly fear? We learned about dogfighting operations and how many of the failed fighting dogs and so-called "bait" dogs ended up at shelters. How was it the year 2001 and yet there were still beings on this earth committing this most craven of crimes? Unbelievable. I became more driven to spay, neuter, adopt, and educate. People had to know about these horrific realities. My admiration for animal control officers in the field grew exponentially that summer as I heard the stories of scenes they encountered and how they had to extricate animals from precarious situations. What a tough job emotionally and often physically, too!

I clung to my dogs a bit harder each time I walked them around our hotel near the shelter. I would rather have died saving my dogs than let anyone lay a hand on them. My faith in humanity slipped that summer, as I felt we were fighting an uphill battle to prevent both over-population euthanasias and crimes against animals, including dogfighting, abuse, and neglect. Those experiences also increased my respect for shelter veterinarians tremendously. I still don't know how they don't blow a gasket with the stress of all the animals they see and the exceedingly difficult decisions they have to make every day. If you ever run into a shelter veterinarian, kennel assistant, technician, or animal control officer, give them a hug because they probably need one. It's a job, I quickly realized, that I would not be able to do for any length of time without a breakdown.

We made one final small detour from Chicago to Wisconsin at the end of the summer before heading back to Ontario. There, we met a new vet friend and animal advocate, Dr. Susan Krebsbach, who would become one of my closest friends. With her encouragement, I searched for a mixed animal veterinary hospital near Madison to do my externship the following summer and quickly found it in Lodi, Wisconsin. The bucolic, rolling hills of Madison seemed a million miles away from some of the things I'd seen in Chicago, Pomona, and Los Angeles. It would be a more peaceful change of pace for me and my dogs.

Before we could return to Wisconsin, there was another year of studying at OVC and still more things to learn from Dallas. I watched Dallas like a hawk, ever since her knee surgeries, to make sure she was doing well. One day as she was standing up from a sitting position, one of her toes on her left hind leg scuffed briefly and didn't straighten out immediately as it should. For the next 24 hours, I stared at her almost non-stop and noticed a repeatable, but only intermittent toenail scuffing as she stood up, which improved once she walked away. Over the next couple of weeks, this mild scuffing progressed to the point where she started losing her strength and would slip on slick surfaces, such as linoleum or wood floors. From the first moment I noticed the single toe scuffing to her first visit with the veterinary neurologist, I strongly suspected that she had a neurologic abnormality or deficit in her spinal cord. I did not *want* my dog to have a neurologic deficit. After seeing so many dogs with similar symptoms, especially at RBVH, requiring back or neck surgery, it was surprising to hear the OVC neurologist's diagnosis. She felt so certain that Dallas did *not* have any neurologic deficits and that all of her gait abnormalities, such as the slipping out of her back legs on slippery surfaces, were secondary to arthritis and degenerative joint disease that she videotaped Dallas in motion for teaching purposes at OVC and later at a national seminar to demonstrate a dog who had osteoarthritis but **no** neurologic deficits. Initially, the neurologist had me convinced that I was just a neurotic vet student who had over-interpreted my dog's clinical symptoms. Veterinary students are encouraged to believe the rulings of a specialist, no matter how strong the vet student's instincts are to the contrary. I was genuinely not trying to be defiant or disrespectful. I just saw something that was *different* in Dallas and was desperate to help her.

As her hind limb weakness advanced and her episodes of slipping increased, it was clear to me that she *did* have a neurologic deficit and that she needed more than just non-steroidal anti-inflammatory drugs (NSAIDs). With some trepidation, I approached the neurologist at OVC again and apprised her of Dallas' situation. She still did not want to believe that the dog she had used as an example of *no* neurologic deficits could be proving her wrong. I repeated to the neurologist that Dallas' current symptoms were distinctly *different* from her years of arthritis. I begged for an MRI because I knew it would be better diagnostically, but OVC didn't have an MRI scanner yet at that time, so a myelogram was performed instead. Even as a veterinary student reviewing the myelogram, I had the sick feeling of being right. Not only did Dallas have spinal cord compression as I had feared, but the compression wrapped around the circumference of her cervical (neck) spinal cord and over two intervertebral disc spaces. The neurologist and now the surgeons reviewing the films together shook their heads in disbelief at the poor state of her spinal cord. As the neurologist discussed the myelogram with the surgeons, both parties agreed that there was too much spinal cord damage in areas that were too difficult and risky to reach to be able to do anything surgical for Dallas. I couldn't believe my ears! The neurologist even had the nerve to say I should just put her on steroids to decrease the inflammation around her spine and enjoy her for the next six to twelve months or so until she couldn't take the pain anymore, as she was already eight years old. I returned to one of my lectures after receiving this blow, blinking away tears of anger and fear. Vet school didn't always welcome independent thinkers and this experience with Dallas' so-called non-neurologic disease that had actually been neurologic all along confirmed it. There was even a saying, "cooperate and graduate" that reinforced the notion of not rocking the academic boat.

This was not a time to cooperate, but rather a time to get a second opinion for Dallas. I had witnessed and scrubbed in on many medical and neurologic miracles performed by the specialists at RBVH and resolved that Dallas would be their next miracle. I called Dr. Salmeri to discuss her situation, FedExed her the myelogram films, and soon heard back the most wonderful words. There was *hope*! I knew that risks, including paralysis, existed for this surgery, but as Dallas rapidly declined before my eyes with no other alternatives offered at OVC, I packed her up in the car and drove 13 hours to see Dr. Salmeri in New Jersey.

We arrived on a Sunday night at the surgeon's doorstep. After gait evaluation and a neurologic exam, Dr. Salmeri agreed that surgery was the only option to treat Dallas. We checked into RBVH that night in preparation for her MRI the next morning. At the time, RBVH did not have its own MRI scanner, but instead used a nearby human MRI facility in the early hours of the morning before people showed up for their appointments. Dogs were anesthetized by the neurologist and his team, and observed for their vital signs through a glass window from the next room. The MRI scans were available shortly after and shared with Dr. Salmeri, who confirmed what she had already seen on Dallas' myelogram. Time for surgery before waking her up from the anesthesia. I had full confidence that if anyone could fix my dog, Dr. Salmeri could.

Dallas made it through the surgery and was walking by the next morning. She was loaded up with pain meds to minimize any discomfort from the surgery. I approached her cautiously in her run to prevent her from turning too quickly or stumbling if she tried to get up, but I needn't have worried. She stood up slowly but steadily with a bit of help from a sling under her belly. Although her back end was a bit wobbly, she was moving forward and her spirits were excellent. I was elated by her steady progress over the next few days while she was hospitalized and when I returned with her to Guelph. What I hadn't anticipated upon our return, as I marveled at her improvement, was the reception by the OVC neurologist and surgeons who had deemed her condition impossible for surgical intervention. I thought they would be thrilled for my dog's recovery and applaud her success, even if it wasn't at their own hands. Instead, as she walked down the halls of the OVC and passed by the specialists who had written her off, there was silence. The ugly realization set in that fragile human egos were bruised. In the next year of clinical rotations, I found it to be no coincidence that my two lowest clinical scores were from the same surgeon who had said she could not perform Dallas' surgery and from the same neurologist who said Dallas was non-neurological. I had no regrets, however, that I had risked my vet student career to save my dog and would do it all over again. Sometimes, if you love a dog, you may just have to fight for her and deal with the consequences, whether it's a contentious custody battle or tacit academic ostracism.

Doubts about Dallas

In my early professional career, the two best days ever were the day I was accepted into veterinary school and the day I was offered a small animal internship at Red Bank Veterinary Hospital (RBVH). Every single day of vet school, my goal was to be accepted for an internship, so achieving this goal was a total thrill. Although the concept of the hard work and long hours seems conceivable beforehand, it is hard to fully imagine how your body and mind will feel while you're experiencing it. Newly graduated vet students are like horses having their first spring romp outside after being cooped up all winter in a barn in Ontario. They have unbridled energy and enthusiasm to start diagnosing and treating their own patients. There is a miraculous second wind of thirsting for even more knowledge than what was already obtained in vet school. All of these factors are the fuel that drives interns.

As busy as an intern is, the year flies by without knowledge or concern for the outside world, a personal life, or anything that isn't pertinent to veterinary medicine. Things that do catch our attention are the immediate needs of our own companion animals, who require a lot of dog sitting and dog walking during this year. One evening after a long day on my surgery rotation, I arrived home at the intern house to find my beloved Dallas in a terrible state. I stepped over a few piles of vomit on the floor before I saw her, then noticed she was lying on her stomach, hanging her head in a most pathetic way. For such a stoic dog to look like she was at death's door was petrifying. She was weak and dehydrated and showed little care for the world or herself. I started to panic, but knew I must get her to the hospital immediately. Almost being outweighed by your own dog makes transporting her very difficult when she can't walk. Somehow, adrenaline kicked in, giving me the strength to carry her to my car.

There is no better time or place in life to receive VIP treatment than with your own dog in an emergency hospital. Like a Formula 1 race car team changing tires and refueling, the technicians can place an intravenous (IV) catheter in mere minutes and administer shock doses of fluids for seriously compromised patients. As I handed over my dog to these skilled colleagues, I felt like a helpless, emotional guardian and not at all like a veterinarian. One of the technicians saw my dilemma and handed me a thermometer, knowing I could not mess that up, even if I was discombobulated. For the next few hours, technicians administered IV fluids and anti-nausea medication, took Dallas' blood samples—normal—took X-rays of her abdomen—normal, except for some fuzziness in the top of her abdomen—and then we proceeded to do an ultrasound. By that point in the day, the internal medicine specialist, who would normally perform the ultrasound, had left. We did our best to look at her vital organs and see if she had fluid in her belly. Dallas had a tiny bit of fluid in her belly, but not enough at that point to be able to safely tap it or even sample it.

Not only had I found her lying on her belly, head hung low, but she also seemed to have more neurologic symptoms, such as knuckling on all four feet. How could she be spiraling downward before my eyes? No one had an answer for me about her diagnosis. A couple of veterinarians suspected pancreatitis, which made some sense, but also seemed a bit odd for a dog who had successfully stomached many naughty treats and surprises without much of an incident. It would explain the severe vomiting, the painful belly, and the haziness on the abdominal X-rays. But how could pancreatitis affect her neurologic status simultaneously?

These questions swirled around frantically in my mind as I watched in fear and frustration, the clock ticking rapidly. Her vomiting was abated by medication. The IV fluids helped a bit with her hydration and blood pressure, but by morning, her blood work was out of whack. Her blood glucose was dropping precariously. Pancreatitis wouldn't normally cause such hypoglycemia, unless there was a pancreatic tumor (insulinoma) secreting an excess of insulin. I didn't have a better answer, but I was questioning the probability of her only problem being pancreatitis. Something wasn't adding up. Low blood glucose shouted "sepsis," but didn't make sense otherwise. The morning shift of specialists had arrived, giving me hope for another lifeline with a different, and hopefully better diagnosis.

It was no time to be shy, so I snagged the internal medicine specialist and begged her to scan Dallas' abdomen as I explained her dire situation. She kindly agreed and realized instantly that I was not exaggerating Dallas' state. Now there was enough fluid in her belly to sample. The internist also saw some nodules on Dallas' liver and spleen; no other obvious abnormalities, but her pancreas did look inflamed. When questioned about her presumptive diagnosis, the internist strongly suspected that Dallas had cancerous tumors in her liver and spleen, especially because Rottweilers are predisposed to certain types of cancer like hemangiosarcomas. She feared that a tumor may have ruptured and caused the fluid in her belly. We prepared a slide of the fluid that we tapped out of her belly and found startling results. Bacteria! Normally, the abdomen is a sterile place, which seems ironic considering the massive amounts of bacteria that are inside the intestines and the stomach. Any breach of the lining of the intestines can result in leakage of their contents into the abdomen, which causes bacterial sepsis and death, if not treated promptly. The sepsis also explained the low blood glucose. Dallas' list of dire problems was growing, as was my concern for her life.

When I asked the internist if Dallas could possibly have something else besides tumors causing the fluid, the pain, and the nodules, she dropped her head, looked at her feet, and replied quietly, "Not likely." Partly because of the pest I am when it comes to my own animals and my stubborn belief that there had to be hope for Dallas, I just couldn't give up on her yet. I pressed further, asking what we could do. Possibly a splenectomy (removing the spleen) because there were nodules on it and dogs can live without a spleen. The internist's concern was if we went to surgery, removed Dallas' spleen, and found she had tumors throughout her abdomen, she wouldn't have much of a chance. I was willing to risk it to just give her any part of a chance.

Dr. Salmeri was not doing surgery that morning, so I approached another surgeon on duty and updated him on Dallas' condition and the urgency for surgery. He gave me a skeptical look that succinctly summed up his concerns about this proposition, but with one eyebrow still cocked, calmly gave instructions for Dallas' surgical preparation. I was on a surgery rotation anyway, so I could scrub in on the surgery. Everyone expected a lot of blood to seep out of Dallas' abdomen once it was opened up because they suspected a tumor on her spleen. We were once again humbled by a curious medical mystery. There was fluid in her abdomen, but there was barely any blood in it; not what you would expect from a bloody splenic tumor or liver tumor. The surgeon elevated her enlarged spleen out of her abdomen through the incision and past all of the retractors, taking care not to squeeze or pull excessively. The spleen is chalk full of blood and one wrong move can result in a volcanic eruption of squirting blood. Even though I was more emotional and less objective than I would normally be with any other patient, I was underwhelmed by the small nodules on Dallas' spleen and liver. I had seen many similar nodules that turned out to be benign in older dogs before. It didn't seem like those little nodules could be causing all of these massive problems. Before we could look deeper into her abdomen, the surgeon had to remove the spleen. Removing the spleen is an exercise in tying off, or ligating, many blood vessels that connect it to the rest of the abdomen without ligating the wrong blood vessels and cutting off the blood supply to the stomach or pancreas. Once her spleen was successfully removed, the rest of her abdomen was explored.

What a shock it was to discover that her pylorus, which is the muscular sphincter that opens and closes the flow of food from the tail end of the stomach into the top of the small intestine, was completely perforated. Finally, we had unearthed the true source of all of her problems. Even though this was a huge, messy problem, I felt some relief, because I knew this was a potentially fixable problem with a good long-term prognosis if she could just get through the surgery and recovery. I was also relieved because I knew Dallas was in excellent hands with surgeons who could perform this challenging surgery in their sleep. The trick with repairing a perforation in that location is that it is more difficult to lift the stomach out of the body because of its deep attachment to the abdomen. Mechanically, it's also a very well-muscled part of the stomach, as one can imagine a sphincter should be, so repairing it to ensure it can still close off without closing it off too narrowly is a very fine balance of judgment and skill. I watched the surgeon intently as he masterfully managed the mess and reconstructed the gaping hole.

During this surgery, I learned to appreciate anew the importance of another surgical mantra: "The solution to pollution is dilution." It means that the leakage of intestinal contents, loaded with bacteria, into the abdominal cavity was a toxic mess that required clean-up, so it doesn't kill the patient. The way to deal with bacteria or "pollution" was by rinsing and removing the diluted bacteria. Dilution is achieved by pouring warmed sterile saline into her open abdomen, gently jostling the abdominal contents to mimic the motion of a washing machine, flushing the nooks and crannies between organs, and then suctioning out the diluted spillage. This process of lavaging, or bathing the abdomen in saline and removing it repeatedly until there is minimal bacteria remaining, is similar to what we did with Oscar, except Dallas' abdomen was already opened up and Oscar's lavage was closed. The difference between washing dirty laundry and washing bacteria out of an abdomen is that bacteria are not visible to the naked eye, so we need to err on the conservative side and rinse the living daylights out of the abdomen to be safe. Before closing up her abdomen, a sample of Dallas' liver was biopsied to check for any sign of a malignant tumor. Then, the three-layer closure of her abdomen began. She had a long zipper of an opening now, but that was the least of her problems. The same surgeon who repaired her perforated pylorus also taught me another surgical mantra: "Incisions heal side to side, not end to end," meaning that no matter how short or long an incision, it will take the same amount of time to heal, so don't fuss about its length.

For several hours after her surgery, I stopped by her kennel as often as I could to check in on Dallas and let her know I was nearby. She was groggy, as would be expected from the surgery and the pain meds, so I couldn't really assess her progress initially. What soon became disconcerting was how her limbs were starting to swell before my eyes. Even when you've learned something in a textbook and have seen it happen in patients many times before, lessons in physiology are never so clearly etched in your mind as when they transpire in front of you with your own dog. How could an abdominal surgery have any effect on her legs swelling? She didn't have any problems with her IV catheter, which was in her leg. Her lymph nodes, which could possibly account for swelling of the limbs, were all in order. One of the miraculous concepts of medicine is that when the proteins responsible for fluids staying inside blood vessels are decreased or leaking outside of the blood stream, surrounding tissues swell with the leaked fluid. When the swelling becomes very significant, you can make a dent in the swollen skin with your finger by pressing down on the swelling. This condition is known as pitting edema, because of the dent or the pit left in the skin or the limb where the swelling is. Dallas was quickly developing pitting edema on all four legs. No massaging or moving her about to help the circulation improved the situation. Instead, hetastarch, a synthetic colloid, which is a type of IV fluid, was initiated. The role of a colloid is to mimic the lost proteins, thus maintaining the pressure within the blood vessels and minimizing the leakage of fluid. It doesn't work immediately and sometimes, even with advanced interventions, the patient is beyond help.

Twenty-four hours post-op, Dallas looked worse than before her surgery. Her limb swelling remained, as well as her nausea. It was hard to see her looking so rough. She had weathered her neck surgery better, but it hadn't involved numerous body systems or a septic abdomen. In the meantime, we received the wonderful news from the histopathologist that her spleen and liver were normal with benign nodules! I contemplated the ideal treatment plan for Dallas, in addition to dozens of other surgery patients. Worrying about her well-being was my moonlighting job in between patients. She was on all of the pain medication, anti-nausea medication, and antibiotics that existed, or that she could tolerate at the time. Her fluids were amended throughout the day according to her vitals. We couldn't give her any NSAIDs, the canine version of Celebrex, because the reason she had perforated her pylorus was due to an adverse reaction to a new NSAID that she had been taking for a couple of weeks. Another surgeon shared with me a journal article that described how Rottweilers have a greater predisposition than other breeds to having adverse reactions, not dissimilar to Dallas', to certain anti-inflammatories. What rotten luck, considering all of her joint issues and previous surgeries, that we would now be limited in her pain medication regime. I was becoming frustrated about everything that had happened to my dog in her life, in great part because of her genetics. The frustration fed my growing impatience as I waited for her critical status to be downgraded to stable. It seemed impossible to pump the brakes on my zeal for her recovery. Just as my parents had kept me busy picking berries as I worried about our dog Rex, the internship duties kept me occupied so that I didn't have time to have a breakdown while worrying about Dallas.

By the next day, I was too exhausted from work and worry to express the relief I felt when I saw Dallas perking up in her kennel as I approached. She still had swollen limbs from all of the protein loss, but her spirit was bouncing back. This time, she nuzzled closer to me as I held her head in my lap and stroked her silken black ears. It was the first time since I found her hunched over at home that she regained some of her personality again. I had to contain my wishful thinking before sharing it with the surgeon, lest I be premature in my optimism. After he looked her over and concurred that her status was much improved, the surgeon confided blankly that he had thought she was a goner for a while; even more reason to exhale, now that she was turning the corner against the odds. Dallas pulled through her most trying surgery, made a full recovery, and resumed her post as companion, protector, and housemate to three other dogs.

Dallas in San Diego

Not every dog could have weathered all the medical setbacks as well as Dallas did, but she was an amazingly independent, resilient, and life-loving soul. Remarkably and thankfully, she loved going to veterinary clinics and interacting with veterinarians in spite of all of her problems because there was always the chance that she would get cookies and/or a back rub. Unfortunately, her tough demeanor could hide some discomfort and pain. Once we moved to California for work, however, her growing discomfort became more apparent with her progressive reluctance to move as far or as freely. Her generalized arthritis had been managed relatively well with the NSAIDs—those that didn't bother her stomach—that she had already taken for years.

When medication no longer sufficed, I investigated canine rehabilitation therapy and quickly became a fan. Initially, she required persistent coaxing with food to learn how to swim. She wasn't an avid or adept swimmer by nature, but she took to swim therapy really well after a couple of sessions. By the third session, this stiff-gaited, slow-moving dog was trotting down the steps to the pool and tugging on her leash to get there faster. As she caught sight of the pool, she emitted a low-pitched contented howl. She waited somewhat impatiently as I strapped on her bright yellow dog life jacket, braced herself as the hydraulic platform was lowered into the water, and paddled off gleefully after her Frisbee. If I hadn't witnessed her progress and that of many of her canine companions with whom she shared the pool, I wouldn't have been as convinced about the merits of rehab, especially swimming. Dachshunds, who had recently had back or neck surgery for intervertebral disc disease and could barely move on land suddenly came to life both physically and emotionally once they hit the water. Their eyes brightened and lost the appearance of apprehension, their facial muscles relaxed, their limbs moved with little effort, and they seemed to delight in the feeling of weightless, independent movement that they couldn't enjoy on land. Even after their sessions, these dogs were changed, just as people's spirits are lifted when their disabled bodies re-learn movement and gain strength and confidence. As Dallas' strength increased, she soon became competitive, trying to race other dogs for their rubber ducks, balls, and Frisbees. She didn't stand much of a chance against Labrador Retrievers or other water dogs, but sometimes she beat a Dachshund or a Beagle, relishing in her victory until the other dog stole the toy away from her again.

While I was relieved about Dallas' progress and recovery, I also had some fear in the back of my mind that her neck pain and difficulty walking would return. During veterinary school, she had already had one neck surgery for Wobbler's disease—neck instability—and the chance of a recurrence certainly existed. There wasn't much time to contemplate when or if Dallas' neurologic problems would recur as I noticed something new happening with her. Twice in one week, Dallas drank water out of the pool, which she had never done before. At home, she didn't drink any more water than usual, so the pool incident was out of context. However, she had one urinary accident in the house, which was highly unusual for her. I started with blood work and a urine sample. She had a urinary tract infection (UTI), which we could readily treat. Her blood work showed that she had elevated liver enzymes and cholesterol, and a few other smaller abnormalities. It looked like she might have Cushing's disease, which was confirmed after running more tests. The next step was to do an abdominal ultrasound to see if she had the more common form of Cushing's disease (85%)—pituitary dependent hyperadrenocorticism

(PDH)—or the less common (15%) adrenal tumor (AT). It turned out that she had the latter, so we soon scheduled surgery to remove the adrenal tumor, which is not a small deal. The adrenal glands are located slightly above and a bit behind the kidneys, making surgical access to them rather challenging. Messing with the adrenal glands risks myriad dangers and complications, so I enlisted the expertise of Dr. Pike for Dallas' surgery, knowing he was Dr. Salmeri's west coast equivalent. He allowed me to scrub in on the surgery and for the first time, I had some trepidation about how things might go for Dallas. However, Dr. Pike made a very challenging surgery look routine, just like an Olympic gymnast makes a somersault between uneven bars look routine. Thankfully, there were no complications and Dallas pulled through yet another surgery with flying colors. The adrenal tumor was benign, as many of them are, and her Cushing's symptoms resolved.

We could now spend time enjoying the warmer weather and some of the dog-friendly beaches. Dallas delighted in treasure-hunting for possible food sources on the beach like seaweed, just as she had in New Jersey where she tried munching on prehistoric-looking horseshoe crab shells. She loved car rides along the coast, extending her nose out the window and sniffing the salty ocean air. She had quickly acclimated to life as a California canine. If only she could surf!

Despite her swim therapy, ocean swims, gentle walks, raised food bowls, and a harness, signs of weakness in her back legs and the pain in her neck returned. We did another MRI and found that her Wobbler's disease had progressed since her first neck surgery. I debated the decision to proceed with surgery, but concluded that Dallas still had gas in the tank and loved life quite a bit. She was not ready to give up, so I needed to get her neck repaired. Surgeons at the specialty hospital did not perform surgery on neurologic cases, so she saw a neurologist who ended up performing her surgery. He also allowed me to scrub in on Dallas' surgery to witness the marvelous miracle. Again, Dallas recovered well and seemed much more comfortable for quite a while. Swim therapy was increased, as was the time I spent with her. She never complained, as dogs rarely do, and was almost always game to go along and do whatever I had on the schedule for her.

One of the biggest thrills she experienced was visiting an elementary school near Lemon Grove in San Diego. The nonprofit Spay Neuter Action Project (SNAP) of San Diego had been asked by the teachers to bring friendly dogs to the school children. We were invited because the SNAP representative knew Dallas loved kids and I figured this outing would be fun for her and great for the kids. A lot of the kids at that school were fearful of dogs, especially big dogs and Rottweilers specifically. One boy asked why my dog didn't bite, as if there must be something wrong with her! He couldn't understand why she was so friendly. I had to explain that most Rottweilers and dogs, in general, don't bite. He was totally confused, yet willing to pet her as she leaned against him and offered him her belly. At one point while I was talking to one group of kids, I looked back to see that another group of kids had surrounded Dallas and everyone was lying on the ground together. As soon as numerous children started petting her, she repositioned herself to maximize the number of hands on her at any one time. She had at least three kids petting her silken black ears, commenting on their velvety texture and how soft her nose was. Many of the kids were feeling and viewing the anatomy of a new species they had never met—a friendly dog—who responded only favorably and lovingly to their inquisitive touch. The only thing that could top the kids' excitement about meeting Dallas was listening to her heartbeat with my stethoscope and then comparing it to their own heartbeats. These kids had never experienced the sound of a beating heart before, much less one of a previously feared Rottweiler. Their eyes widened as they discovered how a dog's heart sounds and realized how similar they both were. I don't think any of the kids felt the same way about Rottweilers after meeting such an amiable ambassador.

As much as I tried to fix all of Dallas' medical and surgical problems, eventually, even her two neck surgeries weren't enough. Her neck pain returned, but this time her MRI didn't show anything that any surgeon or neurologist could fix anymore. It was a severe progression of Wobbler's syndrome pressing on her spinal cord. So many specialists had put their utmost efforts into helping Dallas surgically and medically, but now we would be limited to palliative care in the form of pain meds and steroids. After seven days of steroids and pain meds, I found Dallas in the same position on the floor in San Diego as in the intern house in New Jersey when she perforated her pylorus. This time, my mind skipped over neurologic problems and fast forwarded to a gastrointestinal (GI) upset from the steroids. She had been eating well all week and hadn't shown any sign of GI upset, so this demeanor was a dramatic departure from the rest of the week and even the night before.

I was scheduled to work that Saturday morning anyway, so I quickly packed up both dogs and headed to work. Once at the hospital, we gave her injectable pain meds for her painful abdomen, then they took X-rays of her abdomen to see what was going on inside. I hoped the nervous dog mom in me was overreacting. The X-rays showed evidence of some fluid in her belly, but they didn't spell out a specific diagnosis. We gave her IV fluids and antibiotics, as well as anti-nausea medication, but she declined in front of our eyes. I excused myself early from my shift, left Dijon at that hospital in Rancho Bernardo, and drove Dallas to the specialty hospital, where she had already befriended the surgeons and neurologist on previous occasions. They had an ultrasound, which we would need to further evaluate her painful belly. A sample of her abdominal fluid was removed and examined microscopically, revealing bacteria, which meant she had a septic abdomen again, most likely secondary to a perforation of her stomach or intestines from the steroids—the only thing that had really helped minimize her neck pain. We could try to fix her perforation surgically, but how would we manage her tremendous neck pain without any more steroids afterwards? I vowed that Dallas would only have surgery if there was a good chance of a positive outcome and a good quality of life. For the first time in her life, I doubted that any surgery or post-op treatment or medication could do that for her. But I wasn't ready to let her go. She had enjoyed a great week on the steroids, but I couldn't delude myself to think we could recreate that pain-free existence without them. Her vitals were tanking as I ran through the possible scenarios in disbelief. The surgeon reminded me that I needed to make a decision pronto either way for her.

It was breaking my heart to see Dallas looking so terrible, despite the pain meds and GI protectant meds. I had to be the parent and do the best thing for her. I looked at the surgeon with tear-filled eyes and shook my head "no." No further words were needed. Preparations were made. We moved Dallas outside on a gurney and then onto a blanket on the grass beneath a tree as I tried to hang on to every last moment with my girl, struggling to finalize 12 years of a beautiful partnership. I had to swallow the fear of tremendous loss and push through courageously to do the right thing for Dallas. We had given her more pain meds before going outside, but even so, my tough dog couldn't put up a good front anymore. I cradled her head and rubbed her velvety soft black ears, letting her know how much I loved her and what a wonderful dog she had been. When I tell clients that I understand the pain and anguish that accompanies the excruciatingly difficult decision to say goodbye, I mean I know how it feels like all of the wind has been sucked out of your lungs and you're empty of air and hope. This act of selfless kindness to our companions may be temporarily crippling to us because of its finality. I lay beside Dallas after she breathed her last breath, still warm, with my arm over her neck and my hand between her ears. I kissed her goodbye through blubbering tears and heaving sighs. How could this beacon of light and love suddenly be gone?

The birds chirped outside in the background. New patients arrived at the hospital. Some left with their families. Life was going on all around us. It was hard to understand how this tragedy hadn't forced time and the whole world to stand still. Once I had made the decision to say goodbye to Dallas, I called the vet hospital where Dijon remained, only to have them tell me she could stay there overnight with them so I could go home. There was concern that such a sensitive dog like Dijon might not do well without Dallas. That meant there would be no dog at home, a scenario I hadn't experienced for 12 years. Reluctantly, I peeled myself away from Dallas' still body.

Eventually I drove home only to encounter every reminder of Dallas, including dog beds, toys, and food bowls. I walked by the sliding glass door into my back yard, where Dallas and Dijon played, ran in circles, and relieved themselves. I wished I could have her back with me now just for a moment to enjoy those times. While standing still and contemplating what I wouldn't do to have her back with me again, I felt a warm pressure against both legs at knee level, where Dallas would normally rub against me when she walked by. The sensation caught me off guard, as if a mouse or some other small creature had scurried by. I looked down at my knees, almost expecting to see Dallas again. There was nothing but warmth. Until that moment, I would have dismissed the notion that a deceased spirit can visit us. Yet over the next 24 hours, I also heard the click clack of toenails on the wood floors, even though there was no

81

dog at home. Although I hoped and searched for more signs of Dallas, those visits were her last. I would have to resign myself to the fact that her body was gone, save for her ashes in a cedar box and her paw print in clay. Once it appeared that her spirit was also departed, I would only be able to keep her spirit within me by keeping her memory alive. Filling Dallas' paw prints would be a mighty challenge. She had been the champion of companions, my protector and co-explorer, and a true friend to the end. She had been my inspiration for vet school, surgery, and medicine, my confidante through tough times, and my aging patient whose every boo-boo and ailment I wanted to heal and repair. She made my life so much better than it ever would have been without her. I was grateful for the many years we had together, but devastated that something so wonderful had to end. Her successor, Dijon, who miraculously never missed a beat after Dallas passed away, would be top dog in the house now, offering a very different kind of companionship.

Diagnostic dilemma at Lodi

One of the trickiest parts about veterinary medicine is that cats and dogs are experts at hiding their maladies, however grave or mild they may be. Although it would be a veterinarian's dream, we never hear canine confessions like, "You got me. I ate two pillows, every avocado in the yard, part of the remote control (in an unsuccessful attempt to watch Animal Planet), the birthday cake, which was clearly for me, and then all of the couch cushions, including the zippers." Instead, we hear a relatively vague version of facts from guardians: "Fluffy didn't eat much last night, but she vomited a couple of times today and seems lethargic, which is unusual for her." The list of possible diagnoses for this condition is long, and varies a bit with age. Older dogs tend to develop age-related diseases and get more tumors, while younger dogs often eat something they shouldn't have, aka "dietary indiscretion" or garbage gut.

There are always exceptions to the rule like the 10-year-old yellow Labrador Retriever I saw for similar symptoms as those listed above. A common worry in an older dog would be a more serious disease, such as cancer. Often, pet guardians don't think their older dog is capable of pulling off the same goofy stunts they did when they were younger, so some assumptions are made. Such an assumption almost caused me to miss a diagnosis. The yellow Labrador's owner was convinced that her dog could not have eaten, chewed, or gotten into *anything* naughty. She sang his praises for temperament and behavior, but I asked her for permission to take some X-rays of his belly just to be safe. Lo and behold, I saw the outline of what appeared to be a large rock in his belly! As I approached the X-rays, I thought my eyes were deceiving me, so I needed a closer look. There really was, in fact, a sizable 7-centimeter rock stuck in the dog's intestines. Fortunately, his mom allowed me to perform the surgery to remove it. The lesson I learned from this dog was not to rule out certain things exclusively because of age or a guardian's insistence that their dog could not possibly have eaten something naughty. It's okay to place the possible diagnosis lower on the list of possible diagnoses, but ruling out some things entirely may backfire.

To further complicate the process of accurately diagnosing patients, some diseases that start in organ A only manifest when they are in a completely different location, such as organ B. So began the wild goose chase of a diagnosis for a middle-aged male yellow Labrador-mix dog, "Luke", who presented to the veterinarians at Lodi Veterinary Hospital near Madison, Wisconsin. I was fulfilling my mandatory mixed animal (large and small animals) externship requirement during the summer before my final year of veterinary school. The Lodi veterinarians and staff could not have been more receptive to an inquisitive vet student. They actually welcomed my input and even designated a rubberized, padded horse box stall to house my two dogs during the day while I worked with the veterinarians. Although I was only assisting with Luke's case, he still had such a profound impact on me that I'll never forget him. This boxy-headed young, athletic-looking blonde Labrador Retriever, who should have been bouncing all over the exam room, was feeling lethargic, coughing intermittently, wasn't eating, and had vomited once. Initially, I only got Luke's history secondhand from the veterinarians, who were having difficulty getting straight answers about what had happened in the days before he arrived at Lodi Veterinary Hospital.

On the first day of his hospitalization, Luke's guardians didn't recall him getting into anything. If veterinarians profiled patients, Labradors would be the #1 offenders for polishing off random household goods. Sometimes, we see repeat offenders for whom we wish we could install a zipper for easy access to remove their numerous gastrointestinal foreign bodies. Luke's abdominal X-rays didn't show any signs of a possible obstruction, so that diagnosis seemed less likely. His bloodwork and urinalysis were normal, except for a mildly elevated blood urea nitrogen (BUN), which could either be from dehydration or early kidney dysfunction. His chest X-rays showed a hazy pattern with abnormal whitened areas between the air sacs of the lungs that was not definitive for any one specific disease. This abnormal pattern means that there is a thickening or inflammation between air sacs, making it harder to pass oxygen through the lungs and breathe.

Luke was admitted to the hospital, given IV fluids, IV antibiotics for possible infection in his lungs, and some GI (or stomach) protectants for the vomiting. After 24 hours, he actually looked worse. His family was starting to run out of funds, so they opted not to repeat bloodwork or a urinalysis. Upon further questioning on Luke's second day in the hospital, they explained that they had recently purchased a recreational vehicle (RV) and suddenly recalled that Luke may have gotten into something while they were cleaning it up, but they weren't sure what it could have been. As they recounted this story, they also remembered that he had been drinking a lot of water, a fact they had not shared during initial questioning, and they thought he might have coughed up the water. Neither the history his guardians told us, nor his physical exam, nor his bloodwork provided further clues to solve the mystery of his diagnosis.

By day three, Luke looked even worse. When his family visited this time, they further recalled what he had been drinking: toilet water in the newly purchased RV. One of the Lodi veterinarians questioned the family about anti-freeze in the RV's water lines, which is used to prevent the water from freezing during the cold Wisconsin winters. They nodded in disbelief and asked if the veterinarians thought a small quantity of anti-freeze in the water could make Luke sick. At this point, all of the veterinarians were surely feeling sick inside at the realization of what was going on.

Anti-freeze, which contains ethylene glycol, is highly toxic and most often lethal to animals even in minute quantities. It rapidly destroys the kidneys' ability to function. If diagnosed very soon after ingestion, it can sometimes be successfully treated, depending on the dosage. Veterinarians used to routinely use 100-proof alcohol, usually vodka, administered intravenously to treat these cases, but the treatment is not without risk, as the side effect of too much or too rapid an infusion could be death as well. What makes ethylene glycol toxicity cases so challenging is that pet guardians often don't realize until it's too late that their cat or dog has ingested it and the lab work isn't always clear cut, especially in the early phase of the disease. Diagnostics and treatment can also be costly. Most veterinary clinics didn't stock the 2-PAM antidote due to its prohibitive cost and the relative infrequency with which it was used. Since that summer, it has even been discontinued. Instead, veterinarians may have 100-proof vodka locked up in their drug lockbox for this very reason.

Upon further probing, Luke's family recounted that he initially sniffed around the RV and was seen taking a few drinks out of the toilet. A couple of days later, he started drinking copious amounts of water out of the RV toilet. Soon thereafter, he became very sick and was then brought to us. Ethylene glycol ingestion itself can cause polyuria/polydipsia (PU/PD), which is increased urination and increased water consumption, respectively. His initial few sips would have been sufficient to start causing kidney damage, which could make him thirstier, thus leading to even greater thirst for the toxic toilet water. Anti-freeze has a sweet taste to animals, so it doesn't act as a natural deterrent, unlike some toxins. Cats are particularly prone to fatal encounters with anti-freeze because its toxicity is based on weight and they are generally much smaller than most dogs.

Luke's family wanted to know for sure that he had an ethylene glycol toxicity and wanted to treat him accordingly. The Lodi veterinarian explained that we had long passed the crucial timeline for diagnosing and treating, so instead they recommended that we repeat blood work and a urinalysis to reevaluate his kidney function. Both kidney values, the BUN and the creatinine, were now through the roof. His urine-specific gravity, which indicates whether the kidneys can concentrate an animal's urine, was very low. This poor concentrating capability means the kidneys are not able to rid the body of many wastes, and instead produce diluted urine. These toxic waste products that are now circulating throughout the body instead of being excreted through the kidneys cause stomach upset and even gastric ulcers. Initially, when an animal goes into kidney failure, the kidneys produce excess amounts of urine (polyuria or PU), but as the disease progresses and the kidneys shut down, they produce very little or no urine (anuria).

The cough we had witnessed and the abnormal lung X-rays were most likely early signs of uremic pneumonitis, which is an uncommon manifestation of inflammation in the lungs from end-stage kidney disease. Additionally, Luke now had calcium oxalate monohydrate crystals in his urine, which is another common finding with ethylene glycol toxicities. It takes some time for these crystals to form, so they are rarely found in a urinalysis during those crucial first 12 hours after ingestion of the toxin. Once we knew that we had missed the short window for antidotal treatment and that Luke had end-stage kidney failure and was not responding to IV fluid therapy, it was time to make some very difficult decisions. His kidneys were crystallizing. The air sacs in his lungs were thickening and making each breath difficult. His family had used up all of their funds to hospitalize him and treat him, so considering dialysis therapy, which costs thousands of dollars and would have meant transporting him out of state for treatment, was out of the question. Even if they had been able to make this final attempt, the prognosis would still have been grave.

As they decided to end his suffering, Luke's family gathered around him to say their final goodbyes. He could no longer lift his sweet blonde head or even wag his thick tail in recognition of his family. His warm brown eyes had become dull and lifeless. Even though everyone knew that humane euthanasia was the kindest thing we could do for Luke, there still wasn't a dry eye in the house as he slipped into his final sleep. Seeing his grieving family grappling with the shock of his passing, I couldn't stop wondering how we could have saved him. Those what-ifs keep many veterinarians awake at night. His situation and its helplessness led me to further investigate the details of ethylene glycol toxicities and write up his case as my externship report. The only conclusion I could draw after more research and consulting with the veterinarians at Lodi was that time and a lack of the facts were the enemies for Luke. Although Luke's case was one of the more difficult ones during my externship at Lodi Veterinary Hospital, there were many more uplifting cases with positive outcomes.

Life at Lodi

My preconceived notions of working in a mixed animal veterinary hospital were quickly disabused. Ontario Veterinary College (OVC) demanded that its students become experienced, if not proficient in handling, diagnosing, and treating both large and small animals. While I often questioned the years spent studying the reproductive cycles of horses, cows, sheep, and goats, and how to maximize bovine milk production, I am grateful for the time I spent getting to know these animals and the people who care for them up close and personally. To a Wisconsin dairy farmer in 2002, a Canadian veterinary student, who was a vegetarian, was not only an oddity, but also a bit of an irksome enigma. As soon as I was introduced by the Lodi veterinarians, the dairy farmers would comment on the Canadian government's milk subsidies, as if I had personally levied them. Usually, I could laugh off the teasing that ensued and just focus on the cows. What surprised me most during that externship was the discovery of how wonderful cows are.

Even though I had grown up in the country and had seen cows, steers, and bulls in fields, I never really interacted with them. During vet school, I came to realize that they are very affectionate and social animals, who prefer to lick, rather than kick people. After the hundreds of cows I worked with that summer, I was only kicked once while administering an intramuscular antibiotic injection. Considering the sheer size and strength of that cow, she could have broken some bones if she had tried, but I just got a little scrape. As a needle-phobe myself, I didn't blame her for her response to what was probably an uncomfortable injection, even if I tried the usual tricks to mitigate its sting by pinching her skin and using the smallest sized needle possible, which is tricky to do on the thick skin of a cow without bending the needle. It turns out that cows are the most forgiving and peaceful souls, especially considering what they often endure.

The vast academic investment of time didn't adequately prepare me for the large numbers of beautiful and sweet cows I would meet and try to help that summer at each farm. The science of farming has moved away from individual animal health to herd health due to the sheer volumes of animals kept at most large production facilities. There is a reason that many of these farms are called factory farms. Just as factory workers are often on autopilot to "produce," so are the animals who live on factory farms. The complex physiological disease processes we had learned about in school were now daily manifestations, many of which were simply the result of excess stress and strain being placed on the cows to produce tremendous amounts of milk.

The dairy farmer's goal for his milk-producing cows is to produce large volumes of milk. If a cow were simply allowed to graze in a field and had access to water, once she became pregnant and gave birth to her calf, she would produce about 25 gallons of milk in a day, which would suffice to feed her calf. It is not uncommon for dairy farmers to have a goal of their cows producing 50 gallons of milk per day. This doubled production from what a body is intended to produce has been made possible by manipulating the cow's conversion of feed into milk, and also by keeping the cows pregnant for the majority of their lives to prolong milk production. Becoming pregnant in the dairy cow world is not entirely dissimilar to a fertility clinic for women, with the main exception being that cows are not usually given fertility drugs and women aren't regularly probed rectally to check their ovulation cycles. Cows endure countless rectal palpations by veterinarians and dairy farmers before, during, and after pregnancy, and especially prior to artificial insemination to determine optimal timing. Once their milk production declines below an acceptable level, which varies by farmer, the Madison farmers would say that the cows would be "sent to Milwaukee," which was a euphemism for being sent to the slaughterhouse to be turned into hamburger meat. As devastating as this decision tree was, I appreciated the honesty of dairy farmers. They would state exactly how much they could afford to spend on medical care so they could decide—hamburger or help 'er.

Some of the most exciting farm calls were for cows having difficulty delivering their calves, a condition called dystocia. Although I did not joyfully embrace the large animal portion of the externship at first, by the end of the first week, I had volunteered to be on call to gain more experience. Delivering calves whose mothers were having birthing difficulties was daunting, but exhilarating. As often as possible, we administered an epidural, similar to those given to women who are in labor, to facilitate a successful and less painful delivery. I had learned how to give an epidural injection, which is injected into the lower part of the spine, on surgical cases of anesthetized dogs during vet school. By contrast, dog skin is like supple papier maché and the distance from their skin to their spine very short. A cow's skin is thick and tough, so penetrating it with a needle that is thick enough not to break without causing pain is no simple feat. Lidocaine, a local nerve block, administered bit by bit as the needle passes through the skin and into the muscles, helps numb the sting if given slowly enough. Cows who are straining and struggling to pass their calves don't usually remain motionless, so administering epidurals becomes a bit of a dance routine following the motions of the bellowing cow to prevent the epidural from going astray. At times, even with an epidural, we had to assist the births not just with hands and arms, but also with chains that we wrapped around the unborn calf's feet to help pull them out. The physical strength in conjunction with the anatomic knowledge required to assess the calf's position in the birth canal were tremendous. After my first successful solo epidural delivery, I was euphoric. Seeing the slippery fur-covered little black newborn calf wobble to his exhausted but relieved mother was incredibly rewarding.

Another common call we received that started as a "cow off her feed" (not eating well) was the Left Displaced Abomasum (LDA) cow. The abomasum is one of the four chambers of a cow's stomach. In high-producing milk cows, there is a tendency for the abomasum to fill up with excessive amounts of gas, which is a by-product of the feed they eat. As the abomasum continues to fill up with excess gas, it can stretch and rotate abnormally from the cow's right to her left side. We diagnose this condition with a physical exam when we see a balloon-shaped enlargement on the left side of a cow's abdomen. By listening to the cow's stomach with a stethoscope and simultaneously flicking a finger on the distended portion of the abdomen, we can determine if there is significant internal gas distension when we hear a "ping" sound. It sounds like a tight drum. This practice of listening or ausculting for pings translates well to small animal practice when bloat or a Gastric Dilatation Volvulus (GDV)—a bloated and twisted stomach—is suspected. Once diagnosed, the only treatment for an LDA with a favorable outcome is surgical correction.

For anyone who hasn't witnessed surgeries "in the field," they are life-changing experiences. Whereas in vet school, sterility is of paramount importance and general anesthesia is the preferred analgesic for most surgeries, a different reality exists in the field with large animals. Cows are sedated, but not fully anesthetized, so that they are still standing during an operation. The sedation relaxes them and provides some analgesic (pain medication). Even at the vet school, general anesthesia for cows was a tricky proposition, often only used as a last resort. It slows down the gut motility or natural movement and flow of their digestive tract, which is crucial for their health and can lead to catastrophic metabolic disturbances if not managed intensively.

We administered, via numerous injections along the intended vertical incision line, a nerve block of lidocaine down the cow's right flank. This nerve block needs to penetrate every layer of skin and muscle that will be cut, which is quite deep. While the local nerve block numbs the flank, the "surgery suite" is prepared. A wooden board perched atop two hay bales serves as the "tray" for the surgical instruments. A sterilized surgical pack is opened on top of the tray, covering the hay. Sterile preparation for the veterinarian involves washing hands and arms in a bucket of chlorhexidine solution. Instead of short, snug sterile latex surgical gloves that extend over the wrists, sterilized rectal palpation sleeves that extend to the shoulder are used and clamped onto the shoulders of the veterinarian's coveralls. Just when it seems like there might be a truly sterile moment, a crosswind through the barn blows a shower of hay down from the open loft above onto the surgical instruments. Rinsing them in the aforementioned bucket that is now slightly less clean helps a bit. As for light, there is often a dangling lightbulb nearby, so surgery proceeds more by feel than by sight. A sterile drape is placed around the previously blocked line on the cow's right flank. An incision is made through the skin and muscles with the hope that the block is truly effective. Once the muscles are spread open, there is access to the entire abdomen, like opening a closet door and all of the clothes spilling out. There is also quite a bit of blood from the skin and muscles, but these bleeders are usually superficial and are stopped by the pressure of the arm that leans on them while passing into the abdomen. By sliding one arm through the incision from the right side of the abdomen to the left and bypassing all of the other organs and intestines, the veterinarian can verify the position of the LDA. To mistake any other part of the stomach or intestines for a ballooned abomasum would be catastrophic because the next step involves blindly piercing a hole through it with a tube-like angled wide-bore needle, a trocar, to release the gas. If any other organ is punctured with the trocar, the contents of the intestines spills into the abdomen and causes sepsis. Before successfully penetrating the abomasum, the veterinarian must cover the trocar without puncturing herself or any other organs en route to the abomasum. Once the abomasum has been identified, pierced, and deflated, it must now be pinched off and manipulated without dropping or spilling the stomach's contents, and re-positioned back to the right side of the abdomen, where it is sutured into place (pexied) to stabilize it onto the right side of the abdominal wall to prevent a recurrence. After securing the abomasum in place, the muscles and skin can be sutured back together and the cow can recover. Remarkably, under these conditions, all but one of the cows we performed an LDA surgery on recovered successfully after surgery.

By the time an LDA develops, a cow's metabolic status is already compromised due to the compression of her organs and the decreased blood flow to them, so these cows are at a higher surgical and medical risk. Without surgery, however, cows with LDA will suffer terribly and die. I had mixed feelings about our "saves." I was relieved to help the LDA cows on the one hand, but on the other hand I realized they probably wouldn't need our help if they weren't being pushed so hard physiologically to produce more milk. LDAs are a direct result of this physiologic stress. I pondered this dilemma as the large animal vet and I stopped at a convenience store for coffee after a long day of farm calls and some LDA surgeries. It had not occurred to me that my appearance might be shocking to the general public until the clerk stared at my shoulder. It had a ring of blood stain around it from the perimeter of the abdominal incision into which my short arm and shoulder had been placed. How does one explain such a stain? I was only relieved that we hadn't been performing rectal exams that day or the color of my coveralls would have been different and a lot smellier.

Midway through one of the many LDA surgeries, shoulder-deep in the cow's warm and moving abdomen, alongside the large animal veterinarian and his extended arm, he asked me, "Doesn't this make you want to eat a hamburger?" It was his attempt at vet humor, but I had to reply honestly, saying, "No, I don't think I can eat my patients." I simply couldn't wrap my mind around the concept of treating and then eating a patient.

Although I enjoyed delivering calves and trying to fix LDAs, there was one call to the farm that never sat well with me: the "down cow." To see an enormous, formerly robust animal falling down or unable to stand up is a heartbreaking sight. The cow's soft brown eyes widen as she panics and bellows. Often, cows vocalize in distress and attempt to stand up, but struggle in the process. Footing is commonly slippery from manure and/or urine, further complicating their efforts to move. Veterinarians and dairy farmers employ various methods to help cows get up, mostly without long-term success. Some start off with a pat or a smack on the rump, which, if ineffective may be followed by leaning with both knees into the cow's abdomen, sometimes gently and other times not so gently. Sometimes, they use a cattle prod, which is like a Taser gun. If none of these efforts succeeds, ropes may be placed around the cow to hoist her up. Once a cow has gone down, she usually doesn't have the strength to stand for very long after she has been "assisted" up due to the metabolic inadequacies that tend to cause down cows to remain recumbent. Hypocalcemia, which is an abnormally low level of calcium in the blood, is the main culprit. Being forced to produce excessively high levels of milk sucks the calcium out of cows, causing many to collapse as down cows from this life-threatening condition.

During one farm call, it was clear to the veterinarian that gentle methods would not suffice for this particular down cow. Fortunately, he didn't escalate his methods to kneeing or cattle prodding, or the worst method I've witnessed—pushing a down cow with a bulldozer—which is now illegal in most states. Instead, an IV calcium infusion was started very slowly. The benefit of the infusion, if it's successful, is that it temporarily corrects the precariously low blood calcium that actually caused the down cow to become so weak. The risk of treating them with calcium is that the calcium dose may be too high, even if administered very slowly, because its main side effect is to cause severe bradycardia—an abnormally slow heart rate—which can lead to cardiac arrest. We listened to and diligently monitored the cow's heart rate and rhythm, watching her for any changes. Initially, she appeared a bit brighter and even gave us some hope as she collected her feet and legs under herself. Then, suddenly, her heart rate slowed down dramatically, stopping entirely within a few seconds. I couldn't believe she had literally dropped dead off the tip of the needle—every veterinarian's nightmare. I knew that the effects of our treatment could cure her or possibly kill her, but hoped we would have more of a chance at intervention or reversal. In an outdoor pen filled with tough, strapping men—farmers and veterinarians alike—there was a collective, dark silence. No cardiopulmonary resuscitation (CPR) was administered because it does not seem effective in these cases and is extremely difficult to perform on a 2,000-pound animal. Eventually, the bulldozer was brought out to move her beautiful black and white, but lifeless body. I had to choke back tears and wipe my nose on my filthy coveralls to hide my sadness and sorrow for this poor cow. I started hauling our equipment back to the vet's truck and cleaning up so the veterinarian could spend some time alone with the farmer. It was the only time, and hopefully the last time in my career, that I've literally seen an animal fall off the tip of a needle.

While assembly line workers, machines, and many professionals are ordered to produce more, demanding greater "production" from our cows has cost many their lives with hypocalcemia, LDA, mastitis (mammary gland infection), and foot diseases. I'm not convinced that the mechanization of humans or animals is such a benign undertaking considering the deleterious side effects for both. The case of the down cow that died after calcium infusion later that day provided an opportunity to have an open discussion with the attending veterinarian about the ethics of this notion of production and its possible side effects. He agreed that the dairy cows were being pushed quite hard, but felt the farmers had no other economic recourse but to aim for even higher production goals. As much as I had come to love cows during that summer, I knew it would be too difficult to feel helpless in the face of some of these man-made diseases if I worked with cows and other large animals every day of my career. I would have to focus on working with animals who were considered "worth saving" because of their intrinsic value, instead of the gallons of milk they produced, their first-place purse at the race track, or the amount of bacon sliced from their hindquarters. Aside from some exceptions, most cats and dogs are taken care of because of their intrinsic value.

Toward the end of my externship, I had a chance to help one such dog. "Petey" was in big trouble when I first saw him arrive at Lodi Veterinary Hospital. He was a relatively young Border Collie mix farm dog, who was trembling and showing other neurologic signs like abnormal rapid windshield

97

wiper-like eye movement (nystagmus), drooling, and stumbling. His symptoms had not improved with supportive care that consisted of IV fluids and antibiotics. Based on the veterinarian's notes, his history was unremarkable. However, after losing Luke a few weeks earlier from ethylene glycol toxicity, I remembered that owners' recollections of what their pets truly get into may not be as accurate or imaginative as they could be. For a young dog like Petey to have a brain tumor would be very unusual, so I thought about toxins instead. Living on a farm could present lots of opportunities for trouble. The farm had cows, so there were likely medications—topical, oral, and otherwise—that he could have gotten into. Maybe they had rat poison out, which could explain the terrible neurologic signs, but would also mean his chances of survival were very slim. I decided to risk offending the owner and re-questioned him about Petey's opportunity for toxin exposure. I had to ask him specifically what was on his farm, and by specifically I meant describe the label! Fortunately, I had spent a lot of time on dairy farms by that point in the summer, so I knew what a lot of the preparations and medications looked like.

As I asked about the drugs that I could think of that might cause neurologic symptoms, I questioned the farmer specifically about ivermectin. It is a commonly used antiparasitic medication for large and small animals. However, some dog breeds cannot tolerate even appropriate doses because they have a genetic mutation that allows the drug to cross the delicate blood-brain barrier, which it shouldn't. When ivermectin crosses the blood-brain barrier, it causes abnormal neurologic symptoms, such as those Petey was exhibiting. The breeds that have this MDR1 genetic mutation are mostly Collies and herding dogs like Border Collies, Australian Shepherds, and their relatives. I remembered the motto "white feet, don't treat" when it comes to ivermectin and collies. I was fairly certain that we had an ivermectin toxicity on our hands, but supportive treatment wasn't working, so far. Surely, we couldn't let this young dog die without a fight. It was time to call a lifeline— my toxicology professor back at OVC—to see what he thought of my idea of trying some dimethyl sulfoxide (DMSO), a medication used more commonly for horses, but with some success for ivermectin toxicity. The toxicology professor concurred that there could some benefit with this somewhat unorthodox course of treatment.

As soon as we got the farmer's permission, we initiated treatment on Petey. Sometimes, having a so-called bright idea is an extremely uncomfortable process. Even though the dog would most likely die without treatment and would suffer as his symptoms progressed, there is always the fear of not succeeding, or even of exacerbating the pre-existing symptoms. What good is it to give hope and then to take it away by failing the dog and his guardian? Yet, not to try is to fail outright. Although we weren't asking the owner to trust us to take his dog to surgery, there was still a medical leap of faith that the owner would have to make in an attempt to save Petey's life. For impatient or nervous veterinarians, initiating treatments with low or questionable success rates is a white-knuckle type of ride. Petey's treatment involved injecting a diluted DMSO solution intravenously, so if he had a reaction, we would have limited options to reverse it. Seeing Petey's guardian, a stoic dairy farmer, on the verge of tears increased the pressure to save Petey. He was clearly attached to his young companion and feared for his life. Now was the time to have faith on many levels, but particularly in medicine.

The beauty of Lodi Veterinary Hospital and the veterinarians and staff who worked there was they were small enough and compassionate enough that they could allow me to stay with Petey and monitor him minute by minute instead of making me tend to scut work for many patients at once. By now, I had earned their trust with both small and large animals. They even posted a picture of me suturing a horse's leg from a fence abrasion on their website. I was so lucky to have found a soft landing in a very competitive profession. The more they trusted me, the more I wanted them to be proud of me and to be successful in representing their hospital.

Sitting next to Petey, I placed a hand on his back and tried to reassure him as he trembled and twitched, his world spinning around inside his head. Minutes passed. No change. Self-doubt seeped into my thoughts. What on earth was I thinking that I could be this dog's hero? I was having a hard time accepting the notion that we would never be able to save every animal we treated. But then I noticed that Petey wasn't drooling anymore. Was he just becoming dehydrated or could we be onto something here? Minutes elapsed, while intensely staring at our patient. Then I felt his body's trembling soften to a slow rocking motion. Was he just falling asleep from exhaustion? He rested his head on my lap and as he looked up at me, somewhat bewildered, the eye rolling slowed to a barely detectable beat. His tilted head straightened onto my lap. The sobriety of his spinning world must have startled him because he promptly sat up and slowly stood, wobbly at first. I disconnected his IV fluid line so he could walk freely, signaling the technicians to send over a veterinarian. No one could believe their eyes. As Petey gained momentum, his gait resembled a weak dog more than a drunk dog, which was a huge improvement. Weak we could fix. We let him walk outside as the odor of DMSO wafted throughout the hospital. The chemical-like smell I had found unpleasant took on a more positive olfactory memory now. He could pee on his own and with that burden lessened, he picked up steam, walking back into the hospital. Petey's dad would be so thrilled to see him. He visited his new and improved dog, delighting in Petey's miraculous recovery. Remarkably, he still couldn't believe that Petey had actually gotten into the bad-tasting ivermectin intended for his cows. We were assured that Petey's dad would make it much more challenging for such a smart dog to do such a foolish thing again in the future.

Some of the most important lessons I learned at Lodi Veterinary Hospital that summer weren't just medical facts or surgical skills. Sometimes, hearing a seasoned veterinarian's stories about practicing medicine is better than any classroom education or seminar. "Dr. K.C." shared such an experience with me as we discussed cases one day partway through the summer externship. He regaled me with a tale that started during a very bloody abdominal surgery he had performed on a dog. I nodded eagerly in anticipation, hoping to learn about a fascinating case with a dramatic save. Instead, Dr. K.C. detailed the bloodiness of the abdominal surgery—most likely a splenic mass removal— that resulted in him being covered and soaked in blood from his surgical gown, scrub top, and scrub pants all the way through to his underwear. My eyes widened as I envisioned the dog's precarious condition and Dr. K.C.'s focus to stop all of the hemorrhage. He managed to save the dog, stop the bleeding, and close the dog up without further incident. But that wasn't the point of the story.

What some pet owners may not realize is that veterinarians see emergencies, perform surgeries, and take care of in-hospital sick patients between their regularly scheduled appointments, often trying to overlap and accommodate all of them simultaneously. If you are ever irritated by having to wait for your scheduled veterinary appointment, it could be because your veterinarian is performing CPR on a patient who was just brought in on the brink of death or who needed emergency surgery.

In Dr. K.C.'s case, he tried to sop up all of the blood on himself after the surgery as best he could and changed his shirt and pants before his next appointment. In an effort to absorb the blood that had run down his scrub top and onto his underwear, he used a sanitary pad. In his haste to dart into his next appointment as quickly as possible post-op, Dr. K.C. forgot something that would soon re-surface at an inauspicious time. Donned in his white lab coat, clean shirt, and fresh pants, he was confident that he was ready for his next patient and cheerfully strode into the exam room focused on the dog and his guardian. He bent down several times to examine the dog and stood up intermittently to speak with the dog's owner. Near the end of the appointment, he noticed the owner's demeanor changing as he spoke with her. She was glancing at the floor and then at him as she distanced herself from him inch by inch. The treatment table he was leaning against could no longer hide the forgotten item that had fallen out of his pantleg. At his feet lay the escaped, blood-soaked sanitary pad that must have slid down his pants onto the floor. The dog's owner appeared anxious to wrap up the appointment and exit as her discomfort with Dr. K.C.'s perceived personal hygiene mounted. As he recounted the story, I doubled over in laughter, imagining a very quiet and somewhat shy Dr. K.C. trying to explain away the dubious dropped item to a doubting client, who knew nothing about the surgery he had just performed. It was a reminder to keep one's sense of humor even in the face of ridiculous or impossible conditions and circumstances.

As I drove cross-country with my dogs back to school at the end of the externship, the memories of a Wisconsin summer in my rearview mirror glid by like the lush green hills that I had grown to love. I would miss the Holstein cows that punctuated the rolling hills and filled many barns, and the vets and their staff who had welcomed me into their hospital. If only it weren't so cold, I would have considered returning to work there after my internship.

Vera Heidolph, DVM

Dijon—joie de woof

When I think of Dijon, the song "How Do You Solve a Problem like Maria?" from *The Sound of Music* comes to mind. In their hearts, everyone loved Maria. In practicality, though, she drove them mad at times. Her childlike innocence could test the patience of those who thought she ought to know better or act more grown up. She broke the rules on a regular basis, most often obliviously. Just as you were ready to scold her for misbehaving, she batted her big doe eyes inquisitively, curious to comprehend what the fuss was all about. Dijon shared similarities with Maria. Her joyful state of canine being, or "joie de woof" as I like to call it, was so pure that you often couldn't help smiling just as you were about to scream in exasperation at her antics.

With four petite white feet, slender, long, and springy tan legs, a lean but muscular body, and a soft little white muzzle dotted with pink and black spots topped with two bulging brown eyes, this innocent and darling Boxer puppy quickly captured my heart. Her expressions of excitement or anticipation generally started with the remnant stub of a mutilated tail, which I called her "Happy Meter." She couldn't wag her Happy Meter without her entire back end wiggling rapidly back and forth. Seeing Dijon so overjoyed when she wagged and wiggled and raised her floppy lips, revealing an underbite smile, had a contagious reaction on people and most other dogs. If she was already walking when happiness set in, her gait would change to a prance. If she was already running slowly, she would accelerate to a gallop. Dijon's moods were most often expressed simply and physically. Even when she dreamt, she was running.

Dallas, my Rottweiler, loved being with and playing with other dogs so much, it seemed like a natural progression to expand my canine family to find a companion for her and to have another dog to love. Dallas and I both would have been thrilled with any rescued dog, be it blind, three-legged, or otherwise imperfect, but my opinion was not the final word in this decision. Middle-aged Boxers were deemed "ugly" by the spouse, but I still scoured the East Coast Boxer rescues for a dog that might satisfy his criteria. He insisted that she come from a breeder and had already found one to his liking, which must have meant she was adequately attractive. Dijon was already four months old when we brought her home from the breeder, which should have been a warning sign.

However, it's hard to visit puppies without falling in love with all of them. What's not to love? They are sweet, playful, silly, somewhat gangly, goofy, and so innocent. Puppies make us laugh and smile. They amuse themselves with the simplest of discoveries, like a leaf, a butterfly, or their own tail, if it hasn't been removed. While people read books and sign up for weekend retreats trying to learn how to live in the moment, puppies do it naturally. Watching them explore their world for the first time is exciting and fun because it is a reminder of the many "new" things we take for granted and no longer find exciting. Thunder, wind, and rain, for example, can be exhilarating or intimidating for a puppy, depending on their experience.

At four months old, Dijon was already behind on socialization and basic training. She hadn't been away from her canine pack, so leaving her alone, even briefly, was very difficult for her, and different from my experience with Dallas. Dijon's coping strategy when left alone, was to chew, poo, and pee her way out of wherever she was. Dealing with the sweet little puppy's destructive behavior in response to her separation anxiety became a complex and chronic project for the majority of her life.

I have always maintained that puppies are cute for a very good reason: so we don't lose our patience with them when they do very naughty things. Dijon's cuteness worked well for her in this arena. She seemed genuinely oblivious to many things around her, such as the perils of cars, the presence of food in a bowl when distracted, and the degree of destruction she created when left alone. She earned the nickname Destructo-Dog because of her tendencies to soothe herself by stress-eating objects around her. Doorframes were not an uncommon chew toy. Fortunately, the doorknobs were metal, so she couldn't get very far with them, although I sometimes found knob slobber when I returned home. Furniture, cushions, and the like were fair game, although she soon left couches alone after I placed a mat on them that emitted a high-pitched sound if touched. Just as I constantly had to think of ways to outsmart Dallas when she went through her naughty teenager phase, I tried to find creative solutions to discourage Dijon from being afraid of being alone or thinking I was never coming back again. I was hopeful that positively motivated, brief crate-training and basic obedience training would help make her feel safe and give her confidence, respectively. Judging by the number of allegedly "chew-proof" towels, blankets, and mats that she chewed up in her kennel, she was still expressing some kind of anxiety. Dallas had been a very content canine for the brief training period when she was in her kennel and in general, so this resistance to crate-training was a new phenomenon for me. I alternated between trying the kennel versus a free-range setup, confined to one room, usually the kitchen. One could choose what would be destroyed—towels and mats or a doorframe. It didn't matter if she had a most interesting and tasty treat in the kennel with her. There would be a casualty. Just when I thought she would outgrow these puppy behaviors, I witnessed more debris that was once a solid object. If she had been an artist, we could have created a new genre of dog art called De-Constructionism. She was a pioneer in the art of distressing ANY object of her frustration.

Fortunately, the severity of her destructive ways decreased somewhat over time. However, when she was four years old, I made the mistake of giving her free range in my house while I stepped outside to visit my neighbor on the other side of the street for a chat. From across the street, I could still see Dijon's dainty little white feet perched upon the window sill and her pink, black, and white nose pressed against the window pane. Surely, she had no valid reason to fear that I was abandoning her when she could clearly see me with her own eyes. I was too shocked to react to the mess that awaited me upon my return after only 15 minutes outside, well within her sight. She had completely dismantled a heating pad and its cover that was luckily no longer plugged in. My aching back would miss the comfort of the heating pad, but my mind was more concerned with what its consumption could mean for Dijon's digestive tract as I picked up crushed coiled wires and plastic pieces. I had visions of her abdominal X-rays lighting up with metal pieces resembling Christmas tree ornaments. But that ruination was not insult enough. My "dramatic" absence in Dijon's mind must have literally scared the poop out of her because she left some lovely presents of the fecal variety near the window where she was watching me. Those delicate little white feet had pranced right through it all repeatedly across the pink carpet. It was like a child painting herself out of a bathroom brandishing a dirty diaper.

If it sounds like a mother complaining about her errant child, I may be guilty, but these descriptions aim to depict how lovable Dijon was despite her imperfections. They should also offer hope to anyone who has endured a dog's destructive deeds. It's easy to become frustrated and annoyed by a dog's behaviors that stem from separation anxiety. In retrospect, I wish I had initiated anti-anxiety medication for her and started her on behavior modification earlier, two suggestions I would now offer to clients.

While Dijon detested my departures, she was also particular when it came to choosing a perfect potty place. In New Jersey, she found the grass, beach, and wide sidewalks with greenery adequate for her bathroom needs. In New York City, however, she could not acclimate to the slim city pickings when it came time to relieve herself. I recall walking for blocks and urging her to do her thing with the usual prompts and words of encouragement. Figuring the walk was in vain, we returned home, only to find her freshly wiped paws padding in delicate circles on a Persian rug inside the co-op, as she finally felt a pleasing sensation beneath them and promptly relieved herself. That rug had become a target—first for Dallas' explosive diarrhea bouts and then several stubborn indoor relief preferences by Dijon. I wasn't sad to part with the rug during divorce proceedings!

Dijon was such a delicate flower, so her care required more patience and dedication than I might have anticipated. The destructive habits were usually mitigated by strenuous exercise. Rollerblading with her was the most physically challenging activity I could offer because my running speed would not even have resembled a warm-up for her. Ideally, when she could run off-leash, she burned off anxious energy the best. However, her off-leash recall was spotty in her younger years, in spite of expensive and ineffective training away from home, so there were limited opportunities with fenced-in and secured dog-friendly off-leash areas. The beach was not ideal because she could run away so fast that she would be on the road in a minute. I worked on her off-leash training to help her expand her geographic running range. She was better with another dog to entertain her or chase her and play with her.

She had some habits that inadvertently didn't always bode well with other dogs.

Observing her playing with other Boxer puppies when she was young was enlightening with respect to her innate Boxer habits. Those Boxer puppies literally boxed with each other, albeit in a playful fashion. Boinging up and down like coiled springs, their hind legs provided a trampoline-like bounce as they rhythmically pummeled each other, alternating left and right front paws without so much as a yelp or a whine. Somehow, they just knew the right amount of punch to pack in those rapid-fire blows. No one got hurt and they delighted in this level of play. Dijon's prancing resembled an athletic horse's delicate yet powerful and measured movements, while her full-out galloping resembled a mustang in flight. So many of her natural attributes were expressed in a very physical way.

Unlike Dallas, Dijon's dining habits were rather frustrating for the first nine-plus years. Eating was an afterthought to be considered only when she was finished playing, running, exploring, and fretting. Almost every time I observed her starting her meal, she would look up after taking a few bites only to follow a butterfly outside, a shadow on the floor, or a ray of light reflecting on her water bowl. She might have had an attention deficit, which also made her basic obedience training a challenge. Food was not a great motivator for her, unlike Dallas, who would have climbed a small mountain for some treats.

Trying to get inside Dijon's head was something that occupied a lot of my time and energy for the majority of her life. For a dog who dreaded departures, she was as clingy as one might imagine. She usually followed me from room to room, but I suspected it was more to ensure that I didn't leave the house, rather than to bask in my presence. She did sleep on the bed with Dallas and me. Often, there was little remaining real estate for me, but with those two poochies snuggled on my bed, I was quite content. The presence of another dog was some comfort to Dijon. Dallas was the playmate that I could never be. Sometimes, their play sounded like lions wrestling with one another, although they never hurt each other. Dallas taught Dijon the art of the playful hip check, which she would later teach Bosco, who would use this move to rough-house with other dogs. Once I realized I would never fully understand Dijon's complex eccentricities, I was just content providing her with canine companionship and socialization with people whenever possible.

One rather amusing people encounter with both dogs occurred when I started vet school. The owner of the house I bought needed to stay in the house for the first couple of weeks after I moved in, so I agreed to live in her basement during this time until she could move out. Moretta was an elderly woman, somewhere north of 80 years, but still had a youthful love of animals and, specifically, my dogs. I came home from school one day to find no dogs in the basement, which resulted in acute panic. I hadn't seen them in the yard, so I was baffled about their whereabouts. I climbed the stairs to the main level and discovered the door was open before I could even knock and ask for permission to enter. When I called for Moretta, she beckoned me to come to her bedroom. There, perched atop each of the two twin beds, ears perked up, heads cocked sideways wondering what the next adventure would be, were my dogs! They had invited themselves into Moretta's part of the house and ingratiated themselves into the privacy and coziness of her bedroom. I didn't know if I should laugh or scold them for trespassing. Rather than feeling frightened or intimidated, she was talking to them, petting their heads and telling them stories as if she were putting her own grandchildren to bed. It was a beautiful sight! I was concerned that they might have knocked her over in their excitement to come play with her, but they had miraculously tempered their enthusiasm for this elderly woman. It was such a sweet sight to see these two large and powerful dogs basking in Moretta's attention and being as subdued as they could be with her while she petted them and talked with them.

Watching my dogs interacting so gently and naturally with Moretta inspired me to seek out some opportunities for them to visit residents of a nursing home on a regular basis. Dallas would have a chance to get extra ear rubs and back rubs, Dijon could have some of her curious energy channeled, and we could offer some positive dog-time to residents needing some extra companionship. It would be a new experience for all of us. As a bit of an introvert myself, I was unsure of the best way to initiate such interactions at the nursing home, but as is often the case, my dogs led the way in socializing between all parties. It turned out that they easily had more social graces than I do and didn't have some of the human hang-ups that prevent people from communicating with each other more readily. Although I had some reservations about Dijon being able to dampen her exuberance so she wouldn't knock down any frail residents, she impressed me with her calm demeanor in their presence. She settled in right away, kept all four paws on the ground, and just let people love on her while basking in the attention. I knew Dallas would do well because of her natural affinity for anyone who paid attention to her and from her many experiences with people of all sizes, shapes, and ages in New York City.

What I hadn't anticipated was the impact my dogs might have on some of the nursing home residents. I just hoped Dallas and Dijon would provide a pleasant distraction and a bit of conversation. The interactions turned out to be about a lot more than just petting dogs and chatting about the weather. Most people at the nursing home communicated with Dallas and Dijon to some degree. However, there were a couple of reticent residents who seemed unmoved by their presence or anyone else's. I inquired with the staff about what to do or whether the visit with my dogs was an appropriate idea. They explained that some residents had not spoken to anyone for months and others were taciturn most of the time. Instinctively, Dallas and Dijon interacted differently with those people without me ever instructing them to do so. They would just park themselves beside their chair and lean against them, waiting patiently for a hand to land on their head or back, while looking up calmly at the individual. This befriending effort didn't always succeed the first time, but one by one, the individuals started to warm up to Dallas and Dijon. Some of the men, who were initially silent, spoke directly to my dogs, telling them stories about a dog they had loved in their younger lives. By the end of the stories, Dallas had usually wiggled her head onto their lap while gazing into their eyes. It was a connection I wished everyone could witness, especially those who had a bias against Rottweilers. She brought several people, but especially men, to tears on more than one occasion. They just trusted her and felt her confident and caring soul. I didn't realize Dallas and Dijon would prove to be so therapeutic to so many people.

Most people marveled at the velvety texture of Dallas' ears and Dijon's athletic build, while recalling wistfully the dogs in their lives. Petting the dogs seemed to ease any discomfort they had about speaking or interacting. Fortunately, both Dallas and Dijon relished their visits and could barely be held back each time we returned to the nursing home. Although Dijon was a dog whose physical being seemed to be the main expression of her emotions, those quiet and tender hours of peaceful interactions actually calmed her down. Not only did my dogs love the visits, but several people at the nursing home who weren't "dog people" before, became fans and signed up to have a visit from the dynamic duo of Dijon and Dallas. Those who were initially hesitant to meet them cited fear of dogs as their reason. When they saw how much fun the other residents had with Dallas and Dijon, they wanted in on the visits, too, especially because some of them rarely had family members visit them. When I think of the loneliness that some people in the home felt and how my Dijon suffered from separation anxiety, I wished there could be a program for such dogs to hang out at a nursing home during the day while their guardians worked or went to school, so they could keep each other company. In the same moment of imagining that utopian scenario, I quickly snapped back into the reality of what Dijon might be capable of and envisioned her leading a wheelchair-bound elderly gentleman on a leash at full tilt down a hallway and careening out of control. There would have to be some supervision!

As we got to know some of the people living in the nursing home a bit better, I heard some of their stories. They explained why they were there. In some cases, they weren't completely willing. Several were forced to give up their beloved pets because the home did not accept them. Part of the depression for those individuals was losing the last member of their family that they still had. It was the final straw during a time of life when they could really have used companionship and unconditional love, be it on two or four legs. When I inquired about these rules with the management, they confirmed them and explained that they were standard rules for most nursing homes because they couldn't be managing geriatric patients and their pets. When I asked if they had considered having staff for pets if the residents could pay for dog walkers and similar assistants, they did not have an answer.

In addition to visiting one of the local nursing homes, I sought other methods to engage, entertain, and build confidence in Dijon. The next step was enrolling her in agility training, which was another new and fun adventure and an outlet for her energy. I didn't bring Dallas along for this training because she was still recovering from her second knee surgery. I hadn't seen any miracles from Dijon in obedience training, so I had limited expectations for agility training, even though she was very athletic. Dijon often feared new things, so I worried that she wouldn't want to jump through a suspended tire or venture through a collapsible nylon tube. She loved jumping over things, so that part was easy if she was focused. She could clear a 5-foot fence from a standstill, so I hoped that ascending a wooden plank at a 45-degree angle wouldn't be difficult. Dogs, unlike people, don't usually grow up playing on teeter-totters, so I wondered if that strange sensation of the plank dropping down would be especially unsettling. I considered Dijon's weaknesses and aimed to encourage her to try something new without pushing her to do something that she was not comfortable doing.

It was encouraging to see Dijon build her confidence over time with agility training. She probably would have liked a bit more play time interspersed with the training time, but there was not too much fooling around. Many participants were quite serious about the training and competed with one or more of their dogs. If Dijon had not demonstrated a natural curiosity for or interest in this type of activity, I would have stopped after the first session. However, she became animated with little squeals of delight as we approached the building and would tug on her leash eagerly as we walked inside.

Two years later, I indulged in a Dijon-week so we could spend time together. We drove to Stowe, Vermont to try out Camp Gone to the Dogs. At the time, I didn't know anyone else who had gone to a camp that catered to dogs but thinking back on my camp days as a kid, it sounded like a great idea. The brochures promised lots of agility training, tons of dog-friendly activities all day long, a beautiful setting at the foot of the northern Green Mountains, and the ability to take your dog with you everywhere you went. After paying so much attention to Dallas and her medical needs, it was time to show Dijon some extra love that didn't involve medical attention. It was exhilarating to see so many dog-crazy people and to know I wasn't the only one! Dogs of all types attended, just like their unique owners.

Dijon enjoyed visiting with the dogs we encountered at the camp, provided they weren't too busy obsessing over their own activities or toys. It was rewarding to see her enthusiastically take on a new agility course like it was no big deal from the first day. I didn't push her, but by the second day, I had to hold her back to slow her down. A cool mountain-fed river ran along the edge of the camp property. Although Dijon wasn't an avid swimmer, she loved splashing and running in the river. Once she befriended another Boxer, it was like she had found a long-lost sibling who fully understood her. They romped, chased, and frolicked foolishly and freely in the fields and in the river. By the end of the day, I was ready for bed before she was, only imagining that her doggie diary might read, "Great day!" In addition to meeting new friends and trying out more agility courses, Dijon discovered another new activity.

Campers and their dogs were lined up for something I had never heard of called lure coursing. It involves a white plastic bag, which dogs perceive as a chasable object, attached to ropes on a motorized pulley system that runs along the ground in a large triangular shape over a one-acre area. Dijon remained relatively calm as we waited in line, as she had already had some running and playing time earlier in the day. Dozens of dogs, however, even the well-behaved dogs, could barely contain themselves. They were so antsy to let loose and chase after the seemingly unobtainable object. By the second time around, Dijon was one of the frothing-at-the-mouth dogs eager to engage in a high-speed chase. Her shoulder muscles quivered, her nostrils flared, and her tongue hung out as she drooled with delicious anticipation. I had finally discovered an activity that fully captivated her attention and let her burn off her energy at top speed. Dijon came alive like never before as she ran after the elusive plastic prize at full throttle. It was the wildest and most content I had ever seen her.

A lot of the dogs lined up for their turn at lure coursing would have liked to do it all day long, but the guardians had to be the brains of the operation because they would have started injuring themselves if we let them race at top speed for hours. It was hard to move Dijon away from the course after we finished. As excited as I was to see her love for this new activity, I was sad that we wouldn't be able to continue with it after camp. The only comparable training or activity would be agility training, which was still a source of entertainment and exercise for Dijon. As far as she was concerned, we could have stayed in dog camp mode perpetually. Lure coursing, agility, playing, constant attention—what's not to love? However, school and Dallas beckoned. I would have to try hard to burn off her limitless energy while keeping her safe.

Fortunately, there was a park near the house with natural barriers, such as the Speed River and an embankment, which kept Dijon safe and well-exercised for her off-leash adventures. People at the park would often ask with great concern why Dijon had a mutilated tail and ears and why Dallas had a mutilated tail. I could only shake my head with remorse and sadness while stating briefly, "ex." Some children would start crying when I explained what been done to both dogs before they came into my life. Cutting a dog's ears and/or tail for cosmetic purposes is illegal in several countries. As an aesthetic procedure, I have chosen not to perform it, just like chopping off cats' toe tips and toenails in the so-called de-clawing surgery. If people saw the gruesome reality of what body part amputations for aesthetics entail, they would most likely NEVER elect to have it done. Most tail amputations on puppies are actually done without any pain medication at all, which is a cruel and unusual practice in itself. I relived the guilt and shame of having a dog whose breeder participated in this practice for Dijon's entire life. Kids questioning me deepened my remorse, but gave purpose to the outings in that it afforded me a chance to educate them on canine care and say how smart they were for noticing something wrong with her.

If it hadn't been for my exercising obligation to Dijon and Dallas, I probably wouldn't have gotten much fresh air. After school, I could rollerblade around my neighborhood at Mach speed with Dijon to help get the beans out. This vigorous romp was then supplemented with an evening walk through the neighborhood with Dallas at a much more sedate pace. After back-to-back lectures and hours of sitting and studying each day, I welcomed the opportunity to spend time with my girls and get outside and exercise. As they navigated the neighborhood with their noses and contributed their own input to local news posts, I geared down, breathed in the cool night air, and delighted in their anticipation and enjoyment of those adventures and sniffing missions. Those walks were therapeutic and soothing—a calming interaction with my dogs that reinforced my dedication to helping ALL animals.

As I contemplated how I could help other animals once I finished vet school, an opportunity arose years before graduation. Because of my interest in emergency medicine and critical care, I spent a lot of time in OVC's small animal intensive care unit (ICU). It became evident that, in addition to a constant flow of medical supplies, the patients also desperately needed a reliable and steady flow of blood products. Just as people can donate blood and help save human lives, dogs can help other dogs. It's definitely not for every dog, but I weighed the pros and cons of enrolling Dijon in the blood donor program. Requirements were based on a dog's weight, age, health status, temperament, and blood type. Not only did she meet all the requirements, but her blood type made her a universal donor, which meant it could be used for even more dogs with minimal risk of rejection.

Initially, I thought we could try one blood donation and if she was not amenable, we would stop. To ease donor dogs' anxiety, they were given a mild sedative—valium—before starting, so they wouldn't be nervous and wouldn't be jumping around while they needed to remain calm and still. The sedative helped achieve both the calm demeanor and no bouncing or boxing during the blood draw. As soon as the blood draw was finished, Dijon was offered a bowl of canned food, which she never had at home. My "picky" eater nearly leapt off the treatment table to get her head into the food bowl and chow down. I was amazed by how well she had done. She enjoyed being in the hospital and getting extra attention. She responded well to the sedation, didn't even flinch when her blood was drawn (even though I did a little bit!), and was highly motivated by her canned food reward afterward. Perhaps this was a win-win situation for her and the dogs whose lives she could potentially save.

One whole blood donation could be broken down into a few different products like plasma, platelets, or whole blood. With proper and cooled or frozen storage, it could be viable for weeks or even months until needed. Dogs need blood and blood products for many conditions and diseases. The most obvious is for traumatic hemorrhage, which we saw commonly in the ICU. Dogs getting hit by a car are at the top of the list, as they are often actively bleeding out and need to have their blood supplemented until they can be fixed. Conditions like immune-mediated hemolytic anemia (IMHA) or immune-mediated thrombocytopenia (ITP), in which the immune system attacks its own red blood cells or platelets, respectively, require red blood cells and/or platelets to replenish the cells being destroyed until the condition can be treated and controlled. Patients with certain types of cancer that result in the bone marrow not producing enough red blood cells also need blood products, as do patients with a bleeding disorder, such as hemophilia, which can be found more in male Doberman Pinschers, for example. Seeing patients arrive at OVC's ICU at death's door and ultimately leave in better health with the help of blood products, sometimes even Dijon's, was very rewarding. She truly helped save lives.

Over time, Dijon became one of OVC's most celebrated and prolific regular blood donors. She trotted with a spring in her step each time we entered the veterinary teaching hospital—about once a month—and then the treatment area, where her technician friends awaited her with kind words and affection. She play-bowed, spun around, and wagged her Happy Meter rapidly with excitement. She wanted to jump onto the treatment table by herself, but we helped her up to prevent any mishaps. Soon, she no longer needed any sedative. Curiously, though, the diazepam (valium) we had administered a few times had the side effect of increasing her appetite, thus her intense interest in the canned food. Even without sedation, though, she had become so interested in her monthly canned food that she practically jumped off the table for her post-blood donation treat.

Having my own dog enrolled in the canine blood donor program, I became involved in recruiting other students, staff, and friends of OVC to enroll their dogs, too. I preferred the concept of OVC friends and staff bringing their own dogs in for blood donations instead of using Greyhound dogs, who were housed in the school for that express purpose. Some people ended up adopting the Greyhounds once they realized they had been saved from the horrors of the hellish dog racing world, but those living in a vet school still didn't have a home.

Vera Heidolph, DVM

Our blood donor program sponsored a dog walk to spread awareness of the benefits for any dog in the community who might eventually need a blood product. Dijon's life-saving blood continued to help other dogs even after vet school. During my internship at RBVH, a female Chihuahua, who was in terrible shape, needed blood, but the hospital had just run out of blood and there wasn't enough time to start testing staff dogs to see what their blood type was or to source blood from a nearby hospital. I raced home to get Dijon, which was a welcome change in her day. As far as she was concerned, we were heading to the dog park, but even a trip to the vet hospital was okay if she was going to receive attention. We only needed a small amount of her blood for this little dog, and Dijon started immediately looking for her mandatory munchies post-donation. Her blood donation saved the Chihuahua's life. No one handed out medals or trophies for canine blood donors, but I would have liked to award one to Dijon for being instrumental in saving this little Chihuahua and dozens of other dogs.

When she wasn't frolicking, visiting a nursing home, running an agility course, running beside me while rollerblading, demolishing a doorframe, or donating blood, Dijon had a rather curious pastime. Some dogs have strange eating habits like eating rocks, licking their feet, eating tennis balls, or eating their own feces or other animals' feces. The smell of Dijon's obsession was at least pleasant, but still inexplicable and illogical to me. As kids, we would hear adults threaten to wash our mouths out with soap if we used foul language. The thought of soap in our mouths was most distasteful, but to Dijon, it was a delight. She was indifferent to being bathed, but if she caught a whiff of soap in a bathtub and beat you to the tub, she would hop into the tub and start chomping on the entire bar of soap. She licked and chewed on the edges first, as bubbles formed around her lips and gums. Even though I could surgically remove foreign objects from the obstructed intestines of my patients without any difficulty, it turns out it is remarkably challenging to extricate slippery, slimy soap from a Boxer's mouth. As she sped around the house spewing bubbles and foam, it was apparent that this was an exercise in futility. Adding to the challenge of this chase was Dijon's perception that she had captured a coveted object and was now protecting it with her life. When we traveled and stayed in hotel rooms, she immediately scoped out the shower and the tightly wrapped soap, even as I was still unloading the car, only to trot around the room parading her trophy in her foamy mouth. The only redemption of these "mis-capades" was that, miraculously, she didn't manage to swallow the soap.

My house was Dijon-safe with respect to soap, so I didn't realize that there might be a soap situation when we visited my parents' house. They live about two-and-a-half hours from Guelph. Dallas and Dijon loved the visits because of the vast trees and shorefront on Colpoy's Bay. The dogs could run off leash at full tilt, play hide and seek through the woods, and explore to their hearts' content. On one such visit on a damp day, when much of the ground was muddy, I called both dogs back into the house, but before I could wipe off Dijon's blackened feet, she darted for my parents' bedroom and bathroom. By the time I reached her, she had left a trail of muddy, black paw prints across the light carpet and all around the bathtub, up and down, as she must have fumbled and slipped while trying to bite the soap. She was much more sure-footed on the bedspread as she made herself comfy, muddy feet, bubble-lined lips, and all. I closed my eyes in horror, overwhelmed by how much one dog could deface a space in mere moments. I feared my mom would be ready to relegate Dijon to the roof or the moon once she saw her newly decorated bedroom and bathroom. However, the oddity of Dijon's proclivity may have worked in her favor because my mom was stunned and in disbelief that one dog would do such a strange and naughty thing. I quickly removed Dijon from the scene of her crime and promised to clean everything up. This occasion was yet another reason why they make dogs so cute! Meanwhile, as Dijon was dining on soap, Dallas had returned outside and was dominating the compost pile. I'm not sure why we were invited back after that visit, but it must have been because of my dogs' sunshine personalities and my promise to secure the premises and temporarily re-locate tempting bars of soap next time. Also, they never talked back.

When they weren't rifling through foul or forbidden objects, Dallas and Dijon loved to socialize with my parents, especially if we took them for walks. I bundled Dijon up with an extra layer of jackets because she had shorter hair than Dallas. They romped and frolicked in the snow, which reminded me of the fun we had as kids on the coldest days of winter while playing in the snow. Our dog Rex would race around us in circles, urging us to run faster and chase him or be chased by him. He helped us with our sledding or tobogganing by pulling the rope in front of us to propel us even faster down the long, inviting hill. If his guidance wasn't as steady as we hoped, it didn't matter as we flipped over into the ditch, snow filling our mouths, mitts, and boots. The beauty of snow in the country is that it remains white longer than city snow, dog markings aside.

Dijon didn't have a seasonal romping preference, which made her winter experiences in colder climates more enjoyable for her. When we traveled cross-country and found an open field in Wisconsin or miles of secluded beaches in Oregon, she simply galloped with abandon. I couldn't imagine her in any other state than playfully bounding about at every opportunity and expressing her joie de woof. She continued to act and look like a puppy from the outside, even at nine years old. Around that time, she needed to have her teeth cleaned professionally, which would require anesthesia, so in preparation, I took a blood sample, did an electrocardiogram (EKG), and had some chest X-rays done. I was more than stunned to see her EKG clearly demonstrating an abnormal heart rhythm, which I had not heard when I listened to her heart with my stethoscope. Blinking in dismay at what my eyes were seeing, my veterinarian mind raced to the details and ramifications of her abnormal rhythm. While contemplating these thoughts, her chest X-rays were placed in a viewing box for me to analyze. Her cardiac silhouette, or the outline of her heart, was subjectively large, even for a big dog. I knew that athletic dogs, horses, and humans can all have larger hearts than their non-athletic counterparts due to the increased muscle mass, but I also knew that Boxers are predisposed to heart disease. My mind ping-ponged back and forth between the pogo stick active dog and her obvious EKG abnormality. It looked like Boxer arrhythmia. I contacted a local cardiologist, Dr. Orvalho at UC Davis, for an appointment and an echocardiogram (an ultrasound of her heart). Her dental was postponed so we could first focus on her heart. After working closely with cardiologists at NC State and hearing the same diagnosis and prognosis for many other dogs, it was still a bitter pill to swallow that my dog had heart disease.

The greatest incongruity of her diagnosis was that Dijon lived to run and play. Her unfettered and full-out flow of limbs accompanied by quivering nostrils and lips seemed to be the manifestation of her greatest joys and delights. How could my highly athletic companion be saddled with a condition that could, at best, reduce her energy level or, at worst, kill her? I kept shaking my head in disbelief as I worried about her life being cut short by her most important vital organ misfiring.

Her diagnosis at the age of nine was disconcerting, especially when considering most Boxers have a life expectancy of nine to twelve years, with twelve being generous. I reverently followed every recommendation Dr. Orvalho made, and immediately trusted him to keep Dijon safe and happy. Her examination was followed by a 24-hour Holter monitor, which consisted of her wearing a vest Velcroed around her chest to cover the EKG sticky tabs on her skin. The Holter monitor results confirmed the diagnosis of Boxer arrhythmia, meaning that her heart was having a significant number of abnormal beats over a 24-hour period. The goal with this kind of heart disease is not necessarily to never have another abnormal heart beat, but rather to minimize the frequency of abnormal heartbeats and the heart rate at which they occur. Mammals are quite dynamic in their activities and movements, so our hearts are uniquely capable of accommodating changes in body position, state of hydration, heart rate, blood pressure, and breathing rate. This brilliant capability keeps us alive in many extreme circumstances like running for our lives or temporary starvation, for example. The snag with Boxer arrhythmia is that it can occur very quietly, at rest or at play, and an irregularity of heart beats, if severe enough, can result in failure to deliver enough oxygen to the brain. The higher the heart rate when this arrhythmia occurs, the worse it is because it means that the heart doesn't have enough time between heart beats to fill up again and push out an adequate amount of blood to reach the brain and the rest of the body. A few abnormal beats at a low heart rate may not cause a noticeable or significant problem. As the disease progresses over time, the number of abnormal heart beats in 24 hours can increase, as can incidences of tachycardia (faster than normal heart rate). If the brain doesn't receive ample oxygen, a dog can faint. As long as the heart quickly resumes beating normally and breathing continues, a dog can recover from such a fainting episode, also known as a syncopal episode.

If the syncopal episode is severe enough and the heart does not resume beating normally again, a dog with cardiac arrhythmias can die. This was my new fear for Dijon, replacing the fear of her being hit by a car while running at full tilt. Should I even let her run and play, which could possibly result in a fatal fainting episode? These fears are the normal concerns of a dog guardian. The cardiologist had workable solutions that would allay my fears and allow Dijon to be a normal dog and express her joie de woof. Dr. Orvalho started her on sotalol, an anti-arrhythmic medication, which she tolerated well. The plan was to monitor her meds and re-check her heart on a regular basis to prevent her heart disease from quietly advancing out of control.

Once I had her heart disease under control, it was time to revisit her dental disease. Now, I was more concerned about anesthetizing Dijon. Fortunately, she had two specialists who could take care of her in the same building: both the veterinary dentist who would perform the root canals that we suspected she needed, and her cardiologist, who calculated her anesthetic protocol. I felt as safe as one feels flying into a storm with a reliable airplane and a highly trained pilot. It's still a storm!

Dijon's team did a fantastic job cleaning and repairing her diseased teeth, from which she recovered quickly. An unexpected benefit of her long-winded dental adventure was pointed out to me a couple of weeks after the procedure while we were at the dog park. More than one dog owner remarked that Dijon seemed perkier and had more pep in her step. She had started showing signs of arthritis before her dental, which had diminished afterward. All the bacteria in a dog's or cat's mouth can travel throughout their body, often leading to infection in the kidneys or liver, or the heart valves (endocarditis). There was no evidence of any of those problems with Dijon, but because bacteria can also invade joints causing inflammation and discomfort, it seemed that she may have suffered from some bacterial spread into her joints, which resolved once her dental disease was treated, bringing back her bounce. It was amazing and reassuring to see so many benefits of taking care of Dijon's teeth and following the advice I give my clients. I had saved up funds for Dijon's root canals by starting months before Christmas to knit everyone's Christmas presents. There were at least 20 handmade projects that helped reduce the Christmas budget that year and enabled me to finance her dental fix. What a worthwhile investment in her health it was!

Over the next few years, Dijon started experiencing other health issues, such as suddenly developing a serious appetite and gaining weight. This physical and behavioral change was such a departure from her regular pattern that I had to investigate the cause. She was first diagnosed with atypical Cushing's disease that eventually became Cushing's disease. Unlike Dallas' Cushing's disease, Dijon's was pituitary-dependent hyperadrenocorticism (PDH), which meant she didn't need to have an adrenal tumor removed like Dallas had. At the time of her diagnosis, medical management with Lysodren or Trilostane was the gold standard treatment. Radiation therapy is now being used for some PDH cases in an effort to reduce or calm down that portion of the pituitary gland that is over-active. The pituitary gland is located within the brain and rather difficult to access, so it has always posed a problem from an anatomic perspective. Fortunately for Dijon, she did relatively well on the medication with lots of monitoring and some adjustments along the way. Cushing's patients require frequent monitoring and periodic adjustments to ensure that they tolerate their medications and don't inadvertently become Addisonian. Addison's disease is the opposite of Cushing's—

hypoadrenocorticism, or inadequate cortisol production—and can be life-threatening.

By now, there was a moderate-sized pharmacy in my kitchen to house Dijon's small suitcase of meds. It just became part of our daily routine, like making coffee or opening the window shades in the morning to let the sunshine in each day. Her medication regime kept her heart beating normally, her joints functioning smoothly, and minimized excess cortisol production. Once she reached the point of needing two birthday candles on her dog-friendly birthday cake to celebrate her double-digit age, she was becoming stiffer as is commonly the case with Cushingoid dogs. They often experience an exacerbation of underlying osteoarthritis because the ligaments and muscle fibers loosen and joint stability decreases, causing abnormal micro-motion within the joints, which, in turn, results in inflammation and discomfort.

As I debated how to help and improve Dijon's comfort, I was introduced to cold laser therapy and pulse signal therapy (PST). It sounded a bit hopeful, but my expectations were modest. She had already had a couple of steroid injections into her stifle joints (the equivalent to human knees), which were the main areas of discomfort and osteoarthritis, and had enjoyed mild momentary improvement. Because her condition was not surgical, I had to become resourceful with other modalities of therapy. After her first cold laser therapy treatment, I took her outside for a potty break and witnessed her prancing with a renewed lightness on her feet. I was amazed and overjoyed with her improvement. After a few more treatments and more progress, I took her to a wide-open nature preserve and let her romp and roam as she hadn't for months. She and Bosco raced each other in circles, chasing and edging the other on, slaloming around the tall mounds of grass that had just been fed by a rare southern California rain. They practically quivered with joy as they rounded each corner without slowing down, tongues hanging out and limbs stretched to their fullest with each stride of their gallop. If they had been horses, there would probably have been some whinnying and bucking. Dijon's joie de woof was back in its purest form again! A small part of my brain wondered if she should be exerting herself to this extent in light of her heart condition, but a greater part knew she needed to run free. Her gamboling and galloping were proof-positive of how much we can improve a dog's quality of life even in the face of multiple diseases and conditions. It was such a relief to see a positive outcome for my sweet girl with all of her meds and treatments.

I wonder if dogs seem to calm down in their clown-like or naughty behavior as they age merely because they have some malady or discomfort that prevents them from indulging in their youthful hijinks. In Dijon's case, some of her naughty puppy behavior and mischievousness returned when I wasn't at home. Finding a bashful Boxer with green foam flowing out of her mouth from an avocado raid wasn't funny for long. Unfortunately, her avocado adventure resulted in one of her many bouts of pancreatitis. This time, it was so serious that she had to be on IV fluids and pain meds. Before we could get an IV line into her, several attempts were made, but no one succeeded because her legs started blowing up. She was losing proteins through her gut, so her legs started swelling. We gave her fluids subcutaneously first to improve her hydration status in the hopes that it would plump up her veins a bit, so we could place an IV catheter. While waiting for the subcutaneous fluids to take effect, she was also on pain meds and anti-nausea meds because she was drooling and licking her lips between vomiting. She looked so miserable. What a relief to get the IV catheter into her hidden vein and start her IV fluid therapy a few hours later. Within a day of treatment, she was back to herself and wondering why she was on the bench and not running and playing with her current housemate and younger brother, Bosco.

Dijon needed more medical supervision than in her younger years, so I left her and Bosco at the vet hospital where I was working, rather than with a friend, when I took a week-long vacation. The staff, which was there 24/7, knew and loved my dogs, so I was confident that they would administer medications diligently and monitor Dijon for any possible complications that might arise day or night. Considering no news is good news, I headed to the vet hospital optimistically to pick up my dogs on my way home from the airport late on a Sunday night, delighted to be reunited with them and have them sleep on my bed soon. Both dogs had weaseled their way into the technicians' hearts, laying on the cute factor quite thickly and encouraging them to play and throw stuffed animals for both dogs to chase. My heart raced with excitement as I entered the hospital, anticipating the energetic reunion that awaited me. No other animals were loose in the hospital as I moved toward their run, so it would be safe to let them out. What joyous expressions they both had when I saw their adorable faces! They stood up and snorted, wagging the remainder of their tails with anticipation, while I bent over to pet them and feel their soft coats and heads leaning against me as they circled me and nearly knocked me over in the run. With tongues rolled out and happy butts wiggling, Dijon and Bosco dashed down the hall through the treatment area and veered toward the food room. Neck and neck, Dijon eyed Bosco as she raced ahead of him toward the treasure trove of food bags. I ran after them, knowing that Dijon had tried this stunt before successfully and had managed to rip open a bag of food with her little stumps of teeth that I thought she needed to save. This time my fleet-footed companions beat me to the food room again by a few seconds. Bosco was only along for the run, so he stood back as Dijon pounced on top of a bag of dog food, straddled the shifting kibble, and looked up at me briefly as I entered the room breathlessly, exclaiming, "Dijon!" Before I could even utter her entire name, her face froze, then relaxed as she slipped down onto her right side as if she had fainted. In slow motion, I realized she was having another syncopal episode. She had had several episodes since she was diagnosed with Boxer arrhythmia five years earlier. Some of those spells had sent me into a frenzy, calling Dr. Orvalho in tears and fearing for my dog's life. None had been so dramatic or extreme.

I called for help, even though I knew Dijon's situation was dire. A technician and another veterinarian came running to help me carry Dijon to the treatment area, where we tried to restart her heart, which had obviously misfired. We intubated her to help her breathe, gave her injectable drugs to jump-start her heart in between doing CPR on her, but nothing helped. I looked at her face, still frozen in that moment of ecstasy as she was about to plunder her prey, and knew she was not coming back. I hugged her, signaling that we should stop our efforts. My sweet little girl had had her last hurrah. She had run at top speed like a puppy in a race with her brother, Bosco, to a place of hidden treasures—the food room. Her heart must have missed enough beats that it couldn't restart, causing her to faint, lose consciousness, and never wake up.

The sorrow and sweetness of this moment flowed together as I contemplated how lucky she was to have lived to 14 with a heart condition, and to pass away in such a peaceful way with me by her side. I would never have to wonder or worry about what happened or if she suffered because I saw her and knew she hadn't. I was relieved that she passed while enjoying her joie de woof and never had to languish for weeks or months in a hospital or hospice situation. The mitigating factors surrounding her passing helped to soften the blow of losing my sweet little girl, who remained childlike and joyful until the moment she died.

My Sunshine

To feel that little heartbeat
or cold, wet, pressing nose
against my face or on my arm
warms me to my toes.

There is no greater happiness,
no greater joy or sense of pride
than to gain the trust of man's best friend
that brings her to my side.

Looking for a rub or pat
or just a friendly phrase –
small price to pay for loyalty,
bringing sunshine to all of my days.

Inspired by Dallas and Dijon

My mother, Marietta Heidolph, cradling a hummingbird we nursed back to health

Mama Bear with Baby Bear at a rest area in British Columbia

Lucybelle, my (male!) rabbit lounging in the sun

Wild turkeys wandering on our lawn overlooking Colpoy's Bay

Rex, my first dog, nibbling snow

Dr. Heidolph befriending a horse near Freiburg, Germany,
while studying at the University of Freiburg

Dallas' first day home meeting her godmother, Claire Johnson

Darling Dallas as a puppy looking irresistibly cute

Dallas enjoying the garden in Bay Head, NJ

Dallas delighting in the snow in Wiarton, Ontario

Dijon as a puppy playing with a ball in Bay Head, NJ

Dijon racing at full speed while lure coursing at Camp Gone to the Dogs in Stowe, VT

Dijon pausing long enough to pose with azaleas

Dijon and Dr. Heidolph at OVC Canine Blood Donor Program Fundraiser, Guelph, Ontario (3rd row from top, left)

Dijon and Dallas exploring the beautiful scenery of Mendocino, CA

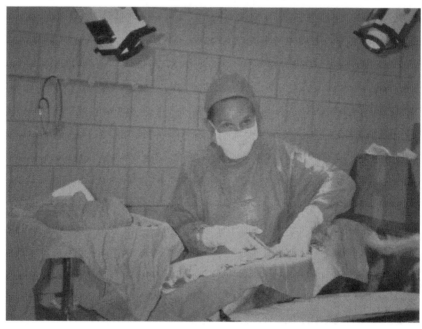

Dr. Heidolph spaying a Husky dog at Chicago's Animal Care and Control

Oscar at home with his new red toy

Bernie mothering her two stuffed puppies

Bosco as a puppy always ready to snuggle

Bosco leaping for joy and a stick into the water

Bosco enjoying a hike

Dr. Heidolph with Bosco hamming it up to showcase his cuteness

Bosco enjoying the drive to Big Sur and the stop at Bixby Bridge, CA

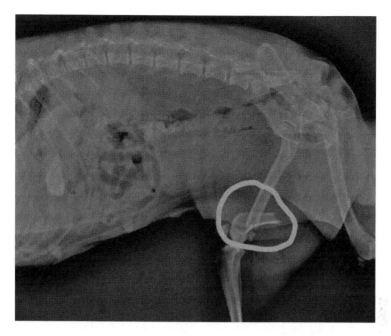

My first 2D view of Coco—a fractured femur (within the circle)

Celebrating Coco's visit with a champagne bottle dog toy

Coco can never have too many tennis balls or squeaky balls

Coco enjoying a weekend sleep-in

Sweet Pea and my mother, Marietta Heidolph, enjoying each other's company

Sweet Pea, my official Under Secretary

Sweet Pea and Teresa Nevarez prepare for their debut
at the American Rescue Dog Show

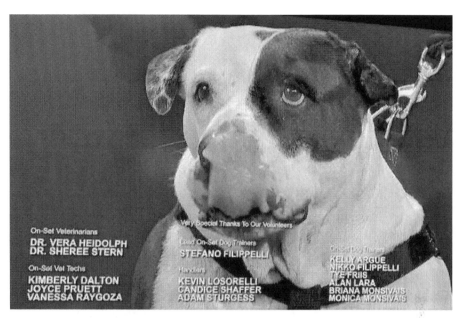

On-Set Veterinarians
**DR. VERA HEIDOLPH
DR. SHEREE STERN**

On-Set Vet Techs
**KIMBERLY DALTON
JOYCE PRUETT
VANESSA RAYGOZA**

Very Special Thanks To Our Volunteers

Lead On-Set Dog Trainers
STEFANO FILIPPELLI

Handlers
**KEVIN LOSORELLI
CANDICE SHAFFER
ADAM STURGESS**

On-Set Dog Trainers
**KELLY ARGUE
NIKKO FILIPPELLI
TYE FRIIS
ALAN LARA
BRIANA MONSIVAIS
MONICA MONSIVAIS**

Sweet Pea and her big tongue featured on closing credits of the American Rescue Dog Show (Dr. Heidolph noted as one of the volunteer veterinarians)

Sweet Pea enjoying swimming while chomping on her squeaky toy

149

Vera Heidolph, DVM

T.J.

Before I arrived in San Diego, I envisioned how my dogs and I would live in and enjoy this new paradise and all of its natural beauty. Part of that lifestyle would also be helping as many animals as possible through new animal activism opportunities. It wasn't long before I connected with the Spay Neuter Action Program (SNAP) that performs large-scale spays and neuters around San Diego County, mostly for pet guardians in financial need. I had never encountered a mobile veterinary clinic equipped for surgeries, which was memorable. The vehicle itself was a bus that had been converted into a mobile veterinary clinic with a surgical suite. All of the equipment necessary for anesthesia and surgery was onboard, including many kennels for the cats and dogs awaiting or recovering from surgery. While a veterinarian performed dozens of spays and neuters throughout the day, the staff worked tirelessly to prep cats and dogs, and then help them recover post-op on the bus. Outside the bus, volunteers fielded questions and provided general information to passersby and individuals whose companion animals were being spayed or neutered. To encourage people to spay and neuter certain breeds, a very low fee was levied for Rottweilers and Pit Bulls. The neighborhoods in which the bus parked were areas of socioeconomic disadvantage and sometimes of cultural divide on issues pertaining to animal welfare and the necessity of sterilizing cats and dogs. Part of my life's vision materialized when I worked with SNAP performing spay and neuter surgeries, and during a regular volunteer gig with a local organization that provides spays and neuters for feral cats.

The narrow focus of my work with animals widened even further one afternoon as I was attending a fundraiser for SNAP hosted by animal lovers in La Jolla. The backdrop of the event was breathtakingly beautiful, the view of La Jolla Cove was magnificent, and the company of fellow animal lovers was inspiring. Then I met "Mr. N." on that fateful Saturday afternoon in La Jolla, who graphically described to me the abysmal state of animal affairs south of the border. While I was actively involved in volunteering at North American animal shelters and vet hospitals throughout my vet school and internship days, I was not specifically aware of the fate that awaited many unwanted and homeless animals mere miles away in Mexico. As I looked around the meticulously groomed grounds and beyond to the tranquil Pacific Ocean, my reverie was rudely interrupted by the explanation of homeless cats' and dogs' fates, be it by electrocution in the Mexican "shelters" or other abuses on the streets in Tijuana, also referred to as T.J. I could no longer simply listen sympathetically and do nothing. I had to act if I wanted to be part of the solution and not just lament passively. It was a very uncomfortable jolt because once I knew the unfathomable, ugly truths and nightmarish realities, the burden of inaction would be on me.

So began the path of involvement with spays and neuters in T.J. I knew from previous visits that laws, religion, and culture were significantly different than in Canada and the United States. Not until I became further involved did I fully appreciate the hurdles that needed to be overcome before spaying and neutering could proceed without appearing to threaten local guardians, authorities, and veterinarians alike. Our first clinic in T.J. was a milestone for so many reasons. There were great cultural differences regarding the sterilization of cats and dogs that would not be easily overcome. Religion played and still plays a role in preventing people from controlling the

Vera Heidolph, DVM

reproduction of cats and dogs, negatively impacting our ability as veterinarians to help prevent the overpopulation dilemma.

Whereas information dissemination in the United States and Canada is relatively simple and straightforward, the methods employed in T.J. to inform people about spay and neuter clinics were word of mouth and drive-by announcements via loudspeakers mounted on cars. Additionally, there were homeless animals we picked up as we encountered them on the streets of T.J. Many locals, veterinarians included, initially resisted the notion of free or lower cost spay/neuter clinics, fearing that they would undermine or undercut their take on the few pesos they could earn for similar services. Last, but not least were financial constraints. Not only did our American-based organization have a shoestring budget, which meant limited supplies, but we were entering a world of significant poverty for most living beings. One of the Mexican veterinarians I met at that first clinic had worked as a bank teller for six years after graduating from veterinary school in Mexico because he could not find a paying job as a veterinarian. With each story I heard and each glimpse into the life of the animals and volunteers I met in T.J., my eyes opened to the challenging conditions of animals and their advocates south of the U.S. border.

A few carloads of enthusiastic and energized volunteers unloaded their gear in front of the appointed building, a small, one-and-a-half-room school building devoid of most forms of light or electricity. Although I didn't expect a hermetically sealed and perfectly sterile surgical suite, I wasn't quite prepared for some of the sights, events, or the rudimentary setting. As we scoped out the circumference of the small structure, we encountered a Dalmatian dog in the side yard, adorned with a wreath of lemons around her neck. In Mexico, some lay people believe this wreath imparts healing properties and even cures distemper in dogs. Veterinarians generally deem

152

distemper to be untreatable and fatal. Whether that Dalmatian ever had distemper or not, she was later rescued and adopted in good health by one of the aforementioned enthusiastic volunteers. Wonders never cease!

After the Dalmatian's situation was discussed in disbelief, surgical preparations began in earnest. The more I saw, the wider my eyes grew. The volunteers and veterinarians evaluated the cats and dogs as best we could, because some were very shy or aggressive. Many of them were underweight, covered in fleas and ticks, and several had injuries that needed to be addressed surgically while we anesthetized them. The volunteers cleaned them up, applied anti-parasitics, manually removed many ticks, and prepared them as best they could for surgery. A Mobile Army Surgical Hospital (MASH)-style unit was created out of virtually nothing. Newspapers were used in place of towels. Anesthesia consisted of an injectable cocktail mixture of telazol, ketamine, and xylazine (TKX). The concentration of these drugs is different when produced in Mexican pharmacies, thus dosing variations had to be considered as each of the aforementioned drugs individually has the potential to knock out a horse.

There was no heart rate monitor, EKG, or blood pressure monitor, and no pulse oximeter, which measures oxygen saturation. If ignorance is bliss, it was probably better not to have monitors because the low heart rates and low blood pressures that would have registered might have been too frightful to fathom. We were fortunate to have a few autoclaved sterile surgical instrument packs, which perhaps provided a false sense of security. Once they were used, they needed to be cleaned and sterilized again, but we had no autoclave or even the electricity to run it. Instead, we set up cold sterilization trays. Although I am an ardent fan of recycling in everyday life, there are instances, such as surgery, in which recycling is suboptimal. A few sterile drapes were also present, again creating a false sense of security. As I made my first incision while wearing my own scrubs, surgical cap, exam room gloves (not sterile, but clean), and no sterile gown, I noticed that every tissue into which I cut bled profusely. This excess bleeding meant longer surgical times when we needed to do surgeries faster than usual because of the limited duration of the injectable anesthetic. I chalked this odd fact up to females being in heat, who bleed more in general, or second-rate surgical blades used for cutting.

It wasn't until several T.J. visits later that I discovered why almost all of the animals we spayed and neutered in T.J. bled much more profusely than on the other side of the border. One of the local T.J. veterinarians informed me that more than 70% of dogs in T.J. are positive for the tick-borne disease Ehrlichiosis. Symptoms can be malaise, pain of multiple joints (polyarthropathy), and most significantly for surgery, decreased platelets, which provide the normal blood clotting function. When I asked why dogs weren't being treated, the local veterinarians explained that doxycycline, the antibiotic of choice used to treat Ehrlichiosis, was considered too expensive for most guardians in T.J. In the United States, doxycycline is considered to be one of the cheaper antibiotics available. Without the benefit of medication to facilitate normal clotting times, we had to work faster against the veritable deluge of blood that greeted our scalpel blades with every incision, every exploration of the abdomen, and inherently bloody fatty tissue.

There were so many challenges to focus on within the routine spay and neuter experience that I was caught off guard by the sudden movements of the anesthetized dog I was spaying. Her injectable meds were wearing off too quickly or maybe had not been dosed quite high enough. First, there were subtle, tiny movements of her limbs, which resulted in my urgent request for a "bump," which is a top-off of a smaller dose of the previously injected TKX mixture when the initial dose is inadequate. Unfortunately, none of the well-intentioned volunteers was able to administer IV injections, which would result in an almost instantaneous response. Instead, volunteers offered to give the bump intramuscularly (IM). We didn't have the 15 to 20 minutes that it would take for this route of injection to become effective, though. As volunteers drew up my requested meds, the dog's movements increased to the point where she was breathing very rapidly, forcing her intestines to be pushed out of her abdomen through the spay incision. While I tried to hold down her chest under the surgical drape with my left hand, I attempted to push her intestines back into her abdomen with my right hand. Finally, the injection was drawn up, but realizing no one else could give an IV injection, I grabbed the syringe, held off her cephalic vein (on the front leg) with one hand, and injected the TKX into her vein with the other. Finally, she returned to her unconscious state, permitting me to proceed with the surgery. As I changed gloves, I briefly looked up and noticed diffusely pale faces on our mostly Caucasian volunteers. If I felt unnerved by this experience, it would follow to reason that they must have wanted to run or to faint. Bless their hearts for sticking it out and even returning for subsequent clinics!

The atmosphere of the day could be summed up by my dismay at one of the fellow Mexican veterinarians as he nonchalantly withdrew his bloodied hands from a female dog's abdomen, reached onto a nearby table with his exam gloved hands, grabbed a non-sterile spool of what appeared to be fishing line, handled it with both hands, cut off a piece of the line with non-sterile scissors, and proceeded with his spay surgery. My jaw must have hit the floor because, soon thereafter, Mr. N. took me aside and assured me that we would have better, more sterile equipment, including suture, at the next clinic. Next clinic? He must have been nuts! Who would willingly enter this environment under these conditions? As we proceeded through more spays and neuters and started to see the rows of recovering post-op animals, my stance on the matter softened. If not us, who else would help the helpless? This work was about as unglamorous as it gets, aside from exclusively shoveling manure, although, in the latter case, one usually has the appropriate tool needed, namely a shovel. As Mr. N. had already pointed out to me at the La Jolla fundraiser, these cats and dogs didn't speak English or Spanish. They were just cats and dogs in need. With this knowledge, I continued volunteering regularly with the organization for several years. There was never an uneventful excursion.

Even though the first clinic had been rather exciting, the trip home and what happened next would prove equally if not more interesting. Not surprisingly, some of the volunteers had discovered and attempted to transport some of the stray dogs back to San Diego. They would be quarantined from other animals to ensure that they had no contagious diseases, given medical attention, and then adopted. What no one had planned for was our reception at the U.S. border patrol. After we declared our mission, activities, and newly acquired canine cargo, we were swiftly pulled over to a secondary checkpoint for further inspection. All of a sudden, all of the women in the car were speaking in rapid, animated tones, becoming very self-righteous about their mission to save four-legged lives. Although I fully empathized with their sentiments, I knew we wouldn't be able to successfully import our recently rescued four-legged cargo into the United States if we presented ourselves in an emotional, rather than a rational fashion. I decided to step up to the plate as the veterinarian among this carload and approach the officers from a health and safety perspective. While this approach ultimately resulted in a successful passage for the rescued poochies, I learned a lesson along the way about the folly of our foray. The border agents expressed their concern about the illegal importation and sale of Mexican puppies into the United States. Most puppies were quite sick, as I would see later when I practiced at veterinary clinics closer to the border. They were often transported in wheel wells or other secretive compartments, resulting in many diseases and deaths. They also explained that the puppy peddlers didn't care a lick about losing several puppies or even a whole litter per carload to some disease or unsafe transportation method because they would just sell more puppies to make their profit. As if the sights of pregnant, injured, homeless, and abused animals wandering or darting in and out of the streets of T.J. were not haunting enough, now the added weight of the black market Mexican puppies being transported into the United States for a fast buck fell on the shoulders of those in the know. It was with quiet humility and relief after the border patrol's admonitions that we headed back home with some extra passengers.

It was not a trip that could be easily forgotten. Over the next several years, many similar trips were made, each with its own individual drama and adventure. Some of the improvements we saw were the increase in donated equipment, such as folding ironing boards, which we used as surgery tables, sterile surgical gloves, and larger clinic venues, such as the local university, which had better lighting, electricity, and cleaner facilities, or the firehouse. Sometimes, we had cultural differences over when to euthanize a terribly sick or injured animal. Sometimes, supplies had been stolen, leaving the hounds and humans with few resources to feed and fix the animals in need. Sometimes, methods were debated, such as the sterilized zip ties that were commonly used by the Mexican veterinarians to ligate or tie off the large ovarian pedicles for spays. The most exciting development over the past 15 years was the widespread involvement of local Mexican veterinarians. With the financial, emotional, and physical support of a growing number of organizations, these veterinarians have worked diligently to spread the word about spay and neuter programs in Baja California, and they have truly made a difference for cats and dogs in this region. It was always a privilege, however hair-raising the experience, to be involved with these spay and neuter campaigns. Over time and with growing safety concerns, I pulled back on my direct involvement with spaying and neutering in T.J. Knowing that life in T.J. is often much more difficult for our counterparts, it especially warms my heart to see so many Mexican volunteers and supporters with far fewer resources than we have in the United States giving freely of their time and talent.

ER

For anyone who has ever seen the TV show *ER* and felt their pulse race as they hear the intro music resembling an ambulance siren, there is a physiologic heightening of the senses at the prospect of a great save in the emergency room (ER). Veterinary staff in ERs feel that same adrenaline rush as they fight to treat and save emergency patients. Although I had volunteered more than 1,000 hours in various capacities at veterinary clinics before starting vet school, being more directly involved in treating patients throughout school was even more exciting. Feeling like you are part of a team with a mission to accomplish a greater good provided purpose and confirmed that I was doing what I loved doing. Team involvement at OVC sometimes meant running down the halls at full speed from the small animal ICU to the large animal hospital to retrieve supplies like specialized blood tubes used to determine a patient's clotting times if they were bleeding out. Sometimes, it would be an errand to procure an oxygen mask for a huge dog like a Mastiff, who would benefit from something used for a foal or calf. Those sprinting missions gave me an increased appreciation of just how much mere minutes matter in emergency cases. The other thing I realized with each emergency case was how important mastery of technical skills can be. If you cannot hit a vein proficiently to administer drugs, draw blood, or give blood, your patient may perish.

Early on in my internship, I had a patient whose situation would test both my technical and interpersonal skills. Waiting in the lobby of RBVH was a black and tan giant-sized dog rivaling a pony. He was a Mastiff, but would be considered large even for his breed, pushing 180 pounds. "Brutus" had just had a seizure at home and was awaiting examination and treatment. The tricky thing about seizures is that they can be unpredictable. Brutus' owner had grown impatient while waiting and was ready to go home. I could see that Brutus was still not 100% normal from his glazed stare and abnormal mental state, but when I explained to his dad my concerns that Brutus could soon have another seizure that might be longer and more severe, he still didn't agree to let me take him into the treatment area for us to place an IV catheter, which is the standard protocol for these types of cases, so we could quickly administer anti-convulsants if he had another seizure. Try as I might, Brutus' dad was adamantly opposed to us placing an IV catheter for some perplexing reason. Perhaps he was convinced that Brutus was now good to go because he had waited in a veterinary hospital lobby. In the back of my mind, I was panicking about the backlog of other ER patients I wasn't able to see yet because I was trying unsuccessfully to explain seizures and their possible fatal consequences to Brutus' dad.

About two seconds after I returned to the treatment area without Brutus, I was paged, urgently, to return to the lobby. As I ran through the door, I witnessed the very scenario I had been pressing so hard to avoid. Almost 200 pounds of flailing and thrashing Brutus were on the ground, frothing at the mouth, urinating, and defecating as he twisted and turned. I spun around, grabbed catheter supplies, and valium from the treatment area, returned within a minute, and got to work trying to place an IV catheter in a seizuring Mastiff. Somehow, I managed to wrestle and steady one limb with all my strength to inject the anti-convulsant and abate his seizure, permitting me to quickly place the IV catheter. By then, the crowded waiting room had become an active audience, momentarily putting aside concerns about their own animals and trying to help Brutus. Once his seizure was under control and he was calmed down, the waiting room looked like a tornado of bodily fluids and excretions had blown through it. My white lab coat resembled the cotton ball used to wipe it all up. Cheers arose as Brutus snapped out of it and stood up again. At last, his dad was convinced that he needed to be admitted to the hospital, where he did, in fact, have subsequent seizures over the next 24 hours, but we would eventually find the optimal anti-convulsant dose that kept him seizure-free. Wrestling wriggling foals on foal watch and working in ICUs had been excellent training for helping such a big, strong dog like Brutus. Only his very public seizure convinced Brutus' owner to treat and hospitalize him. My interpersonal skills would still require a lot of work.

Sometimes, it is quite difficult to persuade animal guardians about medical facts when they have an overriding opinion or feeling about something. One such challenging case arose on a Friday in San Diego. Distraught owners rushed their gasping tabby cat, "Tread," to the veterinary hospital for evaluation. They were somewhat sheepish to state their cat's problem, but because their cat wasn't breathing well, there was no time for secrets or shyness. As I requested that the technicians set up X-rays to look at Tread's chest, the owners finally conceded that Tread had accidentally been run over in their own driveway!

With that crucial piece of information, I thought we could now make headway, starting with pain meds. Yet, I saw hesitation in the family's body language. We needed to act quickly to help their sweet little boy. Once the pain meds started to take effect, Tread became less vocal and seemed to calm down. I requested that the technicians be extra careful in handling him for X-rays because we didn't know what the tire and the attached car might have broken or dislocated. A picture is worth a thousand words, and so it was with Tread's X-rays. Miraculously, he didn't have a single broken or dislocated bone. We determined the cause of his difficulty breathing though. His intestines had herniated through his abdomen into his chest! By taking up space in his chest, the intestines made it impossible for him to fully expand his lungs and breathe normally. It was as if a large potato sack was sitting on Tread's chest. I was relieved to know that he had a fixable problem and quickly shared my treatment plan with his owners. More hesitation. "We can fix him," I repeated optimistically. Finally, their disbelief was revealed. He was 20 years old. They felt Tread should have been dead by now. He had easily used up more than nine of his allotted lives. "How long do cats live?" they questioned. I contemplated saying, "not long with their intestines in their chest." I couldn't give a definitive answer. Instead, I requested blood work to see if Tread had normal organ function in order to handle anesthesia. Reluctantly, the owners agreed. I reviewed the blood work results shortly after and was thrilled to point out that not only were his results perfect, but judging from Tread's meows, he didn't know he was already 20 years old. For better or worse, the pressure of owner apprehension was added onto anesthetizing a geriatric cat with his intestines in his chest.

After calming myself down from allaying the guardians' concerns, I got to work surgically retrieving Tread's intestines from his chest and replacing them back into his abdomen where they belonged. I repaired the hernia in his diaphragm, which had been created from the pressure of the tire trauma. Once his chest was closed up and Tread was breathing on his own again, he was on the home stretch of surgery and on the road to recovery. It had only been a few hours since he was run over in his owner's driveway, but it could have been his last night on earth if his guardians hadn't acted quickly to save him. Tread woke up normally from the surgery and would need to stay at least overnight in the hospital to receive pain meds regularly and to monitor his vitals, ensuring he had no other side effects from his accident. I stayed in the hospital to write up his medical records and complete his orders for his overnight stay. After checking in on him and tucking him into bed, I left for the night.

The next day, I worked at a different veterinary hospital, but thought about Tread intermittently and heard he was recovering well when I called the hospital for an update. I had to see for myself how my poor little geriatric kitty was, so I stopped by the vet hospital on my way home in the late afternoon. Before entering the hospital's elevator, I heard a very loud growling and grumbling noise coming from a cat carrier on the ground. Stepping back to allow the owners and their cat to leave the elevator, I commented on the feistiness of the cat inside. They chimed in saying, "You'd never know he was 20 or that he was run over by a car last night!" I did a double-take, looking up and suddenly realizing it was Tread's family. We looked at each other and had to laugh. "They told us he was getting too feisty to be in the hospital, so we had to take him home." Ultimately, Tread's owners were convinced that his age *was* just a number. Feisty is forever!

In contrast to Tread's known medical history, ER veterinarians must often play a form of charades with their patients and their guardians to obtain a baseline of facts with only a few grunts and groans. Halloween 2003 delivered such a patient—a degu in distress—to RBVH for emergency evaluation. Degus are diminutive rodents that resemble chinchillas and originate from South America. It was clear that Daisy, my first degu encounter, was struggling. From her guardians' description, Daisy had been lethargic, bloated, and hunched over for several hours. She had a fellow degu at home, who was housed with her for companionship. The guardians, a young couple, weren't sure about Daisy's age, but guessed around one or two years old. They provided her with regular dust baths, vitamin C supplements, and her fair share of vegetables and fruits, all of which degus require. The couple was careful when handling her to prevent tail slippage or fur removal.

As I delicately examined Daisy, she became more uncomfortable, which made me worry about trauma or fractures. I had a sudden flashback about the case of a guinea pig earlier in my internship, who came to us in terrible shape and seemed in even more pain than Daisy. The guinea pig's owner had her six-year-old child, who seemed eerily indifferent to the guinea pig's pain and distress, in the exam room with her. All of my internal red lights lit up, which resulted in my secret request to the technicians to get an X-ray of the guinea pig, "Penelope," before euthanizing her, which was the only thing the owner wanted us to do. Full body X-rays of Penelope revealed that she had multiple fractures on her arms and toes. I requested a private talk with Penelope's owner and spoke very sternly with her about my suspicions after establishing that there were no other people in Penelope's house. I theorized that her young daughter had thrown Penelope repeatedly, causing the multiple fractures. Based on the child's lack of empathy for her distraught and broken pet, those suspicions had a high probability of bearing out the truth. It took all of my self-control not to shake Penelope's owner or her kid as my medical imagination recreated step-by-step how poor little Penelope had sustained those unimaginable injuries. As Penelope's mother appeared indignant, I emphatically pointed out the fractures on the X-rays I had somewhat illegitimately obtained.

I should have called the authorities in retrospect, but back then, I may have worried that I didn't have adequate proof or that the protective parent would try to sue the vet hospital for slander, especially because I didn't have permission to take those damning X-rays. Before Penelope's owner left the euthanasia, I made her promise me that her daughter would *NEVER* have another pet. It was probably more out of fear that I was nuts than conviction of her daughter's dastardly deeds that Penelope's owner acquiesced to my harsh admonition. Seventeen years later, we have conclusive data that there is a positive correlation between children who have harmed animals and those who become aggressive or violent toward people. Some serial killers belong to this infamous club of craven criminals. I so regret that I didn't report the suspected abuse.

All of those thoughts sped through my mind as I examined Daisy the degu. Even in her sorry state, she was such a sweetheart. She just wanted to rest her soft little brown head with big ears in my hand as I held her ever so carefully. With further questioning, Daisy's family admitted that her housemate could be a boy, but they were pretty sure she was a girl. This element of doubt and her history and symptoms led me to my diagnosis. She was most likely pregnant for the first time and was having difficulty passing her baby through the birth canal, a condition known as dystocia.

Certain rodents, such as guinea pigs and degus, have a limited window of time to be able to pass a baby safely in natural childbirth because their pelvis fuses permanently by six months if they haven't already had a baby by then. As it fuses, it becomes impossible for the pelvis to widen and expand to accommodate a fetus' head and body. I consulted with other veterinarians about the best course of action with limited funds, and thus diagnostics, and they agreed that the only thing we could do to try to help Daisy was to give her medicine to strengthen her contractions and help her expel her baby degu. I administered oxytocin by injection, taking care not to accidentally inject myself, as it causes tremendous uterine contractions in ALL species. We waited for the drug to take effect and tried to make Daisy comfortable, petting her soft furry little back and belly and cradling her head as softly as possible.

Her owners were unsure of how long she might have been in labor since they weren't even aware that she was pregnant. I worried that Daisy was too compromised to survive. They had no funds for X-rays, fluids, blood work, or possible surgery to perform a C-section and remove her baby. Our only hope was one injection to progress her labor. Daisy's abdomen contracted as the meds kicked in and we felt she might start having her baby. She weakened quickly, however, unable to lift her pointy little brown nose or wiggle her whiskers. Her gums became pale and her breathing slowed down. Then she suddenly just faded before our eyes, leaving her bewildered family to weep for their sweet little degu. If only they had known her housemate was male, they could have spayed and neutered them to prevent her accidental pregnancy and unfortunate demise.

Some ER cases are great saves and others are heartbreaking losses like Daisy. Either way, it takes courage to try to cure what appears to be a lost cause knowing that the lost life will remain on the conscience of the vet team just as it does on the patient's owners. Nevertheless, veterinarians and their ER teams *live* for the lives we might be able to save.

Bernie

If you've ever loved a dog, sometimes you have to reach out and call a lifeline. About a year after finishing my internship and moving to California, my friend Claire called me in a panic from New York. Her sweet, blonde, Buhund-Chow mix rescue, Bernie, was feeling quite sick and Claire was in a pickle about how to help her. As a puppy, this delightful little ball of fluff was found in a parking lot in North Carolina. Claire couldn't help but adopt her and promptly became smitten with her. She nearly chewed her way through the house in her youth, but Bernie finally learned to live calmly, even during brief family absences, with the help of vertically placed plastic snap traps along the walls. As a calm, well-adjusted dog, her anxious behavior was uncharacteristic now. Claire described Bernie's symptoms to me—intermittently vomiting or dry-heaving and acting uncomfortable. Claire had taken Bernie to her local veterinarian, whose X-ray equipment had temporarily given up the ghost. He gave Bernie some pain medication and some fluids subcutaneously and told Claire to bring Bernie back the following day if she wasn't improving.

Some niggling thoughts must have prodded Claire to call me. As I listened to Bernie's list of symptoms, knowing she was an otherwise tough and spunky dog, I worried that we were facing something much more serious than just mild pancreatitis or gastroenteritis. The fact that she wanted to stand rather than lie down was also a tip-off. I asked Claire to do a bit of a telephone exam, wherein I would walk her through some of the steps of the exam and she would report back to me on her findings. It helped that I knew Bernie quite well, and thereby knew her normal baseline. She was far from normal according to Claire's findings. Bernie was panting, anxious, and painful when Claire touched her belly. I offered my top two differential diagnoses: a Gastric Dilatation Volvulus (GDV)—a bloated and twisted stomach—or an intestinal obstruction. A GDV is a surgical emergency that is usually fatal if left untreated. An intestinal obstruction can also be quite critical, depending on its severity and the length of time an animal has been obstructed. My opinion was that Bernie needed X-rays and, most likely, surgery ASAP.

The suggestion of surgery was probably quite jolting, especially because the local veterinarian had told her to come back the next day. I didn't think Bernie could wait another minute in her condition. Most local vet hospitals in that area were closing for the day and wouldn't be able to help Bernie. I suggested Claire drive Bernie down to Red Bank Veterinary Hospital (RBVH) because they are open 24/7 and have board-certified surgeons who could do her surgery if necessary. Then came the inevitable dreaded question: "Will my dog survive this surgery?" If we hadn't lost too much time, yes, there was a very good chance for a positive outcome. If I led her down the garden path, it would be devastating, but without surgical intervention, I feared Bernie was not going to make it through another day and would suffer horribly. Claire would have to make a leap of faith—trusting me and the surgeon to whom I was referring her. I was nowhere near Bernie, but my heart was pounding for her swift diagnosis and treatment. I thought of the thousands of exams we had done in our internship year and how tired we often were in our long days and nights. The ability to sniff out a problem with our eyes almost closed or through the telephone, in this case, was becoming a helpful tool.

I called RBVH in advance of Claire and Bernie's arrival to explain her symptoms and my concerns. Dr. DeCarlo and Dr. Trotter, the hospital's owners, had trained their specialists well. They wasted no time preparing for Bernie, who was quickly diagnosed upon arrival at RBVH with an exam and

X-rays. Her stomach had rotated 180 degrees, thereby pinching off the blood supply to her stomach, pancreas, small intestines, and probably her spleen, too. She was in critical shape and needed immediate help. The beauty of RBVH is the breadth and depth of their specialist teams to address exactly such critical surgical cases.

Double IV catheters were rapidly placed on this fading patient to improve her circulation, especially to her intestines and her spleen. Without IV fluids used concurrently to treat GDV patients pre-op, they can die before your eyes on the way to surgery. As soon as she was anesthetized and intubated, Bernie's dilated stomach would first be deflated. This deflation is achieved by passing a large stomach tube that looks like a clear rubber hose through her mouth into her esophagus and into her stomach, and relieving the excess gas that had become trapped and accumulated in the stomach, stretching it precariously to the point where the stomach or its surrounding blood vessels might tear. In some cases, we insert a trochar (a very large-bore needle) externally to help deflate the bloated stomach even prior to inducing anesthesia, depending on how critical the patient is. The white-knuckling would just begin as Bernie was taken into surgery to untwist and deflate her stomach. Sometimes, the spleen also requires surgical removal if it, too, has been twisted or has become necrotic from the lack of blood flow. Bernie's spleen was still intact and could be spared! The surgeon successfully re-arranged her stomach and any affected intestines, and then secured her stomach by suturing it to the wall of her abdomen, which is called a pexy. Bernie's life was saved, rather narrowly, by her surgery and all of the emergency medicine surrounding her that ensured adequate blood flow to the rest of her body and her oxygen-deprived intestines. She recovered in the hospital for a couple of days until she was stable enough to eat and go home. This near-death experience never shortened her life or her

Vera Heidolph, DVM

joie de woof. I was relieved that I could offer guidance from afar to get Bernie the help she needed via telemergency services.

Trevor the Toggenburg goat

One aspect of veterinary emergencies that keeps them interesting and challenging is the variety. In contrast to general practice where we might see four or five cases of canine ear infections in a day, emergency clinics usher in a vast array of species and their urgent problems. Every time I thought I couldn't be surprised and would be completely prepared for an emergency, something new and different arrived. During one of many overnight shifts of my internship at RBVH in New Jersey, my fellow intern, "Dr. A.", and I were alerted by the technicians that an emergency would be arriving through the back door of the clinic instead of the lobby. The reasoning behind the unusual entry was that this emergency was a goat. "Okay," I thought to myself, "I can handle this. I treated goats during my externship in Wisconsin. Let's get to work!"

As we approached the back door to answer the buzzer, we looked down expecting a diminutive-statured patient. Instead, a sizable, nearly 4-foot tall, 200-pound goat and his owner pushed through the door looking distraught, disheveled, and distressed. Our patient was "Trevor," a Toggenburg goat, which is a breed that originated in Switzerland and was known for its milk production. Trevor was obviously not a milking goat, but rather a beloved pet on his petite British owner's farm. His brown and gray hair was splattered with blood all over his neck and legs. His large inquisitive eyes, framed by white stripes down both sides of his face were glazed over, in shock. What on earth had this poor goat endured?

Through tears and choked up with emotion, Trevor's owner sputtered out his story as we started examining him and planning our treatment. She hadn't witnessed the assault, but heard a commotion coming from the field where Trevor lived. Trevor's mom suspected her two dogs, a Boxer and a Jack Russell Terrier, had most likely attacked Trevor repeatedly. She surmised that her Boxer had probably inflicted the most damage due to his size, and could not imagine how her Jack Russell Terrier could have jumped high enough to bite Trevor. After receiving my own initiation into Jack Russell Terrier Jump-and-Bite 101, I could attest to their remarkable capabilities, and even had a scar on my backside to prove it. A Boxer could certainly apply jaw pressure like any dog, which would make a bite very painful, but the number and severity of the bite wounds seemed more like the work of a narrower, pointier mouth with a perfect bite, which most Boxers don't have.

Our plan to help Trevor was pain med administration, IV fluids to help treat the shock and replenish lost blood volume, and IV antibiotics. We didn't have any goat blood in our blood bank and were too far from any veterinary school that might have had any reserves. Through all of this process, Trevor was such a sweet boy and a brave patient, allowing us to help him and not putting up a fuss. It may also have been that he was so weak from the blood loss secondary to dozens of bite wounds. Dr. A. and I placed an IV catheter into each of his jugular veins on either side of his neck to enable maximum flow of IV fluids and to avoid his legs, which were dreadfully chewed up. He became more sedate with the pain meds, but remained standing as his owner, still weeping through her smudged, thick granny glasses, encouraged and comforted him. Normally, we would have owners leave us to work on our patients, but Trevor truly seemed calmer in her presence and we had enough space in the treatment area to work on him because he was taking up the entire treatment floor.

Dr. A. and I had the technicians open up boxes of suture packs and got to work finding active bleeders and suturing them as quickly as we could. As soon as we fixed one or two bleeders, we discovered many more around the next corner—on his neck, front legs, back feet, and belly. We knelt, we stood, and we sutured and sutured. We cleaned the wounds that weren't actively bleeding and then closed them. Within a couple of hours, the entire treatment floor looked like a helicopter had whirled about blood, boxes of gauze squares, dozens of packets of sutures, gloves, and surgical prep in every direction around Trevor. Surely, we had made progress in reducing his pain, blood loss, and impending infection. Trevor's vitals did not concur with our heartfelt wishes. His blood pressure was tanking, he appeared weaker by the minute, and I feared we wouldn't be able to prevent him from going further into shock.

Before we had a chance to confer with his dedicated guardian, Trevor started sliding down onto the floor for the first time since he had arrived that night. Trevor's mom lay beside him as he panted with increasing speed and effort. We couldn't be losing him after trying so hard to pull him through. I looked at his pale, white gums in disbelief. Cradled by his inconsolable guardian and surrounded by a treatment room full of veterinarians and technicians who had all tried their best to save him, Trevor succumbed to shock and passed away before us.

Silence, then sniffling and shuffling feet followed as we shook our heads in disappointment. We only knew Trevor for a few hours, yet his sweet spirit made us fall in love with him even as his little goatee of a beard dripped blood and he blinked his eyes, imploring us for help. I'll never know if Trevor was attacked by the family's Jack Russell Terrier or the Boxer, or if there was a random or stray coyote that attacked him, but losing him was one of the more difficult and heartfelt losses in the ER.

Vera Heidolph, DVM

Gordo and Frodo

Many veterinarians and technicians have a curious superstition that certain types of cases come in twos or threes, including emergencies. If this superstition were true for minor emergencies, it might be easier to handle, but seeing two hit-by-car (HBC) dogs or cats back to back or simultaneously, for example, is not only stressful, but physically and medically very challenging. I would learn what could make "medicine in multiples" even worse on a Saturday afternoon while working in Southern California several years ago. We received a call that two Golden Retrievers had gotten into something and would arrive at the hospital momentarily. Some of the staff started preparing treatments used to induce vomiting, such as apomorphine, which is administered in the form of eye drops. Instead of two jolly Golden Retrievers walking in, a frantic man ran into the building carrying one large Golden Retriever as we escorted him to the treatment area. He was followed by another Golden Retriever, who was actively seizuring on the gurney that was wheeling him inside.

The medicine in multiples concept had created massive chaos, especially because one of the two Golden Retrievers was unconscious and convulsing. Worried about some terrible toxin, I wasted no time asking the dad what the dogs had gotten into. His gardener had provided the bag of the offending substance—snail bait—and told the dogs' guardian he saw the dogs eating it in their citrus field. Something we didn't worry about in New Jersey or Ontario was the overwhelming presence of snails. Because there is so much agriculture around San Diego and so many snails, gardeners and farmers often use snail bait, aka slug bait or, more precisely, metaldehyde, to kill snails.

Metaldehyde definitely kills snails if they eat it, but it can equally eliminate any other mammals that ingest it, including cats and dogs. Its main method of action is to cause seizures, hyperthermia, and, ultimately, organ failure. If caught early (less than an hour or two) and if the amount of snail bait ingested is very small and the patient is not yet having seizures, metaldehyde toxicosis has a chance of being treated successfully. In that case, we can induce vomiting with apomorphine and administer activated charcoal by mouth, which is tricky because it's like black tar, but it can actually help bind certain toxins.

I had a pit in my stomach as "Frodo," the Golden Retriever on the gurney, was convulsing violently, realizing I may soon have to focus my efforts and attention on only one patient, namely his brother "Gordo." I ordered a high dose of methocarbamol IV for Frodo to try to minimize or better stop his seizures. His body temperature was already through the roof.

As we waited for Frodo's meds to take effect, I assessed the "healthier" of the two Golden Retrievers, Gordo. His face had some mild twitching and his mental status was depressed for a young and otherwise healthy dog—not good signs. "He may only be minutes behind his brother, Frodo," I thought with deep disquiet. As we placed an IV catheter to administer methocarbamol to Gordo, he started having a seizure, too.

I tried to blink away the harsh reality of what I was witnessing, as I realized that Frodo's convulsing hadn't diminished at all with treatment. I ordered a repeat dosing of methocarbamol for him. It was time to speed up Gordo's treatment before he caught up to Frodo. As soon as he got his first dose of methocarbamol, Gordo's seizures stopped—perfect timing to anesthetize him while he wasn't flailing all over. It was too late to induce vomiting because he would probably choke on it and develop aspiration pneumonia. Activated charcoal administration by mouth was out of the question for the same reason. However, we could pump his stomach, aka performing gastric lavage to detox him from the inside out. Once we had a secure and snug tube in his trachea, we passed a rubber tube from his mouth down his esophagus into his stomach. We know we're in the stomach by pre-measuring the distance from the outside and marking it on the tube, and also by scent. Stomach contents have a distinct, acrid, bitter, vomit-like odor. In order to decontaminate him, we would have to rinse and suction out everything in his stomach, which is no small feat. With three people rolling and rocking Gordo back and forth and the suction device attempting to remove his stomach contents, we ran up against chunk after chunk of stomach materials that needed to be broken down before they could be suctioned through the tube. In the midst of our stomach-pumping efforts for Gordo, Frodo started seizuring again, dashing my hopes that we could save him.

As more anti-convulsant meds were administered to him, I looked back to Frodo, whose writhing body could no longer be stopped by medication. Only the weakness of his muscles and the chaos the seizures had unleashed on his poor body were now slowing him down. He must have been going into complete organ failure. Before I could suggest to his guardian that we humanely euthanize him, he became still and lay lifeless near his brother. Gordo's future had only a few minutes, more drugs, and a stomach pumping to be different from his brother's. We hadn't finished pumping his stomach yet, so we just had to continue and give it everything we had, rolling and rocking this large dog with all of our might.

Fear of losing Gordo in my medicine of multiples nightmare prevented me from crying about Frodo as we treated his brother. We knew the toxin. We treated him according to the book. But we knew that even if we were able to wake him up from anesthesia and pump out his stomach, he still wasn't out of the woods. His devastated dad begged us to save Gordo, so we continued with full force. One benefit of anesthesia, which is usually a negative aspect, is that it also helps keep down a rising body temperature. The saline being pumped in and out of his stomach also helped lower his body temperature.

Would we be able to keep him stable once we woke him up? The pressure was immense. The odds were poor. The motivation was huge, but was that enough? As Gordo woke up from anesthesia, he looked completely drunk, but had minimal body tremors. So far, so good. Even though he was not out of the woods, his father was overjoyed to see his only remaining boy looking back at him, somewhat awake. He never even had a chance to say goodbye to Frodo. With his guardian by his side, a glimmer of recognition sparked in Gordo before he laid his head back to rest. We had moved his brother, Frodo, out of the treatment area by that time so it wouldn't be another thing to upset him. He needed calm and quiet and no more seizures if he was going to recover. The multiple doses of methocarbamol had stopped his seizures for the time being. We had removed all of the contents from his stomach in the hope of removing all toxins from his body. If the snail bait had already passed into his small intestines, though, it would be too late.

It's so hard to wait when time may not produce the desired outcome in veterinary medicine. Thankfully, Gordo made it through the night with medication, gastric lavage, and lots of tender loving care. As he returned to himself over the next day, his endearing personality became even more so. It was such a relief to send him home with his father, although it would be a bittersweet return with only one of his beloved boys surviving the snail bait toxicity.

Vera Heidolph, DVM

Jackson the goofy Newfie

In an attempt to find more balance between my work and personal life, I accepted an invitation to join the church choir's Christmas production. Most of the other singers had angelic voices that would make a sung recital of telephone book names sound melodic. Even with their experience and talent, they encouraged me to practice and sing with them. Exercising the pipes turned out to be a great outlet and the more we practiced, the more I looked forward to performing with my fellow choir members on Christmas Eve. All I had to do was finish my day shift, which was scheduled to end at six p.m., and then I could pop home, take care of my dogs, head to church, and sing.

I worked diligently throughout Christmas Eve day in order to keep on top of the dreaded medical records so they wouldn't hold me up at the end of the day. Fifteen minutes before the hospital was supposed to close, a small moose, or rather a mammoth-sized black Newfoundland dog named "Jackson" arrived. He was walking in on his own, so that gave me hope that we could sort him out and be on our way in short order. When I inquired about the nature of his emergency, I no longer felt quite so hopeful. He had been vomiting on and off for several hours or at least trying to vomit. Depending on the dog's history, a vomiting dog usually requires abdominal X-rays to make sure he doesn't have a GDV/bloat or an obstruction or foreign body. As I sized up this huge, hairy, slobbery boy, who still looked happy as a clam, it was clear that his X-rays would take a long time because we would have to shoot multiple shots to get the equivalent of one shot on a Beagle-sized dog, similar to photographing a Sequoia tree that requires a dozen or more shots to capture its

178

enormity. We would also need all hands on deck to lift him and hold him while gowned up in our protective lead gear.

My mind was calculating the number of hours it might take to diagnose and treat Jackson and whether his treatment and singing in the Christmas choir would be mutually exclusive events. First things first. We needed to help him. Being bright and alert was good for him in that his prognosis was better, but a bit of a challenge for everyone involved in handling and holding him because he was still playful and trying to be rambunctious. His vomiting had gone on for hours and the owners didn't know what or if he had eaten anything out of the ordinary, so it was too late to give him medication to induce vomiting. I was considering what toxin he might have ingested as I pondered the many geographically-specific toxins, plants, and objects in California, not all of which I had learned about in vet school in Ontario or in my internship in New Jersey. The first time someone showed me the pretty flowers of a plant that their dog had eaten and I researched the plant, I discovered why Morning Glory is so named—it's LSD! I can no longer look at the previously romanticized image of a sago palm tree without thinking about its liver toxicity. Toxins and naughty dog indulgences ran through my mind as we took multiple X-rays of Jackson's abdomen.

The beauty, or perhaps the frustration of medicine, is that it's so often not black and white, even if the X-rays are black and white or shades of gray. Because Jackson was such a champ, he was still eating, even though he was vomiting. His X-rays ruled out a GDV and showed food-like material in his stomach and parts of his small intestines, but there was a loss of definition in his small intestines that made interpretation challenging. Could he just have pancreatitis from eating something naughty or could he have an obstruction? His owners couldn't imagine *anything* forbidden that he might have eaten.

While I explained the uncertain X-ray findings to Jackson's owners, the vet techs were busy wrestling with him to place an IV catheter so we could administer fluids and give any other medications intravenously to avoid oral medication. After showing Jackson's guardians his abdominal X-rays and sharing my concerns about his stomach not being empty after vomiting, I offered a few options. The most conservative plan would be to hospitalize him on IV fluids overnight and to monitor him for ongoing vomiting or abdominal discomfort and re-check his X-rays in the morning. We could also send him to the specialty hospital for an abdominal ultrasound, which might give us more insight into what was ailing him. The most aggressive approach would be to perform an abdominal exploratory surgery, aka an exploratory laparotomy, to visualize and palpate his stomach, small intestines, and all other organs. Jackson's family was so sure that he had not eaten *anything* out of the ordinary that surgery was out of the question for them. I wasn't 100% convinced that he needed it either at that moment, so we agreed to hospitalize him overnight, where he would be watched by a technician, and re-check his abdominal X-rays in the morning.

I wrote up his treatment plan, tucked him into bed, and tried to catch the tail end of the Christmas church service, even though I was pretty sure it was long over. By the time I reached the church, it was not only over, but there weren't even any cars in the parking lot with church members talking among themselves after the service. I felt so badly that I had had to bail on them and was sad to have missed the service I looked forward to so much. I headed home to my own dogs, Bosco and Dijon, and was grateful to be able to spend time with them. I thought about what we could do together on Christmas Day— sleep in, go for a hike, or take a ride in the car.

But then it dawned on me. I was on duty the following day. My big friend, Jackson the goofy Newfie, was waiting for me, along with several other hospitalized patients and boarders, all of whom needed exams, medical treatment plans, and so on. I brought my dogs with me to work on Christmas Day in case the quick and easy morning that I was promised turned into something else, as it had the night before. As I contemplated Jackson's case, I felt uneasy on a visceral level. We repeated X-rays of his abdomen, which were again quite a feat of strength and wrestling skills. By the time his X-rays were completed and I reviewed them, I knew why that niggling gut feeling existed. It looked like Jackson had an intestinal obstruction, which was not as clear on Christmas Eve, but much more convincing on Christmas Day. He needed surgery to remove the obstruction and possibly to repair any damaged intestines. His guardians were still in disbelief as I explained his situation to them. I offered to do the surgery myself at the hospital or to send him to a specialty hospital to have a board-certified surgeon do it. All roads led to surgery.

Once Jackson's family decided that I should perform his surgery, I had to ensure that we had enough manpower on Christmas Day to get him prepped, into surgery, through surgery, and then into recovery. Handling him required more bodies than usual, not because of his demeanor, which was quite sweet, but because he was a 140-pound wiggly, young dog. Just to hold him for exams and treatments was like wrestling with a wild foal. Lifting him onto the gurney to get into surgery involved several people, too.

After he was safely anesthetized, which necessitated massive amounts of drugs for a Goliath of a dog like him, I could get to the real work of fixing him surgically. It's not like opening a box of chocolates and having a small surprise. There are so many possible surprises one can encounter when performing surgery to repair an intestinal obstruction—rocks, dog toys, GI Joes, underwear, socks, cassette tapes, hair elastics, Disney bandanas, or solid-packed grass, just to name a few treasures I've surgically removed from dogs' and cats' intestines.

My curiosity was certainly piqued by the time I palpated his small intestines and started running his bowel. I saw with dread some discoloration of his intestines and felt a firm thickening. As I opened up the injured area of small intestines, careful to prevent any toxic spillage back into the abdomen, the fetid smell hit me. I had to know what this thing was causing a terrible traffic jam inside Jackson's intestines. I saw brown and green and grayish food-like substances, but they were covering a firm object. My palpation indicated that this object was long, so I would have to plan the intestinal opening and foreign body removal carefully and strategically. We probably had at least 16 inches of something firm and solid, which is a bit worrisome because pulling some things out of the bowels, such as cassette tapes, Christmas ribbon, or tinsel, could actually cut the intestines like a sharp rope. As I worked around the food particles to grasp the object and started to manipulate it, a light went off—it was a hand towel! Why on earth had the goofy Newfie eaten an entire towel? I would never have guessed.

Part of Jackson's bowel was discolored, indicating that the tissue was dying off, so that would have to be removed. The procedure is called an intestinal resection and anastomosis, or R&A for short. It means a piece of the intestine is cut out (resected) and then the remaining two unconnected ends of intestine on either side of the cut-out piece are sutured back together again (anastomosed). This can be a tremendously messy surgery on a good day with a small dog, but everything about Jackson was bigger, including this part of the surgery. It would have been helpful to have an assistant in surgery to lend a sterile hand by holding off part of the bowel as I sutured it back together, but it was Christmas Day and I was already using every available body in the hospital just to be in surgery with Jackson. Oh, to be an octopus and have additional, dexterous limbs! All things considered, Jackson's surgery went very well, despite some personnel limitations. I couldn't wait to tell his guardians about what he had been hiding. I would save the swallowed object for them because I suspected they wouldn't quite believe me until they saw it with their own eyes.

After prepping Jackson for surgery in the treatment area, relocating him into the surgery suite, and removing some of his intestines and a towel, and rinsing out (lavaging) his abdomen and suctioning it out with a pump, the surgical adventure had left behind a trail of massive messes throughout the hospital. We had practically exhausted the hospital's supply of certain controlled substances, which were under lock and key due to concerns about humans misusing them. We would need even more of those drugs in the post-op phase for Jackson in order for him to have a pain-free recovery with his newly rearranged intestines and long zipper of an incision that I had created. There were also other patients in the hospital who might need pain meds and would be left short if we didn't replenish our supplies promptly. At my behest, the technicians called the hospital's owner to request controlled drug reinforcements, which were at the owner's house. We settled Jackson onto some custom-designed comfortable horse-sized bedding in the middle of the treatment room for post-op observation because there were no cages or runs large enough for him. At that moment, the hospital owner's wife, who was also the manager, passed through the treatment room with the much-needed controlled drugs. I was relieved to see our drug supply replenished, knowing we could safely provide Jackson with all of the meds he would need for his post-op recovery.

The hospital was quite the sight, because we had left a tornado of pre-, post-, and intra-op items in our wake, focusing on getting Jackson into surgery and safely through it. Although we were all physically weary from the heavy manual labor of treating, lifting, and moving Jackson, everyone felt like they had done a good job. I praised them for working so hard to help pull off this large medical and surgical feat. Expecting the owner's wife to offer the same praise, we were all rather stunned as she simply walked by the exhausted team and grumbled resentfully, "I hope we made some money for all of this," glaring at the storm of supplies, hair, and slobber scattered about. Silence followed. No "Merry Christmas." No "Good job, team." Nothing. We had all worked so hard, sacrificing Christmas Eve and Christmas Day only to be questioned about the bottom line.

Fortunately, Jackson and his family were all much more grateful, albeit dumbfounded that their goofy Newfie had eaten a hand towel. We surmised that it might have had scraps of food on it from someone's hands and, therefore, enticed him to gulp it down like a magic trick. Although I missed singing in the choir on Christmas Eve and had worked fervently and diligently on Christmas Day only to be chastised, I felt blessed to be able to help Jackson and his family. He was my ER Christmas gift that year.

Love at first sight

After losing my beloved Dallas in 2005, I was grateful for Dijon's constant canine companionship during a difficult time of grief. Although I was initially concerned about such a sensitive dog becoming depressed over her housemate's passing, she didn't exhibit any overt sadness or diminished joie de woof. On the contrary, Dijon seemed to relish receiving all of my attention and love, like a child whose older siblings have moved out of the family home. She had played second fiddle to Dallas for nine years, which had its benefits of older sibling protection, but now it was her time to enjoy the solo spotlight at home. At the dog parks and beaches, she loved playing with other dogs and would seek out playmates as soon as we arrived. Her boundless energy was more readily burned off by goofing off with and chasing another dog than by me trying to run around with her or rollerblade off her excess exuberance. I encountered dogs in need of a home on a daily basis through my work and was often asked if I could adopt this adorable puppy or that senior canine citizen. Each one of those dogs was wonderful and worthy of adopting. They might have been a good playmate for Dijon, but I just didn't feel that any of the dogs was the perfect companion for her. I was looking for a dog who would let Dijon be the top dog and would still be active and energetic enough to be her playmate and companion.

One day while working at a veterinary clinic in El Cajon, which is about 15 miles east of downtown San Diego, the right opportunity presented itself. This clinic served many lower-income clients, so it was not uncommon for pet guardians to have insufficient means to treat their pets' ailments or to hear a technician advising the veterinarians that there was a stray dog or cat that had been dropped off and needed attention. As I faintly heard that familiar request, I was in the middle of an operation and, therefore, couldn't jump in right away to help. It wasn't until a few hours later, after I finished with surgeries and examinations, that I found myself mindlessly, instinctively, wandering toward the back of the hospital, where the dog runs were located. When I reached the run that housed the so-called stray dog, I was immediately drawn in by the dog's shy and sweet demeanor. I entered the run slowly to avoid frightening him, and realized he was still a puppy. He looked like a mixture of a Boston Terrier and a Pit Bull, who was completely unaware of his incredible cuteness. The moment he looked up at me with his innocent and curious, but shy big brown eyes, my heart melted. His eyes were encircled by a dark brown mask-like pattern on a white background. The brown mask matched the tuxedo-like seal brown color over his back that was demarcated by a white "collar" around his neck. His legs were mostly white with some brown patches and spots. The only other colors were the pink spots around his soft muzzle. His head was relatively big and boxy in comparison to his skinny little stumpy legs. Although it was hidden between his hind legs at first, as he became more courageous, his long dark brown tail with the narrow white tip started beating rapidly in anticipation of something good.

I remember being speechlessly in awe of this wonderful little creature as he sniffed me and let me pet his head. For a scared little guy, he warmed up to me quickly, so I sat down, stretched out my legs in front of me, and soon had a puppy flopping onto them. He became more animated and encouraged by a few reassuring words and some belly rubs. Within a few minutes he had rolled onto his back and wiggled his entire body to position his head on my stomach. He beamed up at me, delighted, as he wiggled his belly to a spot where I could rub it and his big, blocky head simultaneously. In that moment, I knew with certainty that I had found love at first sight. The name Bosco just came to mind and seemed to fit him right away.

I immediately felt an intoxicating love for this little guy I had just met. One of the wonderful characteristics of dogs is that when they're into you, most are not shy about demonstrating their feelings. I was almost in disbelief that there could be such a fast and furious connection with a dog, even though I had met and loved thousands of dogs before him. Bosco just looked at me like I was **IT**! I took it as a sign and set about determining how to give this so-called stray dog a forever home in my house.

The policy at the time for a "stray" dog was that he must first be brought to a shelter so his rightful guardians could have the opportunity to find him. I promptly placed my name on the top of the waiting list to adopt him in case he was not claimed, and was tremendously sad to have to let him go back to the shelter before I could take him home. Somehow, I knew that he would never be reclaimed because I suspected that he was actually *dumped* at the vet clinic where I was working. If owners surrender their dog to a shelter, there is a surrender fee, but if someone claims they found a "stray" dog and leaves the dog at a vet clinic as a Good Samaritan, there is generally no fee. Once Bosco had spent five long days at the shelter and no one claimed him, it was obvious to me that this four to five-month-old puppy was dumped. Any normal, concerned guardian would have checked local shelters and made an effort to find their baby.

I thought it would be a straight-forward adoption because I fancied myself an ideal dog guardian with an ideal dog home—a veterinarian with another dog, who would be Bosco's playmate. To ensure that Dijon would get along with this new puppy, I brought her to the shelter to meet him. I didn't have expectations that she would fall in love with him the way I had or even be best friends, but rather just wanted them to be compatible, which they were. Each time I visited Bosco at the shelter, I just wanted to bust him out because he seemed so scared and lonely amid the din of other nervous, barking dogs. It's tempting to want to adopt multiple animals because all that faces a visitor in a shelter are homeless, helpless dogs and cats, who are depending on good-hearted visitors to bail them out and save their lives. In the best-case scenario, they are adopted soon after arrival and find a loving home. If the shelter is a no-kill shelter and they are not adopted, they remain there for life. In the worst-case scenario, dogs and cats are not adopted and because of inadequate space or funds to care for them, these innocent souls are sentenced to death and killed due to our overwhelming pet over-population dilemma in North America.

Although it broke my heart knowing I couldn't get them all out, at least I could do everything possible for this one dog. It turned out Bosco's adoption would not be the slam-dunk I had envisioned. I was called by a shelter worker, who informed me a few days before I would have been able to adopt Bosco that I could not have him. To my astonishment, it was not because his original guardian had picked him up, but rather because I had admitted that I had another dog in my home, evidenced by my previous visit to the shelter with Dijon. The shelter worker explained to me, as if I had never interacted with a dog before, that because Bosco was a Pit Bull mix, he would not be allowed into a house with another dog. She expanded on her ill-conceived and erroneous theory that ALL Pit Bulls, regardless of environment, training, and neutering status (he was neutered while he was waiting at the shelter) would become aggressive toward all other dogs and could not be trusted with another dog at home. She claimed that, as soon as he turned two years old, I would come home one day to discover my other dog, Dijon, had been viciously killed by him! To say I was dumbfounded is an understatement. No clarification of my qualifications or experience satisfied her or dispelled her rigid and predetermined errant beliefs. However, she was now Bosco's gatekeeper. To prevent a gang banger from snatching up this sweet little Pit Bull mix as a bait dog for dogfighting, I knew I had to act fast. I had people in the animal rescue world write and make phone calls on my behalf, even though it struck me as a ridiculous necessity. All someone had to say to adopt him away from me was that they didn't have any other dogs at home. I was so furious about the misconceptions already assigned to this puppy without him ever having done any harm to anyone or any other dog. I didn't feel that the shelter was doing its job of "sheltering" him at all. He was being condemned for a crime he might commit in the future. What kind of justice was at play? Breedism literally kills dogs.

Fortunately, justice eventually prevailed for Bosco. After five drama-filled days of negotiating, pleading, and convincing, I was allowed to adopt him and bring him home. I am happy to report that the individual who tried to convict Bosco and all of his relatives of uncommitted crimes based on breed is no longer at the shelter. Before leaving the shelter, I paid my $40 adoption fee and gave an additional donation because I had noticed that the corrugated tin roof covering the dog runs didn't extend to the end of the runs. I still remember seeing one darling male Rottweiler shivering in the rain because he was not covered. I begged them to extend the tin roof with my donation and packed Bosco up to leave.

As we pulled away, I felt relief for him, but profound sadness for those left behind, knowing that the statistics were not in their favor. However, it was time to celebrate the adoption of my new little guy. It occurred to me as I drove home that it had been a long time, nine years in fact, since I'd had a puppy in my house. There would be a lot of fun and excitement, but I reminded myself that something or several things were going to be destroyed and I couldn't be upset about it. That's what puppies do.

When we stopped at a friend's house on the way home to meet her dogs and socialize, Bosco just wanted to play and love on the other dogs the entire time. I wasn't seeing any part of the ferocious beast he was purported to be by ignorant naysayers, but I saw a lot of personality that was just ready to blossom if given the opportunity. As soon as we arrived home, he got reacquainted with Dijon and won her over right away by being playful, but submissive to her. I had no idea how he would be in a home environment, so I watched him like a hawk to facilitate house-training. He caught on very quickly. After his veterinary clinic and shelter experience, landing in a home must have been a sweet refuge. It was clean and dry and quiet. All he needed was a safe place to sleep and the day would be complete. Before I could argue, he had joined me on my bed and was snuggled up against me and looked at me as if to allay any concerns I might have about any bad behavior.

From the very first day I had met him, he looked at me as if we had known each other for a long while. That sensation was a bit unnerving at first, as if he were an old friend who knew my heart already, but then it was oddly reassuring. I debated whether or not I should allow him to sleep on my bed for a while, as I envisioned a house that would be redecorated overnight by a destructive puppy. He would have to sleep in his own kennel beside the bed for the first night. Even though it was outfitted with soft and warm blankets, I felt terrible that he couldn't snuggle with me because he was still a baby and just seemed to crave closeness and love. The second night, he laid on all of his innate charm as he jumped onto the bed with me. Because he had been so well behaved the first night, I attached his leash to my wrist, so if he needed to relieve himself, I would feel him move beside me and could let him outside without incident. I don't believe he moved an inch all night! The sweetest little face greeted me joyfully as I awoke the next morning, as if to say, "This is how we should always sleep." It's probably not a mystery that, from then on, he always slept on the bed. On the third night, the leash was superfluous. He just wanted to stay by my side.

By day, Bosco was playful with Dijon and any other dogs or people we encountered. We enrolled in puppy training and had so much fun in the process. The classes were held in a large pet supply store with other puppies. The biggest challenge for him was resisting the urge to play with the other dogs and paying attention. Fortunately, this training used the modern positive reinforcement clicker training method. No one got hurt, choke-chained, "corrected," or bullied. At the end of the course, he graduated with a little doggie cap and a diploma. I couldn't have been prouder. My little boy from the other side of the tracks, dumped at a vet clinic was now a canine college graduate. It was refreshing to see how much fun dogs could have and how quickly they could learn while being trained with the right methods.

What is difficult to anticipate with a new dog, be it young or old, is what sort of issues or phobias he or she might have. Bosco feared water, and especially the bathtub. We'll never know exactly what happened to frighten him, but for the first six months, he wouldn't even enter the bathroom, unless I carried him in. Bathing him was tantamount to torture, even if it was done slowly and gently. It was one of his few hang-ups, considering his house-training was going well. He had a few accidents in the first weeks at home, but only while he was playing. He would become very excited and animated, and would suddenly squat to urinate while running around the house, even if he had just done it outside in the garden 10 or 15 minutes earlier. I decided I would avert the accidents by setting the oven timer for 15 minutes. When it chimed, I let him outside and encouraged him to do his business by saying, "Hurry up." He obliged and then resumed playing between the garden and the house. I used paper towels to soak up his accidents and then placed the soiled paper towels in the garden to encourage him to pee there. After a few days of the kitchen timer trick, he would hear the timer and then trot outside on his own to the soiled paper towels and relieve himself. How smart he was!

Although Bosco loved meeting new people and dogs, not everyone was convinced about his intentions. Whether I was near my house or in another city, people often crossed the street in a hurry when they saw him. It was often the most ill-informed individuals who had the greatest bias. Former neighbors with an energetic and, at times, aggressive Rat Terrier were the perfect example. It was okay for their dog to bite me—"he's small, so it's okay!"—but as their dog lunged toward Bosco, who kept wagging his tail to encourage the Terrier to play, all I would hear them mumbling as they yanked their snapping dog across the street was, "That's a mean dog. Bad breed." Really? I have been bitten, or narrowly avoided being bitten, countless times in my practice as a veterinarian by many of those so-called angelic *non*-Pit Bulls. A Pit Bull is actually the last breed of dog on whom I use a muzzle for protection. For the record, I have never been bitten by a Pit Bull.

While some people clung firmly to their prejudices about Bosco's potential parentage, others were dramatically converted. It was especially encouraging when individuals who had been bitten or whose dog had been bitten by a dog similar to Bosco could befriend him and see how their experience was not representative of the whole species or breed. He could have an intimidating look with his very large jaws that hung open like a beluga whale when he was excited, revealing a mop-sized tongue. I could appreciate a healthy amount of respect based on his sheer size. Some onlookers actually inquired as to whether I "trained" him, as in strength training, because he was so muscular, especially his back legs and butt. He received so many compliments on this part of his anatomy that he became conditioned, upon hearing the word "booty" to swing around to offer his back end for a back massage. If his admirers didn't oblige, he swung his head around looking backward to invite ANYONE to give his back end a massage. He still enjoyed his massage so much so that in the morning, while I prepared coffee and breakfast, he would saunter into the kitchen, turn around and back up his booty for a massage over his back. Any visitors were invited to do the same. His requests for massage from strangers proved to be quite an icebreaker and myth buster. It's hard to fear a dog who is wiggling in your hands while stretching out his long tongue in a very relaxed fashion. Part of his charm was his sometimes embarrassing habit of kissing people.

I warned kids, especially, that he might give them a kiss, so they wouldn't think that his big head was going to swallow them up. At first, their eyes got very big as they received a lick on the face. Once they realized he was playing, most of them burst into fits of giggles and asked for more of the same. Ideally, he shouldn't have licked people in the face, but of all of the bad habits he could have, that wasn't one I was going to change. It was hard for him to fully express himself sometimes the way he might like to because of his size. A little dog can express exuberance by jumping onto your lap or jumping up on you every now and then. This behavior would knock people over and cause full leg numbness if he sat on you for any length of time. So, the dog kisses stayed, as long as visitors were okay with them.

Another characteristic that usually won over people and dogs was his desire to befriend every person and dog he encountered. Especially as a puppy, he would make a complete fool of himself just to engage another dog in play.

He threw himself on his side or back, licked the other dog's lips submissively, or hip-checked them to initiate play. He would pick up the other dog's stick or ball, in which he actually had little interest, only to run away in hopes of the other dog chasing him. If challenged, he would always give up a toy. It was not uncommon to have small dogs sniffing him and humping his back legs as he trotted onward, unfazed by their antics, just as Dallas had been. The little dogs' guardians were often petrified that he might hurt their dog, especially in light of the humping, but it never bothered him.

On one of our outings to the dog park, Bosco was enamored of a new puppy and played with him nonstop. For a moment, I knelt down to pet and play with the little puppy just a few feet away from Bosco. From across the dog park, someone who must have known Bosco and was watching him during this interaction cried out, "Bosco's lying down!" I turned around and discovered he was lying on his side. At first, I thought he was just tired, but then I realized he looked worse than tired. My veterinarian mindset kicked in, so I checked his gums—pale. Not good. I quickly attempted to feel for a pulse on the inside of his back leg. On a big, muscular dog like Bosco, this pulse should practically jump out at your fingertips. I could barely feel any pulse. I wanted to scream but felt paralyzed. My beloved Bosco was in huge trouble and barely had any vital signs. My first instinct was to pick him up to get him help. Even pumped full of adrenaline, I struggled to lift his solid and virtually motionless 75 pounds. As I attempted to stand with him in my arms, another dog owner regular from the park swooped in to lift him up and, without missing a beat, ran with Bosco in his arms to my car. He was breathing, but barely. He had a heartbeat, but it was weak. He didn't respond to my voice or my touch. He was checking out and my panic was setting in completely.

I jumped into my car and sped out of the dog park toward the highway. I called the veterinary hospital where I used to work to warn them that we were on the way. I hadn't spoken since Bosco passed out and didn't realize it would be so difficult in this state. I believe I was hyperventilating a little bit as I tried to blurt out the details of my problem and why I was coming to the hospital. As the receptionist heard me speak and figured out that I was in shock, she asked if I was okay to drive. Well, considering I was hyperventilating and sobbing uncontrollably by that point, the answer was probably no. However, I didn't have the luxury of time or an alternative driver, so I tried to steady my grip on the steering wheel and intermittently stretch my right hand back onto Bosco's barely moving body on the back seat.

When I arrived at the veterinary hospital, I was met by an assistant, who immediately scooped him up and marched into the treatment area of the hospital. I was relieved that we were safely inside and felt that he had a chance of making it. That is, until the receptionist told me that they were short on technicians, so I would have to be the person treating him by placing the IV catheter and administering fluids and injections to him, and so on. I was a bit stunned, but there wasn't time to think. In retrospect, I know why my internship training was so intense. As a veterinarian, if you hesitate to think about an emergency in a time of urgency, fatal consequences can occur. We literally have to be able to do certain things in our sleep. Being able to place an IV catheter in a dog with barely any pulse is one of those things. We grabbed all of the supplies needed for an IV catheter and fluids. As I rapidly prepped his leg and he lay limp on the treatment table, I feared the worst. I had to be fast and not falter. I shaved his leg and held the vein steady to insert the catheter, squinting to better visualize his veins because tears were pouring down my face so fast and I could not use my hands to wipe them away. The assistant's face had the look of sheer panic. Clearly, I was not instilling confidence in her with my emotional state. Normally, I would not have been crying while treating a patient in this condition. However, she knew Bosco was my dog and my objectivity had officially gone out the window. She was not trained to place an IV catheter, therefore, the best she could do was to hold off the vein to help it pop up for the catheter placement, while comforting Bosco with a hug and some kind words.

Miraculously, the catheter placement succeeded on the first attempt and I quickly started the IV fluids at a shock dose bolus. I pulled up dexamethasone, a steroid used to treat some types of shock, and injected it. Bosco was in very critical condition, so I also gave him a dose of epinephrine to jump-start his heart. We also give Benadryl (diphenhydramine) to act as an antihistamine. I suspected a sting by a bee or some insect was the catalyst in this whole disaster, because his clinical signs occurred within seconds. We held an oxygen mask in front of Bosco's nostrils the entire time we were working on him to improve his oxygen intake. For a few minutes, there was nothing but the slow sound of the EKG monitor (we had placed EKG leads on him to monitor his heartbeat and rhythm) and my sniffles. I was praying so hard that this little bundle of love would jump back to life that I think I squeezed off circulation in my own clenched fists.

After what seemed like an eternity, but was probably only a few minutes, he lifted his head. I wasn't going to be greedy. ANY sign of life was good. I could work with that. As he flopped his head back down, I watched his heartbeat speed up on the EKG monitor. Oh my God, he was responding! I had to cry some more now out of sheer relief and happiness. I wasn't even going to pretend to be tough in this instance and because my emotions were so raw, there was no chance of tempering them. Over the next 30 minutes, all of his vitals improved and we started seeing a more lifelike demeanor. I knew he had turned the corner when I felt a warm (no longer cold!) tongue on my hand as I held his leg and watched his vital signs on the monitor. It was as if he was saying, "I'm good now." Once he was stable, we got him situated in a comfortable kennel and we could all resume breathing a bit more normally. I never found a stinger or specific bite anywhere on him, which is a common occurrence for insect bite-related anaphylaxis. Sometimes, the specifics are less important than the treatment, and this was one of those times. It wasn't the first or last time I would have to fight for my dog's life, but it was one of the most terrifying times because he came so close to dying.

Another frightening Bosco escapade occurred when he was in the car on a summer's day en route to the beach. The windows were cracked, but did not appear to be down too far. At a traffic light with four lanes of traffic in all directions, Bosco decided to jump out of the rear window and run toward the sidewalk, and then into the road to the right of my lane. I jumped out of the car shouting his name, only to realize it frightened him and made him run even farther away from me. What I wouldn't have done for a lasso at that moment! He was oblivious to the perils of the traffic around him, but also confused about where to go. Fearing that drivers might not stop for a dog or might not be able to see him because he was crouching low to the ground, I ran out in front of him and put my arms up and waved them around like a crazy person, begging people to stop. I didn't have to beg too hard. It was clear that I was no longer in New York City. Everyone stopped and several drivers got out of their cars trying to help me round up the stray mustang who had gone for a romp down the road. We circled around him and looped a slip leash over his head. He was so scared he refused to walk, so he had to be carried to the car. Again, some kind stranger helped out until he was out of harm's way. Someone was really watching out for him that day. He jumped out of the car one more time a few months later, upon arrival at Dog Beach in Del Mar. Fortunately, he jumped out onto the beach side, which was adjacent to the car park area, and ran directly to the beach. That was the last of his premature vehicular exits. Thankfully, he was cured of the desire to jump out of moving objects.

A veterinarian's dog will commonly have a few special behavioral or medical quirks by definition. In addition to food and environmental allergies, which were treated with a specially formulated diet and allergy shots, respectively, Bosco had a hard time hiding his exuberant feelings about people or dogs he liked. This quality was endearing until he whacked his wildly wagging tail into a wall and made it bleed. For months, we went through a cycle of bandaging the tail, which is a very challenging part of a dog's anatomy to bandage effectively, and treating it medically. Each time it seemed that the tip of the tail was completely healed, some new joyous encounter made him wag so vigorously that he beat it and it broke open again. I had stopped noticing the diffuse blood spatters at knee level on the walls throughout my house until guests arrived and commented on the alarming blood stains. I didn't see the point of repainting when it was likely to recur. When it seemed like the only prevention to reinjuring Bosco's tail was to make him stop wagging it—a highly unlikely possibility—or having him roam where there were no walls or horizontal objects to hit his tail, I reluctantly proceeded with something I dreaded doing—a partial tail amputation. It was so ironic that, as a staunch opponent of cosmetic canine procedures like prophylactic tail docking and ear cropping, I was forced to perform a potentially painful, but necessary surgery on Bosco to prevent him from hurting himself repeatedly.

For anyone who thinks a tail amputation is a quick snip-snip, that's not the reality. Pit Bulls and many other large dogs, especially, have very thick tails loaded with blood vessels, nerves, and bones, namely the tail vertebrae, or coccyx, that have to be cut off in order to remove the affected part of the tail. A tail is sturdily designed to remain intact, even with some pulling, perhaps by a predator back in the days of wild dogs and wolves, thus removing a piece of it goes against the very nature of its design. I gave Bosco a nerve block around his tail before starting any incision so that even while under anesthesia he would not feel much of anything during the procedure and for some time afterward. A tourniquet was placed at the top of his tail to help minimize the amount of bleeding, but could only be left on for 15 to 20 minutes before it would have the highly undesirable effect of causing problems after the surgery, such as loss of innervation, blood flow, and, ultimately, necrosis (tissue death) and sloughing (falling off) of the skin on the tail. I have seen it happen to other veterinarians and had learned my lesson from them. Lots of bleeding during surgery would be better than a sloughing tail afterward. As much as I gritted my teeth during the entire operation, the outcome of a shorter and healthier tail was exactly what Bosco's ailing tail had needed. His tail healed well post-op. I hoped he felt relieved after it healed not to have any of his joie de woof subdued again by a nervous mom. When I returned to my house after the surgery and regarded the circumferential view of what appeared to be a long, drawn-out crime scene with flailing blood splatter, I was reassured that fixing his tail was the best solution for him.

As soon as Bosco recovered from his tail repair, he resumed his role as my companion and mascot for my mobile veterinary clinic, the VetBus. He would sit up front when we parked the bus and greet patients and their guardians with a very loud and enthusiastic bark, which was difficult to modulate. At home, he would patrol the house and any possible point of entry if there was a knock or suspicious sound outside, but he generally followed me from room to room to be by my side. So many potential adopters think they're doing a dog a big favor by rescuing them. That is certainly true, but the added bonus is that our adopted pets do even *more* for us, without ever being asked. Many guardians have reported that their dogs have come to them when they were sad or in tears to offer a paw to hold, a belly to rub, or just close companionship. Bosco was definitely in the devoted companion club. He loved sleeping in so he could practice more of his Olympic snuggling technique, which involved occupying a disproportionately large percentage of the bed. Maybe math is not a dog's strongest suit. Anytime I was sick, he would never leave my side. If I had a dog walker come by to walk him when I was unable, I had to get out of bed to accompany him out the door with the dog walker because he refused to leave my side.

His bedside manner was especially comforting when I shattered my wrist in 2015. I was rollerblading at the park on a Saturday and was as shocked as anyone would be after wiping out on the sidewalk to look up and see a disfigured wrist hanging off the end of an arm that was mine. The weeks and months that followed with doctors' visits, surgery, physical therapy, and not being able to work were painful and frustrating. Yet, instead of complaining or becoming antsy at the changed situation, Bosco never left my side. I was amazed by how patiently he waited for me to recover and would have stayed by my side in bed if I had never made it out of the house again. His loyalty stretched beyond anything I had ever seen. I was bored with being a patient all day and couldn't imagine anyone else putting up with a frustrated version of myself. The more anxious I became about not being able to work, the more closely he clung to me. I never had to ask him to be there for me because he was always there offering his strength and protection should I need it.

Shortly after fracturing my right wrist, I felt a lump on Bosco's underside with my left hand, and normally would have aspirated it promptly to investigate. However, I could barely move the tips of my fingers that protruded from the cast, much less perform any medical procedures. I hired another veterinarian to perform surgeries for me while I was convalescing and was very grateful for her help, especially because there was a new lump on Bosco that I wanted checked out immediately and a few others that needed to be rechecked. He had had many other lumps and bumps aspirated, so I was not alarmed or worried by this new discovery. However, the lab reported that this new mass was a mast cell tumor, which is a common but malignant skin tumor in dogs. Mast cell tumors can often be surgically cured if removed with wide surgical margins, but they can potentially also spread to other organs in the abdomen. Thankfully, Dr. Radtke was able to remove the mass surgically. She did a beautiful job of excising it with aggressive margins and leaving behind an incision that healed perfectly.

I scheduled a consultation with Dr. Proulx, a veterinary oncologist, to determine what the next steps were. I had met him at the NC State Veterinary Hospital in 2000, when Dallas started her radiation therapy with him. To be safe, we had the radiologist perform an abdominal ultrasound on Bosco to look for any evidence of metastasis to his abdominal organs. The radiologist took small samples of his spleen and liver, two favorite organs for mast cell tumor metastasis, with a fine needle aspirate. Like the perfect patient he always was, he could not have been braver during this visit. Normally, veterinarians don't want pet guardians present for most procedures and certainly not for invasive ones for safety and mental health reasons. A benefit of being a veterinarian is being able to be present with your dog for such a procedure. With one hand in a cast, I could only pet him and comfort him with my left hand, but that was all he needed to cooperate for the brief, but undoubtedly uncomfortable procedure. Everyone was impressed with what a sweet boy he was and how he didn't cry or show any untoward sentiment. We could learn a lot from dogs like Bosco being such a good patient. How easy it is to help them! Fortunately, the cytology reports for his spleen and liver came back negative, so with a grade 2 mast cell tumor completely removed with wide surgical margins, he was cancer-free.

Now we could take care of some other issues that needed attention, like his shoulder that had been acting up more over time. I think the underlying problem with his right shoulder was that as an adventurous puppy, he had explored some of the higher cliff ledges at Dog Beach and before I could stop him, he leapt down from a 10-plus-foot peak as if he could fly. He landed with more weight on his right front leg than his left. He had some shoulder pain for a couple of weeks thereafter that got better with rest and anti-inflammatory medication. This time, I took him to Dr. Pike, the same surgeon who had seen him for the same problem when he was much younger. Dr. Pike recommended arthroscopic surgery for both his shoulder and elbow. I was hopeful because the recovery from an arthroscopic procedure wouldn't be as long or painful as completely opening up the joint. Bosco seemed sore for a few days after the procedure, but not much more than before the procedure. As the days passed, it seemed like he was improving. I could focus on my wrist healing and pushing hard through physical therapy to get back to work as soon as possible.

A month or so after his arthroscopic surgery, we were at home when I noticed a slight bit of nasal discharge from his left nostril. He sneezed a few times, shook his head, and then seemed unbothered. I tried cleaning up the blood initially, but there were more drops. Once he rested, the dripping stopped. My first thought was that my dog had a tumor. Then I had a quiet talk with myself and reminded the doubting doctor that just because he was a veterinarian's dog didn't mean that only the worst-case scenario could happen. After all, he'd had a foxtail encounter when he was younger and within a half hour of his initial sneeze, he sneezed the object out again. Once the bloody drops stopped, so did my fears for that night. The next day, there were a few drops of blood, and then nothing. By the end of the day, there was just some thicker nasal discharge that started when he got excited or breathed harder and faster, but stopped when Bosco quieted down. Although I hoped a day or two of this pattern would be the end of it, the third day was a repeat of stopping and starting. His symptoms weren't typical for a foreign body, like a foxtail, which was what I was hoping for. I called my technician to see if we could meet at the VetBus to sedate Bosco and look up his nostrils for the source of the discharge. She was busy rescuing cats, so it wouldn't be until ten thirty at night.

Ever the willing patient, Bosco let us give him some good sedation so I could look up his nose. My hand was now in a hard splint, so I could move my fingertips a few millimeters, but found it very difficult to grasp an otoscope (a scope normally used to look into a dog's ear) to look up into his nostrils. No time to complain. If I could just find that pesky foxtail or other plant, we could pluck it out and be done with it. But I couldn't find anything other than irritated and red nasal tissue, probably from the sneezing. As brave as you sometimes need to be to do surgery, I felt the wimp in me come out very strongly as I inserted the scope into his nose. Even though Pit Bulls have medium-length noses, I felt like I was about to poke through Bosco's brain as I gingerly advanced the scope into his nostril toward the back of his head. I checked both nostrils to be safe, but woke him up soon after, dissatisfied with the lack of a result. A couple of days later, I had Dr. Radtke recheck his nostrils when she was working on the VetBus again. We both arrived at the same conclusion: further testing was required.

It was time to see the oncologist, Dr. Proulx, again for a consult. This time, he recommended a CT scan of Bosco's head to determine the source of the nasal bleeding and discharge. At this point, there wasn't any more blood, just occasional clear discharge, so I convinced myself that we were on a purely academic mission. As Dr. Proulx's words hit me that Bosco's CT revealed a nasal tumor, I wanted to burst into tears and simultaneously hug Dr. Proulx, knowing what a miserable task he had. How could my dog have another tumor in such a short period of time? Actually, the odds of a dog his age having more than one tumor were about 1 in 4. I clung to hope again as I waited for the histopathology report of the nasal biopsy. Couldn't a nasty infection or an abscess look like this? I began bargaining and rationalizing that there must be a mistake.

Prophylactically, we planned to start radiation therapy as soon as possible while we waited for the biopsy results. The most common nasal tumors in dogs are adenocarcinomas. The best way to try to treat them is with radiation, but there is generally no permanent cure. Bosco decided not to read the standard veterinary textbook for dogs because the growth in his nose was a malignant chondrosarcoma, a type of tumor found most commonly on the ribs. We had no time to waste in starting radiation, but needed to plan and schedule carefully. Dr. Proulx recommended Cyberknife radiation for this type of tumor. From my perspective, it looked more like cyberspace, but, essentially, its advantage over traditional radiation therapy would be tissue sparing of the surrounding organs and structures, while focusing more narrowly on the tumor itself. Nothing would be too high tech for my Bosco. The beauty of the treatment is that it is only three consecutive days versus the twenty days my

Rottweiler, Dallas, endured for the tumor on her head. Bosco was a stellar patient, who received a bandana and a teddy bear from the oncology team when he finished his final radiation session.

It was exciting to be on the healing and tumor-fighting side of the equation now. Survival times had mixed reviews for nasal tumors, and with a less common nasal tumor, there was more uncertainty, but like any hopeful guardian, I just heard the best possible scenario and added a few years onto it. Three years tops? Let's make it five and make medical history with Bosco. I was up for the challenge and ready to do whatever it might take to beat this beast that had invaded my dog's nose. As expected, the radiation caused some irritation at first, but then the nasal discharge subsided to virtually nothing and I felt victory was within our grasp. Time to let Bosco's radiation work and get back to work myself. The appointment list was building up, in spite of additional help in the form of another surgeon.

Once again, Bosco and I were a team on the VetBus driving to different neighborhoods to help animals. He liked the camaraderie of the other patients and being my copilot. As he resumed regular activity and started walking more again, he began to limp on his right front leg again. I couldn't believe that his shoulder was on the fritz after everything he'd already been through. Time to go back to see Dr. Pike, the orthopedic surgeon. While waiting in the exam room with my niece, Alexandra, who was visiting from Canada, I noticed one of his toes seemed a bit swollen. I examined it and thought it felt soft and squishy, so I wanted to dismiss it as a benign fatty mass, but then remembered what I had just been through with Bosco's nose. While Bosco was being sedated for stem cell therapy to be injected into his shoulder and elbow, we aspirated the swelling on his toe just to be safe. As I awaited those lab results, I talked myself into believing that there was no way lightning could strike a third time. The lab results showed otherwise. The mass on his right hind leg pinkie toe was a poorly differentiated sarcoma. Unbelievable. Why had my poor Bosco been dealt such a lousy hand? Now I was really mad. Tumors on toes can be very aggressive and, depending on the type of tumor, can metastasize to the lungs. His toe needed to be removed pronto. At the same time, I had been wanting to repair Coco's elongated soft palate for a while because her snoring had worsened, but I had been focusing on Bosco, so I didn't get around to it. What better time than this to have a surgeon come to the VetBus and take care of both dogs on the same day?

Once Coco and Bosco recovered from their surgeries and were acting like themselves again, it seemed like we could all breathe a bit easier, until Bosco threw up several times one November morning all over the house. Flashbacks of Dallas perforating her GI tract filled my head with fear. I looked at his gums to see if he was pale or dehydrated. Instead, I saw that his large top canine tooth was purple. What on earth was happening to my dog? Then it dawned on me that it could be from the radiation. To be safe, we returned to see Dr. Proulx, who repeated a CT scan at my request. I wanted to make sure he didn't have a tooth root abscess. Normally, if a dog has a purple tooth, it indicates that the tooth is dead, but it also means there may be disease in the tooth secondary to trauma or infection. Bosco had been living in a protective bubble under my care, so he was not prone to any of the perils of trauma or lack of dental care.

Dr. Proulx explained that the radiation had probably deadened some of the nerves and blood vessels associated with the canine tooth because of its proximity to the nasal cavity. The upside of radiation damage to the nerve roots and blood vessels is that the nerves are deadened, thus eliminating any pain. The frustrating part is thinking you can or should do more, but knowing that extracting such a tooth would be a mistake because it would drag tumor cells with it as it's pulled out and then there's also the potential risk of bone tissue dying off in a process called necrosis post-radiation for the surrounding bone. The last thing I would want to do is to cause more pain and undue trauma, so I just let the purple tooth be Bosco's signature mark, like a pirate with a gold tooth. Fortunately, the CT I had requested to check for a tooth root abscess also gave us more information about the tumor. It had shrunken significantly and was withered down to almost nothing. Victory was going to be a bumpy road, but I convinced myself it was the only road I would travel.

I honestly stopped worrying about Bosco and his nasal tumor after that CT. It was such glorious news that there was no reason to waste energy on any negative thoughts. It was time to focus on work and a remodeling project on my house. The house had become very comfortable and functional over the years, but mostly it was comfortable because the dogs felt comfortable in it and their happiness is my happiness. Urine and vomit stains on the carpets from my dogs and visiting dogs had resurfaced after each industrial-strength cleaning, leaving me to wonder if I would ever live in a house that had any part of it clean or unadulterated. With encouragement from friends and family, the renovations proceeded. I wondered how Bosco would feel about his turf being invaded every day by men who would probably be wearing hats. He had a bit of a phobia and I didn't want him to be freaked out every time tall, hat-wearing guys arrived. After the contractors arrived each day, I took Bosco and Coco to the dog-sitter for the first week and then to a dog day care and friend's house thereafter, so they wouldn't be subjected to the noise and dust during the day. Soon, my very protective Bosco knew and trusted the crew and was begging for butt rubs from them. It was exciting to envision the rooms taking shape and seeing where Bosco and Coco and I would hang out as the renovations progressed.

As the details of my house were coming together and I prepared for my mother's annual visit to California, Bosco's nasal discharge ramped up again. It wasn't bloody, just thick mucus. Greeting the contractors with excitement upon their arrival made him pant, setting off a gag from the post-nasal drip. All I could do to help him was to stroke his throat to help him swallow and pat his chest to clear the mucus. Once my mom arrived, Bosco had another person to love on him, but also someone else to notice his gagging episodes and dripping nose with me. Watching Mom watching Bosco, my concerns were magnified and confirmed. At the risk of being a nervous Nelly, I brought Bosco back to Dr. Proulx the last week of February. I didn't mind if he was going to tell me I was overly concerned, but I wanted to help Bosco because the pain meds and the antibiotics that he'd been on for months weren't slowing down the gagging episodes or the nasal discharge anymore. He acted normally in terms of his energy level, appetite, and love of life, but I couldn't ignore the dripping nose. We repeated another CT scan. I needed to confirm that there was simply some unanticipated oddity causing the discharge. Maybe this backup of gunk in his nose had caused some kind of infection that we could manage with different medication. If Dr. Proulx had smashed a brick over my head, however, his words couldn't have been more crushing than when he quietly told me that Bosco's tumor was back and even bigger than before. No amount of kindness or compassion that Dr. Proulx always exercised could dampen this blow. Instead of affecting just one nostril, it had now spilled over into the right nostril as well, which explained why he had so much discharge from his right nostril.

The statistics for radiation and nasal tumors raced through my mind. I thought we had more time. Now he had months, not years. I was stunned to learn in one sentence that his life expectancy had been truncated so severely. "My poor dog," raced through my mind. Imagine feeling confident that the enemy was a continent and an ocean away and you had a fully functional arsenal to combat them if they approached any closer, only to open your front door and there is the enemy. The only weaponry left to try to thwart this enemy was another round of radiation. We had already hit him with a significant dose in August, so palliative radiation, which would be a lower dose, was the only option left. Less radiation also meant a much less optimistic prognosis than the initial one.

I had tried to put on a good face inside the specialty hospital after hearing the dreadful news of Bosco's tumor coming back, but I finally fully lost it as I drove Bosco home. He was still drowsy from the anesthesia for his CT scan, so I hoped he didn't notice the pilot's breakdown in the front seat as he snoozed on the back seat. I could barely hear any sound or perceive anything but the road as I drove numbly through a tunnel of disbelief. He's only 10 years old, I argued in my head. He should live until 15. His spirit was still strong. From his eyeballs back, he was healthy, other than some shoulder issues, which could be solved with another surgery. We had beaten the cancer on his toe by removing it, and his mast cell tumor on his prepuce by removing it. This news and its implications disturbed everything about the natural order and progression of things in my mind.

Upon arriving home, I tried to maintain normalcy by feeding Coco and Bosco and going through the motions of a regular dog evening. My mom inquired about Bosco's CT scan and what Dr. Proulx had found. As I explained the devastating news to her, I burst into tears, realizing with each word the heavy weight of Bosco's latest diagnosis. We really didn't have much time anymore and there wasn't much I could do about it. Bosco's breathing was punctuated by intermittent coughs from his post-nasal drip that first night. All of his symptoms worsened overnight, which is a common symptom with nasal tumors. The nights were rough on him and, by default, also on me because I was stressing over him. If you've ever loved such a sweet, helpless soul and seen any suffering or discomfort, it is impossible to sleep soundly. Until this latest news about his tumor, I had been his cheerleader and kept an upbeat demeanor to encourage him. It would require an Oscar award-winning acting job and some lying to go about life cheerfully in the face of this worsened reality. For his sake, I tried, but didn't always succeed. The weekend before he started his second round of radiation treatment, his nasal discharge caused multiple gagging episodes each day, to the extent that I didn't want to leave him alone for any extended period. By Sunday night, dread and fear occupied the space that hope had previously filled.

Some hope remained, though, as I dropped him off that Monday morning for his first of five palliative radiation treatments. I asked for reassurance from Dr. Proulx that we weren't doing anything deleterious to Bosco for only limited gain. He convinced me that was not so. All day, I worried about him and what the radiation might or might not achieve. The drive to pick Bosco up was through pelting rain, which was interrupted as I absent-mindedly lifted my gaze from the road to the hills in the distance and the heavy clouds forming over them. The appearance of a brilliant, full, double rainbow caused my jaw to drop and my tears to halt. Surely, this double rainbow was a sign of hope and promise for Bosco's recovery.

On the second day of radiation therapy, I dropped Bosco off from my VetBus and proceeded to work with Coco, my Boston Terrier, onboard the bus as one of my dental patients. Hopefully, a full day of work would distract me from worrying about him. Working with animals has always been an excellent distraction, as I could fully become engrossed in surgeries or treatments. Coco's dental, however, proved a bit more exciting than anticipated. Although everything about her heart and lungs sounded normal before we anesthetized her, after 20 minutes or so under anesthesia, the monitors she was hooked up to showed some abnormal heart rhythms on her EKG. Sometimes, there is only so much cumulative bad news that is manageable. I couldn't have anything happen to *her* now. She was the healthy dog. But the monitors clearly indicated that she had a first-degree atrioventricular (AV) block. It's a common heart rhythm disturbance in dogs, which is generally treatable with atropine. The veterinarian mind raced through all of the possible scenarios of what might happen if her rhythm worsened to a second- or third-degree block, or if she didn't respond to the atropine. If things worsen or can't be treated, her heart could stop. It was not going to happen today, was my thought. We are fighting back! Once we gave her atropine, her heart rhythm shaped up back to a normal rhythm, easing yet another fear. Perhaps the worry about Coco's heart stopping prevented me from spending all day worrying about Bosco. By the end of the day, I was relieved just to be able to spend the evening with both dogs. They were very precious moments that I relished with each breath, however noisy or gurgly it was.

On the third day of radiation therapy, my mom accompanied Bosco and me to the hospital and marveled at how well he behaved in the waiting room full of other dogs and then in the treatment area. He didn't want to be taken away from me by a technician or oncologist to the treatment area, but gladly proceeded if I led him. From there, he walked over to the scale on his own, fully aware of the routine. My mother couldn't believe her eyes because her own dog, Honey, a rescued Lab-Beagle mix, requires two or three people holding her and struggling with her against her protestations just to be placed on the seemingly life-threatening scale. She remarked what a cooperative and trusting patient he was. For those reasons, he was also such a good candidate to have such advanced treatments. My mother's dog would not have fared so well going to a vet hospital every day. I was reassured by Bosco's reaction to the technicians when they brought him out to me at the end of his treatments. Seeing him give them big sloppy kisses meant that he felt safe and comfortable with these professionals. It made me proud to be a veterinarian, knowing that others in my profession took their jobs so seriously and cared so much about their patients. Considering how fast his tumor must have been growing to first shrink almost into nothing and then grow back bigger than before in such a short time span, it is very likely that he never would have lived to see the New Year if it hadn't been for the radiation and the oncologist's expertise. Each day of radiation therapy was like a solemn gong, sounding the time running out on the clock in spite of those potent light beams doing their best to penetrate the monstrous tumor cells.

Until my mom left for Canada again, she watched over Bosco any time that I worked away from home. He loved snuggling on the couch with her or joining her in the garden, sometimes squeezing her out of her spot on the couch outside only to tuck in tightly beside her like a lap dog. Both Bosco and Coco accompanied us to the airport to drop off my mom when she returned to Canada. I couldn't watch as she kissed Bosco goodbye, fearing it would be her last visit with him.

Home alone with Bosco and Coco again, I waited anxiously for the results of the radiation therapy to kick in and help Bosco's nasal discharge and episodic choking. It is like watching water boil, except the water will eventually boil if the stove is on and it's obvious when the water is boiling. Like surgery, entrusting radiation is another leap of faith because the proof is often internal with only minor external evidence to confirm its efficacy. But within a week or two of starting the radiation, his nasal discharge improved. Hope was budding again as he perked up and appeared livelier than he had in a while. This second round of radiation brought with it another round of hope, but it was hope with a finite timeline this time, knowing the aggressive nature of his tumor and that we had used up our final chance at radiation. Additional radiation would only damage all surrounding tissues, including his entire nasal passage inside and out. Collateral tissue damage would be worse than the tumor. I could have spent every minute of every day running down the list of medical possibilities and statistics, but as I watched my dog it became ever clearer that he just wanted to live each day, as most dogs do, so now it was my job to make each day count more than it ever had before.

I couldn't quite accept the news that there were no more treatment options, so I made inquiries with a few Canadian and American veterinary oncologists. I knew the chances of cutting-edge breakthroughs or experimental trials were slim, but I had to try. What if there was a clinical trial in Switzerland that had success that no one else had experienced? Oncologists must have a long line of desperately hopeful family members, willing to do anything for another chance at prolonging life. I was one of them, and they all had to tell me the same thing: there wasn't any other viable treatment option for Bosco's nasal tumor. My research attempts were fruitless, so maybe it was time to do something that Bosco would really love that wouldn't jeopardize any of the progress he was making with the radiation. We took a somewhat impromptu road trip from San Diego to Monterey, a place he had already visited and we had enjoyed tremendously together.

Vera Heidolph, DVM

Bosco had always been a fantastic travel companion, not just because of his easy-going nature and his innate protective capabilities, but because we just always had a good time together on the road. Any time we drove even to the grocery store together, he would eagerly await me in the garage sitting expectantly beside the passenger side back door where he knew he would hop in, ready to go anywhere with me. I don't know too many other beings who can make every single trip and simple outing a fun adventure the way he did. On our trips, short or long, he loved being the passenger when I was driving, and the sitting pilot when I was parked and popped in somewhere. Passersby would remark at what a cute driving dog he was. Bosco slept soundly or looked out the window for the long drive. He seemed a lot less impatient than I was about reaching our destination. Upon arrival, he jumped out of the car in Monterey to be greeted by his best dog friend in the world, Max, the exotic Labradoodle. What was Max doing there? Bosco appeared at once perplexed and delighted to see his dear friend in a different town that they had not yet experienced together. The last time Bosco and I had visited Monterey, we had stayed at Max's house, but Max wasn't home then. Now, Bosco was so thrilled, he squealed and wagged his tail madly as if he'd been reunited with a long-lost love. My worries about his long-term prognosis dissipated in that instant.

Dogs really seem capable of living in the moment much more effectively than humans. I needed to learn from my dog how to optimize those moments for him. Even though Max always played the reluctant bride in terms of reciprocating Bosco's affection, just being in his presence was enough to make Bosco happy. He would perk up every time he walked into a room and saw Max there. We walked together on the beach, walked around town, and visited Carmel and its many dog-friendly establishments, which we had enjoyed a few

214

years earlier. This time, it was with Max's owners, Mindy and Arnie, who also loved Bosco. When I worried that he would ruin their couch with his nasal discharge, they just covered everything with blankets and said not to worry, which was very kind, considering the amount of nasal discharge that he was producing. We strolled the many inviting small streets of Monterey and Carmel with both dogs together and then sometimes just the two of us. Watching Bosco enjoying the expansive sandy beach on Carmel just made me so happy as he sauntered and trotted without a care, sniffing other dogs, seaweed, and anything he wanted to sniff on this off-leash beach. The views were breath-taking, with the famous golf resort on one end of the beach and rugged cliffs and crashing waves on the other. The cove-like nature of the beach felt like a protective cocoon that kept out all other ills and fears and encircled life's beauty and tranquility in the midst of a jaw-droppingly beautiful setting.

The pace of our days was leisurely because I was away from work and we could modify our itinerary at any moment. Maybe that's why dogs don't need 85 or 90 years on earth to live fully. They live in the moment **every** moment. Humans are so busy making and doing that the "being" part is often neglected until we are forced to gear down our pace and smell the flowers, appreciate beauty, hear our own breath, and feel those feelings that we have suppressed. That's probably why I love dogs so much. This time together with Bosco helped me to be a bit more like him in the sense of living in the moment and enjoying every moment with him.

We drove to Big Sur one day for the spectacular views and the stunningly beautiful drive. We stopped a couple of times on the way there to take pictures in an effort to capture the magnificence of what we were seeing. Smelling cool, salty air and hearing thunderous crashing waves on craggy shores was refreshing and invigorating, even though we lived near the ocean in San Diego and could see the beach any day. Something about the rugged nature of this particular coastline was raw and invigorating. The absence of other people in some spots may have helped, too. Along the way, I stopped to eat a banana that I had brought along, anticipating that the restaurant at Big Sur was long on burgers and short on veggies. As I peeled it, I felt Bosco's warm breath on my shoulder leaning forward from the back seat. I unbuckled my seatbelt to turn around and share the banana with him, one bite for him, one for me. After a couple of bites, he seemed so thrilled about this banana sharing that I had to give him the rest of the banana, but in individual bites since he kept waiting for me to take a bite in between. Ever the gentleman, he kissed my cheek when he finished eating and licked every finger. We proceeded along the curving coastline to Big Sur until we reached the lookout point and restaurant, which were not so secluded. After securing a parking spot, I let Bosco stroll around to stretch his legs and have a potty break. He filled up on some water and then we shared some pasta salad before I left him in his shady spot in the car for a brief look at the shop inside. The views all around were equally impressive, but the menu at the restaurant confirmed my suspicions that Bosco and I had shared our lunch al fresco and spent a lot less on simple but delicious food.

On the drive back to Monterey, we stopped by Bixby Bridge. I took in the majestic views of the bridge, while marveling at the feat of architecture undulating gracefully between precipices, and then tried to capture some images of Bosco. He has always been camera shy and tried to look away for photos. In many of his pictures, he looks like he's going to run away and hide, unless he was in mid-play or unaware of the photographer. If only he knew how handsome he looked in those pictures, but I know he still wouldn't have cared how he looked or how others looked. After a week of this leisurely schedule and dog-centric existence, we headed back south to work, life, and home. This time together had become one of the highlights of our life together, so I contemplated how to do more of those types of things when I returned with Bosco.

The first day back, he slept almost the whole day after such a long drive. Coco, his housemate and companion, was happy to come back home after staying with the dog-sitter and sitting out the road trip. We got back into our groove of daily walks, while pacing ourselves to Bosco's energy level. It wasn't until my return after being away for a few days that I realized how much evidence there was throughout the house of Bosco's tumor. Nasal discharge gets into and onto all kinds of things, but I didn't care so much at the time and just wanted to be with Bosco as much as possible and not worry about cleaning up every five minutes. We enjoyed our walks and our short play times, but especially snoozing and snuggling. Bosco had definitely become more easily tired since his radiation, so we worked around that. We walked at his pace, stopped if he started sneezing or coughing, and waited to see how much or little he wanted to do.

Much to my delight, right from the beginning of our walk on Tuesday evening, April 19, only four days after returning from Monterey, he started trotting. Uphill! Woohoo! "I'll run right along with him if he wants to trot," I thought. Coco kept up and seemed to enjoy the accelerated pace. This was turning out to be an excellent outing. Even after the hill, he still tugged energetically on the leash. Alright! We continued at this brisk pace for a few more minutes until we were on the street and he stopped in his tracks to sneeze explosively. As he shook his head post-sneeze, I saw it: as plain as a billboard's large letters along a highway—Bright Red Blood. Seriously? Maybe it would be just one big clot and that would be it. But the next sneeze brought more drops of blood. He regained his composure and plodded ahead as if nothing had happened. Was I supposed to be the doting mom or the veterinarian? I let him walk a few more steps and didn't see more blood. Now he wanted to trot again, but I thought if he trotted, he would breathe faster and increase the chances of having more nasal bleeding, so we walked. Then I saw it again. Drip. Drip. Tail wagging. Drip, drip. What to do? Drip, drip. I hesitated, but then let him walk a few more steps, certain that it must stop soon. We were now about a quarter mile from home. He showed no outward signs of distress, but his nose bleed wasn't diminishing. Time to head home.

As we re-traced our steps on the concrete sidewalk, I could see every drop of blood he had been shedding. Drip, drip, drip, drip. Somehow, it was even worse seeing it on the sidewalk than just coming out of his nose. This impartial, factual writing on concrete was impossible to ignore or misinterpret. Drip, drip. Trouble had arrived and it wasn't going away. As we continued home to the metronomically predictable drip-drip, all I could think of was how to stop it, while I knew that a dog's nose bleed and a human's are very different management dilemmas. Most dogs don't let you put things up their noses to stop the bleeding. Also, a bleeding nasal tumor is expanding and compressing all sorts of tissues around it, rendering those tissues more sensitive, especially after radiation. I already had been using, with some success, a decongestant. For weeks, I had been treated like a card-carrying methamphetamine dealer when trying to buy decongestants to help my dog to breathe better because it turns out that meth entrepreneurs use some medications we need to actually treat patients with diseases. I was not permitted to purchase more than a certain number of tablets in a certain number of days and had to have my information stored on a national registry. I explained that I was a veterinarian and that this medication was for my dog with a nasal tumor. Blank stare. She's a drug addict. What? Ridiculous. I even tried to reason with the pharmacist, after displaying my Drug Enforcement Administration (DEA) card that I have access to drugs that would knock out an elephant. Unimpressed. Medication denied. But now we had to contend with something worse than congestion.

Once we were home and resting, I hoped the bleeding would stop, but even with calming and resting, it continued steadily. He ate his dinner as I called the specialist's office. I requested a Yunnan baio, Chinese herb that can help mitigate bleeding. I explained that Bosco, normally an extremely compliant patient, who offered his leg to technicians when it was time to place an IV catheter, wouldn't even allow me to touch or place a covered ice pack on his nose. There was nothing short of knocking him out that would enable me to get near the source of the bleeding. We were going to have to battle this enemy from the inside out. Before I left to pick up the Chinese herbs, he started sneezing again, this time more violently than before. Blood spewed everywhere and Bosco gagged on it as he tried to swallow the remainder. I had to stop the bleeding. I took him with me in the car to pick up the meds, afraid to leave him alone even for a minute. Fortunately, the meds could be easily administered because he would still take Tofutti cream cheese-covered medications. Amen to that!

Waiting for a cure to kick in that is not instantaneous is torture. How could I explain to Bosco that the gagging, coughing, and choking would soon be over? My thoughts raced between being a veterinarian and knowing things were dire to being Bosco's guardian and wanting to be brave for him. I gave him more pain meds so that he would be more comfortable, but his nose still had a slow bloody drip that wouldn't cease. I spoke with an oncologist technician, Jo, who knew Bosco very well and knew that I wouldn't want him to suffer. She suspected that the bleeding would stop with the help of the meds

219

and then I could spend time with him when he was not in distress. All night, I wrestled with difficult decisions and looked for a sign to make the right one. I propped Bosco's head up on the couch to make him comfortable. He seemed to like it best when I had my arm over his back, just close enough and touching, without bothering his head or nose. All night, I waited for his bleeding to stop completely, only to be disappointed when he sneezed or coughed and it started again. I didn't dare move him off the couch to go upstairs to sleep, for fear that the exertion from going up the stairs would set off another sneezing fit with more bleeding.

By morning, I felt like hell had arrived. I noticed his bleeding had finally stopped. For half a second, I was relieved, but immediately looked at his gums as I had done many times overnight, and now saw that he was becoming pale. He had lost a lot of blood, even for a 75-pound dog. The couch was sprayed with explosions of bloody sneezes. The staircase had sprays of blood from the night before, even though I had cleaned up the biggest messes. The blankets that I had kept changing out around him were soaked with crimson crusts on their edges. I was plugging a dam. Ineffectively. Yes, the bleeding had stopped. But the next big bleed was surely around the corner. The smartest veterinary oncologists in North America couldn't concoct an alternate solution for Bosco. There was no way I could let him go through another night like the last one. I fed him breakfast and he actually ate well, but sneezed and choked a few times afterward. We went outside into the garden together and then I noticed how weak he was as he chose his corner to pee. He sat down on the mulch after he finished, patiently waiting for me to inspect and clean off his feet in case he had stepped into anything that required cleaning. It was our little routine that he still managed to do, without me asking, in his weakened state. It just made me love him even more, if that was possible. I saw the sweetness and light in his face, but I needed to know if he was putting on a good face for me. I gazed at him and in my feeble human English implored, "Is it time? Have you had enough?" and knew from his reluctance to look at me and the way he hung his head a bit lower that it was, and that he had.

You are never prepared for this decision or this morbid moment. I remember occasionally when Bosco was a puppy and I was overwhelmed with love for him and sometimes dreaded the notion of being without him. Through 10 fabulous years of daily experiences and a steady, harmonious cohabitation, we had been each other's best friends. How could this blissful union come to such a tragic end now? So many things in life that are unpleasant last so long. Was I letting him down in his hour of need or being selfish for wanting more time with him? His sadness in the garden was the subtle sign that I needed to be there for him to help stop any more suffering. We had officially tried everything and our enemy was at the front door, fully armed. It was time to lay down weapons and find peace in a time of heartache and sorrow.

After helping ease thousands of animals' suffering in so many ways over the years, I knew one of the most important ways to do so was to say goodbye in a humane and peaceful way for both the patients and their people. I had to become my dog's veterinarian now because Vera the dog mom was falling apart in every possible way and fighting with the harsh reality of having to say goodbye to her beloved boy. I changed into my green scrubs to reinforce this notion. I drove to the warehouse where my VetBus was parked in order to gather all of the supplies I would need. Max's mom, whom I had just left in Monterey not a week earlier, called me to see how Bosco had made it through the night. I fell apart on the phone, telling her what had happened. The scrubs weren't helping. She reminded me of some of the things I remind my patients' guardians who are making similar decisions—let him have dignity before things progress any further. Of course. Sometimes, even as you are doing the right thing, your mind questions and fights the correctness of those actions. I contacted my technician, Anna, to see if she could help me say goodbye to Bosco. We would have a few hours together and then she would come to my house.

I prepared everything we would need as soon as I got home, so I could just spend the rest of the day with Bosco and not fuss with any more details. I told him, like so many times before, how much I loved him and how wonderful he was. His bleeding had stopped, so we retreated upstairs to the bedroom to snuggle for the next few hours. I tried to breathe in every bit of his love and sweetness, even more than I had done for the past 10 years. I didn't want him to see me sad and blubbery. I wanted him to remember this happy and peaceful time together. I reminded him of what a good boy he was and how sweet he was. It was a relief that he had no more bleeding and that he could rest, but any time I tried to convince myself that he'd get better, I flashed back to the previous night and convinced myself again that I had to be the one making the most heart-breaking decision that day.

We lay in the garden on the chaise longue together. Anna, the technician, gave him a sedative injection into his lumbar area, while I fed him lots of cookies with his beautiful big head on my lap. I pet his head as he was chomping on the cookies and touched the side of his mouth where his soft, pink lips came together. I tried not to cry, but doubt I succeeded. Soon, the sedative made his head heavier in my lap, so I knew he was resting easier and not scared or in pain. This sedative helped me, too, knowing that he wasn't hurting or anxious. I told him all of my favorite stories about him, but mostly how much I loved him and that I would see him again. He never even noticed that Anna sedated him because he knew and trusted her and was also being distracted by cookies. As Anna gave him his drugs, I was so grateful to be able to love on him and hold him for his final moments on earth as he fell asleep and gently passed in my arms. Now the sorrow would begin in earnest. I had to touch those soft pink lips one more time and that naked radiated pink nose, too. I kissed his face and inhaled his dog aroma. Those soft floppy ears. The big clunky feet. I knew every inch of this cherished boy and couldn't imagine parting with even one piece of him, much less all of him. I hugged him and cried heartily, shaking and sniffling. How could my best friend leave? Why couldn't I go with him? I didn't want to stay. Everything was better with Bosco. Even a banal trip to the grocery store was more inviting when you had a willing and eager companion for the trip. How would I go on without him?

This question was soon answered by my other dog, Coco. Normally, when saying goodbye, I recommend that all of the pets in the house have a chance to be with the pet who is passing, both before and after. When I placed Coco beside Bosco, she sniffed his still body momentarily and then hopped off the chaise longue in search of crumbs elsewhere. She has not missed a beat since. I didn't want her to suffer from depression, but she barely acknowledged the news outwardly. On the contrary, she easily stepped into Bosco's large shoes. After Bosco's passing, she was soon anxious to make tracks for a walk. I just wanted to take her somewhere quiet, peaceful, and beautiful. I didn't have any expectations of anything exciting. Within a few minutes of walking numbly along the beach with her, my eyes blinked repeatedly to verify what they saw—breaching whales close to the shoreline at the lagoon in Cardiff! It was the most uplifting thing we could have seen, short of Bosco's reincarnation. I would like to think it was a sign from Bosco, even if it was just a happy coincidence of something I hadn't seen in 12 years, but such a relief to witness these magnificent creatures frolicking and content in their world in order to briefly distract me from my sorrow.

Sadness in the face of such a tremendous loss was a theme that would not be readily erased, even with concerted efforts to look for beauty in nature and in life. In fact, the sorrow overshadowed everything I did and felt. Initially, I couldn't stop crying and thought that if I cried five more minutes, my head and face might explode because they were already so swollen and congested from hours of daily tears. I wanted the pain to be over right away. I didn't want to have to go through any more. I had already been through the loss itself. Why should I have to feel more? I thought of so many injustices that existed and how Bosco's loss was on the top of the list. I felt robbed of this most precious and beloved soul. Take my house, my car, whatever. But not my Bosco. I couldn't believe how unjust his death sentence with cancer was. No stay of execution. Cancer really is the enemy. It takes on every kind of opponent big or small, rich or poor, old or young. It's a non-discriminating equal-eradicator. How could I reconcile my hatred for the cancer that had claimed Bosco's life? How does anyone reconcile with a vicious enemy after losing the war? No amount of screaming, shouting, hating, and hurting would bring Bosco back again.

So, I shared my very personal feelings about the love of my life, first in a letter to friends and fans of Bosco, then with a therapist, and now in a book. The letter read as follows:

Hi Guys,

It is with great sadness and some disbelief that I'm sending you all this letter to let you know about my beloved Bosco. After a brave battle against a nasal chondrosarcoma, we had to say goodbye yesterday, April 20, 2016. As many of you know, he had a tough year medically. He got through a mast cell tumor on his prepuce (thanks for your surgery, Dr. Radtke) last May. He got through a toe sarcoma (thanks for removing his toe, Dr. Hughes) in October, he had his shoulder and elbow scoped and then treated with stem cells in the summer and fall (thanks, Dr. Pike). He had radiation twice for his nasal tumor – Aug. 2015 and again in March 2106 (thanks, Dr. Proulx). His nasal tumor was a beast, though. There was reason to be very optimistic between the statistics and his three-month post-radiation CT, which showed the tumor shrinking to almost nothing. But then, like the biological terrorist that cancer is, it just kept growing in spite of treatments. Prednisone helped him breathe more easily for the last few weeks of his life, but it was a sign that even more radiation couldn't beat the cancer. During our walk on Tuesday evening, Bosco started trotting on his own, which made me feel so relieved and happy to see him feeling so good. But as he slowed down, he sneezed repeatedly and with the sneezing came spurts of blood from his nose. The bleeding continued slowly but surely for the remainder of the brief walk, leaving a trail on the sidewalk that we will be able to follow in the future. When we got home, he had several sneezing fits, each producing more blood than the last. Keeping him quiet and resting didn't help. He was also not agreeable to any cold compresses or epinephrine and tissue or anything else that might stop the bleeding. I got some Yunnan baiyo, a Chinese herb used sometimes for such cases to help improve the blood clotting. I don't know if it was the herbs or Bosco's own body finally clotting, but by morning the bleeding had stopped. Bosco was pale, weak, and had gurgled blood in his nose, mouth, and throat throughout the night. It was a night I will never forget and hope never to repeat. By the morning, I knew that even if we briefly stopped the bleeding, this monster in his nose would keep progressing. As I reluctantly realized Bosco's temporary improvement was just temporary, I remembered the week we had just spent together.

Knowing time was running out, we set out on a road trip to Monterey, CA, on April 9th. He always loved any travel adventure and this time would be special because he had another chance to see his beloved boyfriend, Max, a Labradoodle, and his parents, Mindy and Arnie, who have always been so kind and welcoming to Bosco. He got to sleep in late, eat some special foods, which he hadn't done much because of his food allergies, go for car rides, and enjoy walks in Big Sur, and the beaches on Carmel and Monterey. Having the opportunity to enjoy this beautiful and serene part of California one more time with Bosco was a tremendous gift.

All of Bosco's life, though, has always seemed like a gift to me. From the moment I first met him, it was love at first sight. He had so much love in his little (75 lb.) body that it made me want to be a better person. He was my protector, my best friend, my companion, my confidant, and my playmate. His favorite thing to do when I came home was to be chased around the house—up the stairs, over the bed, down the hall, into a different room, down the stairs, into the garden, around and around the garden. Then he would flop on his side, waiting for me to rub his soft belly. If I wasn't careful, I would get the mandatory thank-you kiss with that famous, long tongue. At night he was an Olympic snuggler. First on the couch, then on the bed. He just wanted to be next to me. I was never afraid with him by my side. I was also never worried about him with Coco, even though she gave him some Boston Terrier attitude on occasion. Bosco was everything you could possibly want in a dog, and so many things that would make people better humans.

I miss him with all of my heart, just as I loved him every day with all of my heart. I'm so glad now that I told him at least once if not a dozen times a day how much I loved him and what a good dog he was. My only regret is that he couldn't have another 10 or more years on earth because we need more Boscos! Thanks to all of his supporters and friends for your love, support, medical and surgical attention, belly rubs, head pats, and for accepting his sloppy kisses if he got you. Please send a prayer to him.

Love, Vera

It was a difficult letter to write because I relived so many memories of Bosco's life as I wrote it and longed for those experiences to be recreated or to share more experiences with him. It was sobering and saddening to read the words describing my heart's loss, but also beautiful to hear back from the Friends of Bosco group who were touched by his life. Some people commented that they had suffered similar losses and pain when their dogs had passed, so they understood the immensity of Bosco's passing. Still, the expression on paper, the sharing with a therapist—none of it could pull the knife out of my heart as I ached each day trying to come to terms with the reality that he was never coming back and that we would never be together on earth again. What is life without your soul mate? Yes, I still had another dog— Coco—and family and friends. As I looked at Coco and longed for Bosco, I thought "I'm not a little dog person." This feeling was not meant to detract from Coco's character or even her size. But part of me just didn't know how to put the mountain worth of love that had enveloped Bosco all of his life into a little dog who definitely didn't think I was the alpha and the omega like Bosco did. It would be like the artist Christo taking all of his golden fabric used to encircle the Pont Neuf and trying to wrap it around a Mini. Coco would look at me blankly as I contemplated how to love her more and find a new home for all of my feelings for Bosco. I couldn't love my patients more. There is only so much love you can give a dog or a cat in a 30- or even 60-minute exam. The day Bosco died, I wanted to go to the shelter and bring about 10 Pit Bulls home to try to fill the void. I knew it would take at least that many dogs at that moment to come close. But even 20 or 30 rescued dogs couldn't have dusted away the gritty despair of heartache that would consume me for quite some time as I mourned for my boy Bosco.

I was grateful for work to keep me busy throughout the day and as an outlet for compassion for other animals. Every day, I suffered Bosco's loss anew, barely able to cope with the grief. My only consolation some days was knowing that it was better that he died before I did because he would have suffered even more if he had lost me instead. He loved many people in his life, but I was his number one. He was such a sensitive boy, too, in that he fussed over others, whether they were people or dogs, when he perceived that they were hurting. When Dijon passed away, Bosco barely ate one whole meal a day for three solid weeks. He moped around the entire time, having lost his playmate, even though she was five years older and not quite as playful as he was. In fact, the saddest part about losing Dijon after she enjoyed such a wonderful long life, was seeing Bosco missing her so much. I wouldn't have wanted Bosco to suffer losing me, so now I had to be the one who endured the loss.

Although we know there will be sorrow when we lose our beloved dog or cat or horse or rabbit or turtle or whichever companion we lose, it's impossible to foresee how this loss will manifest or exactly what our companions meant for us and did for us. For example, while he was alive, I could always snuggle with Bosco whenever I felt down or overwhelmed by life. But in my saddest moments after his passing, my comforter, my snuggle buddy was gone, leaving me alone to suddenly feel all of the pain, unshielded and unbuffered by his unwavering presence. Let me be clear that just because a dog or a cat or a person, for that matter, lives in your house with you, it doesn't always mean they are there for you. Bosco was always there, however, as that emotional support system for me and for anyone else who seemed upset. Even if we were watching a movie or a heated topic on TV and people in the room were excited or animated, he would become concerned that there was discontent and try to lay his head on their lap or feet to comfort them. His calming, soothing presence was exactly what I needed to overcome the gaping hole in my heart left behind by his passing.

As I walked numbly, in slow-motion through my daily activities, I doubted I would ever feel joy again. I wouldn't see that happy dog-smile that greeted me every morning from the moment we woke up together to the moment we fell asleep together. Now, Coco literally snuggled into Bosco's spot on the bed with utmost authority and purpose. It was some comfort. We developed our own routine, which was all about Miss Coco. She clearly won't suffer for too many minutes if I leave this earth before she does. Even small tasks that I used to enjoy like watching the birds and plants in the garden each morning as I drank coffee and saw Coco and Bosco sniffing about couldn't bring any joy. Losing Bosco had resulted in losing most of my sensations, including smell, hearing, feeling, and taste. Logically, I knew that Coco needed my attention and care, but I only went through the motions dutifully and mechanically. I barely wanted to speak with anyone because I knew it would result in more tears, which I preferred to share only with Coco, who didn't seem to mind or care.

A month after Bosco died, my friend and neighbor, Cindy, invited me to her house with her in Hawai'i to get away. My tormented mind couldn't imagine how that was going to help bring Bosco back, which was the only way I could envision overcoming his loss. She convinced me that I could do my own thing and just hang out, so I gathered my accumulated flying miles and booked a flight, unsure about how such a trip might have any positive impact. As the plane approached the Big Island and I peered down onto the turquoise coastline, I only wished that Bosco could be with me. While I normally might have some trepidation with turbulence, this time I just thought that if we went down, I could soon be with Bosco. Sometimes, in the following months, when I was driving and someone would cut me off or nearly hit me, I just didn't care and had the same thought about being with my dog. I had no plans for a premature exit, but I often thought if something happened to me, I would be so happy to be with him again. I knew Coco would be okay, but this life of torment without my Bosco was consuming me every day. How could a change in scenery possibly mitigate the grief?

From the rugged volcano fields to the friendly geckos, there was something new and intriguing to look at every day that didn't have a specific memory linked to Bosco. I still thought about him all day, but after about three days, as I overlooked the ocean through the numerous flowering blossoms of my friend's garden and suddenly saw a double rainbow, I noticed myself breathing. I inhaled mindfully, slowly, actually feeling air filling up my lungs, and then consciously compressed my diaphragm to exhale. Who knows if it was the change of scenery or the departure from the scene of the crime, but I started to feel again. Slowly.

When we snorkeled, the other-worldliness of the ocean and its tranquil inhabitants helped buffer tormented, grief-ridden thoughts. If I hadn't been concerned about getting sunburned or turning into a prune, I could've stayed in the water for hours, floating in a world of creatures involved in their own reality, unconcerned about ours. I've always marveled at how immersion in undersea life instills peace. There is a harmony and calm that transcends our experience on terra firma. Whether it was watching the Hawai'i state fish, the Humuhumunukunukuapua`a (triggerfish) and not getting nibbled by them, or following the darting angelfish on their travels, or watching the manta rays feeding at night, I was mesmerized. These wonderful creatures captivated my mind and filled my heart with more love for other animals. Cindy's vibrant and eclectic garden was also a feeding station for wild turkeys, hummingbirds, and many other birds that graced us with their presence and their songs throughout the day. We traveled to some of the beautiful local spots, including the bay where Captain Cook landed and ultimately perished. We went to hear local bands play music, enjoyed some school kids performing hula dance, and took every opportunity to get into the water and enjoy the scenery below. It was truly another world.

One constant reminder of Bosco, however, was Cindy's neighbor's dog, Pono, who was also a Pit Bull, so every chance I got to say hi to him, I visited and gave his huge blocky head a rub and told him what a good boy he was. He exuded that aura of happiness that Bosco always had, too. He was the four-legged deliverer of the aloha vibe on a daily basis. Between Pono, Cindy's hospitality, and the bountiful natural wonders of the island, I started to see beauty again. It was a turning point in my grieving process for Bosco. I still missed him dreadfully every day and felt terrible anguish and physical pain, but slowly I regained my connection with the natural world again, which had seemed very surreal and unimportant during the most profound sorrow. As with any loss, it is hard to accept that we're not going to get over it, because it will be a part of us forever, but rather, it is vital that we somehow get through it. The "through" part of that saying is what's so difficult, because it's like passing through a ring of fire without adequate protection each time those memories resurface.

By sharing Bosco's story, it's not only possible to relive many wonderful parts of his life and the people and animals he touched, but for those people who knew him to remember how he touched them and for those who didn't know him to realize what profound joy a dog like Bosco can bring into one's life. Sometimes, I wondered how a little bag of bones can touch one's heart so deeply. Bosco embodied the concept of love. What was it about Bosco that made him even more lovable and dignified, even as he turned gray over the years, lost hair all over his nose due to the radiation, and spewed sticky nasal discharge like a diseased whale? Objectively, he was no longer as strong as he had been. Even with moderate exercise, he limped sometimes on his right front leg, in spite of stem cell therapy and arthroscopic surgery. His will to enjoy life and still please me grew more dogged. If he couldn't run as fast and frolic limitlessly, he would become an even more devoted companion and guard. Then I thought of some of his boo-boos. The list was pretty short. He liked to hump male dogs, he ate part of my stick shift in my car while waiting for me, and he sometimes stepped in his poop in my back yard, so I had to clean the poop off his feet. How I wish my own list of lifetime infractions were that short! Memories of him were really all very positive. I just wanted more of them.

A few weeks after Bosco passed, I was scrubbing some tiny encrusted blood droplets from the tile on the stairs that I had missed initially and was suddenly reduced to a rag of raw emotion. I was amazed I'd missed these flecks of blood but saddened by the removal of another remnant and memory of my beloved Bosco. Moments like those caused me to float and flounder aimlessly. During the deepest sorrow, I thought I didn't want to be a veterinarian anymore. If I couldn't save my own dog's life, what business did I have trying to help any other animals? What was the point? Who was I without my dog? He was the best part of me. But then I thought of how Bosco would have reacted if he saw me moping about. He would have been equally dismal. It occurred to me during my more objective moments that I wasn't honoring him and his relatives to the best of my ability if I just hid in sorrowful seclusion perpetually. So, I pushed through the pain and have tried to honor Bosco and all other animals by being their advocate and, in some cases, their personal veterinarian. Any time I have the chance to share his story, I do. It helps me, but more importantly, I hope it sheds light on an exemplary ambassador for dogs, and especially Pit Bulls. Bosco was the love of my life, without whom I still feel incomplete. But for others, there are many Boscos out there, just waiting to be adopted, hoping to find their forever homes, and possibly become the love of your life. Give them a chance and let yourself find love!

Bosco

Muscles and bones and tongue and ears
My love grows stronger over all the years.
Belly rubs, tail wags and romps in the park
Always feel safe with a poochie after dark.
Looking for my shadow, who is also my light
When we hang out together the world is right.

Vera Heidolph, DVM

Coco-Puff

Coco announces her arrival with coos, howls, and exuberance as she races up the swimming pool ramp to start her beloved swim therapy. She pants and stomps her little twinkle toes in anticipation of her delightful first plunge. Her physical therapist barely has time to don her own hip-wader rubber suit because Little Miss Impatient cannot wait to get into the water. Coco leaps from the bottom pool step into the water in pursuit of her squeaky toy that's been tossed to the other end of the pool. Once she has chomped down on the squeaky rubber chicken, eliciting squeaks and gurgles, she kicks off the pool wall, returning to the submerged step with her prey securely clamped between her teeth. The swim coach encourages Coco to use both back legs by making her swim in circles between stretches of swimming straight laps. Even though her body type isn't exactly that of a natural swimmer, such as a Labrador Retriever, between her determination and her little flotation device around her neck, she paddles on eagerly.

Occasionally on these outings, she is joined in the pool by an English Bulldog, Body, who is paralyzed in both hind legs, yet swims for 45 minutes at a time. They ignore each other because they're so intently focused on their own swimming pursuits. Toward the end of Coco's half-hour swim session, she tires, but refuses to give up, even as fatigue sets in and her eyelids and head droop between laps. Sometimes, the swim therapist has to perform several tricks to extricate the toy from Coco's mouth because she doesn't want to surrender it. At the mention of exiting the pool, she jumps back into the water, unwilling to stop, stubbornly clamping down on her squeaky toy. As I witness Coco's indomitable spirit in action, I can't help but beam at the progress this little soldier of a dog has made in terms of physical rehab and fitting into her new life. It's especially delightful to watch her joyfully swimming around because this 13-year-old Boston Terrier very nearly didn't make it to her seventh birthday.

Restlessly, I shifted in my chair while waiting in the doctor's office in November 2013. It was only my annoyingly incessant cough and my friends' insistence that forced me to seek medical attention. I didn't have time to be sick while trying to help animals who needed my attention. I scrolled through the list of emails on my phone, scanning for any urgent matters that could be addressed while I waited. The question, "Do you do leg amputations?" caught my attention. Attached to that weighted question was an X-ray image of a dog's femur, snapped into two separate pieces and now in the shape of an "L" instead of a straight line. Even from the limited 2D view on my phone, I could immediately see the problem that needed to be fixed. I called the rescue person to inquire about the details. Not surprisingly, based on her injury, this poor dog had been hit by a car. But now she was at a shelter in Palm Desert, a two-hour drive from San Diego. The shelter had a limited drug supply, especially controlled substances, which are used for pain management. It was just after four p.m. and I learned that the only medication this broken dog had been give all day was meloxicam, a non-steroidal anti-inflammatory drug (NSAID), comparable to Motrin for people. When you've been hit by a bus, the equivalent of a Motrin just isn't enough!

I could have cared less about my stupid cough because now I was getting worked up about this dog's suffering. A three-way conversation with the shelter employee, the Boston Terrier rescue, and me ensued. The shelter was technically already closed for the day as of four p.m. There was no veterinarian on-site or available to do anything else for this injured dog for the rest of the night. She had no bandage or splint and her horrific fracture had not been set or "reduced," so the rest of her leg was dangling down without any support or stabilization. How she hadn't died of shock yet was beyond me, and that was before I knew more facts about her story.

If you've ever loved a dog and fought to save one, you know that sometimes you have to get creative and grovel for help. The shelter employee seemed genuinely concerned and willing to help, but had limited resources, be they veterinary, medical, or pharmaceutical supplies. I begged her to help with a plan to bust this broken Boston Terrier out of the shelter. If she drove the dog home with her and kept her at her house until I could drive up to Palm Desert, I could give her my "Cadillac" controlled drugs for her pain, place a heavily padded bandage around her leg to stabilize it, and drive her back to my home in San Diego that night. This way, she would get all of the medication and treatment she needed without waiting another day.

With minimal arm-twisting, the kind shelter worker agreed to the plan. My head was racing as I plotted my to-do list before I could leave town with the appropriate supplies. At that moment, my doctor walked in to examine me. I barely had the patience to stick around long enough for his exam and consultation because I felt the urgency of this dog's dilemma. The doctor recommended that I get X-rays to rule out pneumonia, which had practically flattened me in the past, so it was a prudent call that I decided to heed. Fortunately, I didn't have to wait long for the X-rays and could fit in one more call to the Boston Terrier rescue about our plan. As much as an amputation can be the right procedure for shattered bones or mangled limbs that can't be pieced back together again surgically, I explained that I was quite hesitant to consider it as an option for an uncomplicated fracture in a six-year-old dog. It was explained to me that the price quotes from surgeons at the local specialty hospitals were out of the rescue's budget. Therefore, they sought my help for a more affordable surgical amputation. We could worry about those details once we got the dog to San Diego, but first she needed pain meds and a ride home.

Once my chest X-rays showed no signs of pneumonia, I was free to head to the warehouse, where my mobile veterinary clinic, the VetBus, was stored. At 33 feet in length, it would be over-kill to drive it all the way to Palm Desert to transport a dog weighing less than 20 pounds, who could easily fit into my car. I packed up all of the supplies I imagined I might need, which was something I did frequently for my house calls as a mobile veterinarian.

As I wound around unfamiliar and unlit roads, my mind meandered back and forth from the events that had led to this dog being hit by a car to fretting over her condition. Knowing less was probably better considering how mad I was about the facts I did know. This little Boston Terrier had escaped from the owner's yard on Friday as one of the owner's relatives was dog-sitting in their absence. After being hit by a hit-and-run driver, she was left to perish on the side of the desert road for three days and nights without pain meds, food, or water. We knew about this timeline because alleged attempts were made by Animal Control to rescue her. They failed because they claimed she was vicious and had tried to bite them. Once Animal Control finally procured the "tools," like a towel, to handle her, she was collected and her owners were contacted. The owners refused to have her leg fixed, but instead asked the veterinarian to euthanize her. Thank God the veterinarian declined to end her life for a broken leg! Instead, she directed them to surrender their dog to the local shelter, where she might be rescued.

Fortunately, my mounting anger with the situation didn't find a negative outlet, such as tracking down the previous owner's home address to express my displeasure with their decisions. Instead, it fueled me in my sickened, coughing state to retrieve and return her quickly and safely back to San Diego. Upon arrival at the shelter worker's home, which appeared to be a canine oasis, I felt instant relief that this sweet little dog's misfortune and misadventures had landed her in a safe place. We lifted the dog bed she was lying on onto the pool table to better examine and hold her. She trembled in fear and pain. "Coco," as she was called, was not quite the ferocious, feral dog that she had been declared to be by Animal Control. Her darling smushy face with a black mask around her wide and frightened eyes and a white stripe down her nose was the epitome of cuteness. The moment I gave her pain meds, all four little black legs relaxed into our arms as she allowed us to gently bandage her broken right hind leg. We tucked her into a softly padded dog bed "nest" on the foot of the passenger seat of my car for her ride back to San Diego. I trusted my co-pilot Bosco for this late-night adventure, and with any dog I brought home either after a procedure while they awaited their owner's pick up, or for an exam. He always demonstrated kind and gentlemanly behavior. His demeanor with Coco was no different. I placed her and her dog bed nest on the floor downstairs when we arrived at home and prepared to sleep on the couch beside her. I didn't want to risk her falling off a bed or down the stairs, but also didn't want her to be in a kennel with a broken leg. Both dogs sniffed each other and then Bosco settled on the couch near Coco as we watched her doze off into a drug-induced, peaceful sleep, probably for the first time in three days.

I still had serious reservations about amputating an otherwise healthy leg on a young dog, but fasted her the next morning in case it was our only option. Technically, Coco was the property of the rescue, so her care was not my sole decision. She rode in a well-padded kennel on the VetBus all the way down to Spring Valley where we had surgical procedures scheduled, while Bosco assumed his usual shotgun position on the passenger seat. My technicians were pleasantly surprised to see me with a second dog and immediately doted on Coco and tended to her as if she were their own dog. Still, her ferocious nature was nowhere to be seen. I performed several surgeries on a variety of cats and dogs until early afternoon. My hope was to find an alternative solution that would be less invasive than the amputation, while still repairing Coco's broken leg. Before starting the next round of surgeries, the Boston Terrier rescue called with an update. They had found a local board-certified surgeon, who would give them a significant rescue discount. Excellent news! I offered to bring her back to my house that night so she could continue receiving the Cadillac of controlled pain medication, and then I could drop her off at the rescuer's house for her surgery the next morning.

Now that anesthesia was off the table for the day, I could finally feed Coco. For a dog whose meals had been almost non-existent the past few days, I anticipated that she would eat almost anything. However, it might have been the opioids that made her snub regular dog food. I hadn't eaten my own lunch yet, so I offered her my plain tortilla to start. Now she was getting interested. She ate the tofu and veggies that were supposed go inside the tortilla next. It didn't matter that I was out of a lunch. Coco's leg was going to be saved, she had eaten her first meal with me, she finally had adequate pain meds, and the rescue would find her a great home, as they had with hundreds of Boston Terriers already.

News of her upcoming surgery was dampened with more details about her previous owners. Once they discovered that she was taken over by the Boston Terrier rescue, they had the gall to request reimbursement for the money they had spent on her X-rays. From her looks, it was obvious that she had been used over and over for breeding purposes, so they had had plenty of opportunities to profit from her puppies. Not only had the previous owners not bothered to spay her, which significantly increased her chance of developing mammary cancer, but when the surgeon spayed her after fixing her broken leg, she discovered Coco's uterine horns were filled with pus, a potentially life-threatening condition known as pyometra. Unspayed female dogs commonly develop pyometra, also known as cystic endometrial hyperplasia (CEH), which is yet another reason we recommend spaying them. How crazy was it that Coco was almost killed by the car that ran her over, but her life was inadvertently saved because she would have died from untreated pyometra!

After only 24 eventful hours of being with Coco, I was already starting to miss her as I said goodbye before her surgery. She had already wormed her way into my heart and Bosco's heart. He couldn't have been more thrilled with his cute little canine companion. Coco spent the next month after her surgery recovering at a foster family's home near Brea, California. When I saw pictures of her new digs, I was reassured that she was very well-loved and cared for. The rescue reached out to me, inquiring if I would be able to dog-sit Coco for a couple of weeks while the foster family left town for some college football games over the Christmas and New Year's holidays. Of course! I was delighted to be reunited, because we often do surgeries or send pets for adoption and don't get a chance to see them again. I wondered if she would remember much of her brief drug-induced sojourn with Bosco and me. She acted like we were old friends and readily made herself at home, sharing Bosco's big dog bed with him and sunning herself on the warm patio stones.

She was moving fairly well for having a big fracture repair only five weeks earlier. I enjoyed spoiling her over Christmas and spending time together with her as she and Bosco got re-acquainted. He was trying to be her protector and best friend, ready to play or snuggle if given the green light.

Coco most likely hadn't had many canine companions or interactions except for being bred and tending to her puppies, based on her behaviors. On the VetBus, we spay and neuter many kittens, so she had the opportunity to see those babies up close and personal. Coco quivered with anticipation and excitement, pushing everything out of her way to get closer and then, finally, with our supervision, we let her sniff her first kittens. She acted like the kittens' long-lost mother, licking, cleaning, and fussing over them fastidiously. Every subsequent cat or kitten that she has seen on the bus has elicited the same reaction. Her ideal home would probably have a few dozen kittens for her to mother, something that would land me in a hospital with an inhaler and an oxygen tank due to my severe allergies to cats.

During our time together, Coco grew accustomed to the routine of walks and feedings, going to work on the VetBus with me, and even enjoyed sporting some of the dog sweaters the rescue had sent with her. At work, she would fret if she thought an animal was in pain or distress and sit by them or even on their dog beds to comfort them as they awoke from surgery in a confused state. So, when the Boston Terrier rescue checked back with me to see how long Coco might stay with me, I wanted to say forever, but I hesitated only because I still hoped that she would develop more of an interest in Bosco. Every day, he would go to great lengths to bring her toys and sniff her and try to snuggle with her when she was resting on his dog bed. Coco's idea of playing with Bosco was that he retrieved a ball or some other toy, and then Coco played with the toy by herself. When Bosco tried playing with the returned ball, she growled at him briefly, sending my 75-pound Pit Bull into a respectful retreat. In my perfect dog family picture book, Coco would have shown more interest in actually playing with Bosco the way he liked to play.

In February, my mother arrived for her annual migratory visit from Canada and instantly took a shine to Coco. She was the perfect size for my mom, who enjoyed walking her every day. Upon returning home from those walks, Coco immediately looked for Bosco, which seemed to be her subtle way of showing that she *did* care about him. I had to remind myself how her life must have been before she was rescued. She wasn't allowed to be a normal dog with other dog companions other than her own puppies. Her job was to propagate for profit. I don't think she was harmed or under-fed in her previous home, because she showed no signs of human fear or malnutrition. If offered an assortment of small squeaky plush toys, Coco would gather them up and assemble them in her dog bed, where she would tend to them as if they were her puppies. These mothering characteristics made me wonder further about the circumstances of her time with the puppies that she was expected to produce. I could tell she must have been an attentive mother, but I hoped she was able to be with her puppies long enough to nourish and mother them before they were sold off.

Two months of dog-sitting had turned into three by the time the Boston Terrier rescue checked in again to see how Coco was doing at my house. I hesitated once again, and only because she didn't share Bosco's overt affection for her and his desire to run around and play with her. I worried that it wouldn't be fair to him. As the months passed and I pondered this decision, I saw a relationship develop between them that answered the question for me. In contrast to my expectation of two dogs frolicking and racing around while playing together as Dallas and Dijon and then Dijon and Bosco had, Bosco and Coco were more silent partners, exploring my garden, dog parks, and sidewalks together side by side. It was a relief to see them sharing a dog bed for a snooze during the day, usually at Bosco's insistence. It was time to make it official and adopt Coco.

Part of the vetting process of joining our family was testing her ability to come to work with me on the VetBus and getting along with all of my patients. Coco was bulletproof. Even if another dog growled or barked, she remained unfazed. She would briefly greet and sniff a new patient and then search for the all-day entertainment of her squeaky ball or rubber chewing bones. She has the same reaction to a little 5-pound Chihuahua as she does to a massive 150-pound Mastiff or Great Dane looming over her. Size or breed doesn't matter. They're all mildly interesting for a brief sniff and a greeting, and then she's off to the next adventure, or preferably a squeaky ball or toy.

She could also be left in the house with Bosco for a few hours at a time while I worked without having a meltdown or destroying the house. After Destructo-Dijon's separation anxiety antics, I was so grateful that she was not at all disturbed by my departures. She seemed quite happy when I returned, instantly howling and cooing a gurgled greeting for me to pet her and play ball with her as I admired her Pelé-like ball handling skills. Although I see it and hear about it from clients and friends whose dogs are fussy eaters, our partnership was not going to work if it took an hour to cook for her, and half a day for her to decide if she was going to eat her food. Fortunately, her appetite has always been healthy to the extent that her internal feeding clock is more precise than a Swiss watch. When we turn back the clocks an hour in the fall, I have to re-set her feeding time gradually because her stomach is still on summer time. Unlike Bosco, who wouldn't want to bother me with a food request, Coco not only solicits me or whomever is around for food, but she actually tap dances around her bowl beseeching her person to fill it promptly, and snorts impatiently if they don't. So, after passing my basic tests of playing well with others, being comfortable at home without supervision, and eating well, Coco's assimilation into the pack was under way.

Perhaps it was her willingness to go along for any adventure that obscured the fact that she was a special needs dog. It was easy to focus on her abilities because she didn't seem to be left out of any action or fun due to her previous injuries. Her repaired femur had healed well according to the surgeon and the follow-up X-rays. She ran for her ball, albeit with a bit of a hitch in her giddy-up as she extended her right leg sideways. If she heard the crackling of a bag of dog treats downstairs in the kitchen all the way from upstairs, her little feet would fly down the carpeted stairs while sliding her right leg along to the side. She readily chose to hop onto the sidewalk from the street instead of taking the flatter, easy-access approach when given a choice. She got around so well that I was surprised and disappointed to discover that she couldn't fully bend her knee. Subsequent X-rays and consults with different surgeons over the next few years revealed that although her fracture was repaired and fully healed, the soft tissues around her knee joint were now stuck, preventing her from being able to fully bend it. Barring surgical intervention that couldn't guarantee a complete fix, we would most likely not be able to restore full range of motion to her right hind leg. I started her on physical therapy to help improve her range of motion and strengthen her surrounding muscles and soft tissues.

Fortuitously, Coco has taken to swimming like a fish to water. Her inflatable neck ring elevates her head, preventing her from taking in too much water as she scoops up her squeaky rubber chicken like a whale feeding on krill. After half an hour of this high-energy swimming, Coco often resists relinquishment of her aquatic trophy. With eyelids half-closed, she stands elbow deep in water, teetering in a semi-trance, fatigued, but unwilling to let the party end. We have tried many tricks to remove the toys from her small, but strong mouth, such as substituting a treat for the toy. Those attempts have not always been successful. Once she has swum to her heart's content, the next half hour of her spa treatments consists of cold laser therapy, massage, stretching, shock wave therapy, and ultrasound. As her therapist cradles her on her lap, Coco's eyelids finally relax shut and she dozes off, completely spent and content. Even though her gait is mechanically imperfect, her weekly physical therapy has improved her mobility and always lifts her spirits to their highest.

Although Coco obviously came with some special physical needs and even required a couple of additional surgeries to enable her to breathe better, it didn't seem like she needed much more than a soft landing in order to fit in and make herself comfortable in my home. Her soft landing was both literal with three to four dog beds per room and figurative in the sense of being there and making her feel comfortable and loved. She takes being a canine couch-potato, resting, and sunbathing quite seriously. All she needs to feel comfortable wherever we are is a soft and comfy dog bed, couch, or blanket. In the absence of a proper bed, she has made a habit of finding comfort in almost any position on any surface while basking in the sun. I've often found her belly up, rolling left and right on the flagstones of my garden while luxuriating in the warm California sunshine.

One day, I was moving from room to room in my house and suddenly realized Coco was not with me. I searched every room frantically, checked the garage, and then surveyed the back yard. How could she have escaped the dog-proof fence? I hadn't opened any doors. In a panic, I was trying to figure out what could have happened to her as I stepped back inside. A creaking sound from outside drew my attention to my old wood dining table outside the window. There, on the top of the table, was my little sun worshipper, Coco, rolling to and fro on her back, kicking up her legs in wild abandon. She must have jumped up onto a chair and then hopped onto the table to bathe in the sun puddle. I didn't realize the lengths she would go to for her vitamin D therapy, but was relieved to find her safe and sound.

Not only does Coco find creative ways to do things she enjoys, but she must also have developed an instinctive coping mechanism during her years of being bred repeatedly. I had never had a dog who had this dirty habit, so my experience with it was limited to client descriptions and stories from friends. Seeing it in action was like watching a train wreck in slow motion and not being able to stop it before it happened. While it's a great relief to see a rescued dog exhibiting self-confidence, it's quite another matter to see not only no shame, but extreme pride in one's self—body, spirit, and all. Coco's extreme self-confidence manifests occasionally when she demonstrates that her own poop doesn't just smell good, but she acts like it's quite tasty! The name of the canine culinary crime Coco commits is coprophagia, aka eating poop. German Shepherds are known for having coprophagia. Many small dog breeds also find their self-produced tootsie rolls to be a delectable delicacy. How could it be that a dog with every food source and chew toy available would find her own poop palatable? I was mortified! Fortunately, prompt poop patrolling on my part prevents forbidden potty pilfering on Coco's.

It was previously posited that nutritional deficiencies caused dogs and other species to consume their own droppings, but today's more balanced diets and evidence of behavioral influences have reduced those deficiencies to a minority of cases of coprophagia. Some dogs eat their own feces to avoid being scolded by their guardians if they accidentally defecate indoors, thus literally hiding the evidence of their crime. Coco's crimes were committed outdoors, so that theory didn't apply to her. Other dogs have coprophagia due to stress, boredom, lack of play activity, or separation anxiety, some of which may have applied to her earlier life. When puppies are placed in crates for extended periods of time during their first few months of life—the crucial timeframe for socialization—and don't socialize enough with other people or dogs, they can also develop coprophagia. Being exposed to a breeding environment in which Coco was the mother of several litters of puppies, she may have witnessed her own mother cleaning up her feces and that of her littermates by licking their bottoms. This behavior is a normal maternal instinct that cleans puppies and stimulates them to defecate at an early age. Both repeat mothers and exposed offspring can subsequently develop a habit of eating feces, even if it isn't in a maternal setting. Coco's coprophagia may well have developed from those influences and/or crate confinement, which is common among dog breeders, especially puppy mills. For a dog who likes eating some disgusting things, she has been blessed with a pretty sturdy constitution, rarely exhibiting diarrhea or vomiting.

In light of her tough tummy, it was all the more worrisome to find a puddle of poochie vomit on the floor one August morning in 2016 and a despondent looking Coco, barely lifting up her head from the couch. She didn't even want to get up. Her face couldn't suppress a pained look, which was very uncharacteristic for her. Mornings are usually her snuggling time when she leans against me to solicit a head rub or a belly rub. She hadn't even made it to bed the previous night. Her head was flaming hot to the touch and she tensed when I slid my hand under her belly to lift her up. I carried her outside to see if she needed to relieve herself. She peed and then plodded heavily back inside, where she vomited again, weakening further. I grabbed my stethoscope to listen to her heart and lungs. Her heartbeat was double the usual speed and her pulses felt weak. My dog was at death's door!

I rushed her to my neighborhood veterinary hospital, where I had brought Bosco back from the brink of death with his anaphylactic reaction to an insect bite. The veterinarian and the technicians swiftly placed an IV catheter and started her on IV fluids, pain meds, and anti-nausea medication between X-rays and blood work. Her temperature was 103.6 degrees F, whereas a normal temperature should be under 102.5 F. She was burning up as she lay almost motionless. My veterinarian mind ran down the list of differential diagnoses and fretted over the worst-case scenarios. The night before, she was fine, but the next morning she looked like she had been run over for the second time in her life. Her darling little squishy face that normally radiated joy and serenity winced with discomfort. Soon after the pain meds were administered, the pained look was replaced by a look of just feeling lousy. The radiologist would arrive soon at the hospital, as previously planned, so he could add her to his list of ultrasound patients and scan her belly to answer some questions that the X-rays couldn't answer definitively. I left her at the hospital while I attended to some house calls.

Upon my return, I met the radiologist in the lobby. When he suggested we step outside to discuss Coco's ultrasound, I had a sinking feeling in my gut. She didn't have an intestinal obstruction, but he found a mass on her spleen. How big? How bad? Was she bleeding out? What to do next? She wasn't bleeding into her abdomen at all and the mass was "only" 1.5 cm in diameter. To determine its nature would be too risky right now, according to the radiologist, considering it involves inserting a needle into an extremely bloody organ that can result in unseen and uncontrollable hemorrhage. For those of us who are nervous Nellies and need to know the facts NOW, this answer wasn't entirely satisfactory. I understood and agreed with the logic, but knew my impatient side would be antsy for the entire month that he suggested we wait to repeat and compare Coco's abdominal ultrasound. Her fever, nausea, and pain all resolved with medical treatment in the hospital. They suspected that she had severe gastroenteritis from some unknown dietary indiscretion, possibly sniffing or licking something naughty during her walk near the ocean the night before. During those four weeks of waiting to repeat the ultrasound of her belly, I had to leave town for my niece, Alexandra's, wedding. As much as I wanted to celebrate with her, my mind kept returning to Coco and her well-being.

Finally, the four-week wait was over and we could repeat her ultrasound. The radiologist confirmed that her splenic mass had grown and was looking rather plump, which is worrisome. The spleen has a thin capsule surrounding it that is similar to snug-fitting Saran Wrap. A growing mass can be painful because the spleen and its thin covering are well innervated. Even worse than the pain is the concern of the mass bursting through the capsule, rupturing and bleeding quietly, or even fatally, into the abdomen. It was time for surgery.

I've removed plenty of spleens, but now that it was my own dog's, there was additional worry about the nature of the mass attached to it. Fortunately, Coco is an excellent patient, as all of my dogs have been. My technician and I set up everything in advance for her surgery and recovery, and fortunately had a most uneventful surgery and anesthesia. In the middle of her beautiful spleen was a knob-like projection with a tightened splenic capsule around it that was threatening to burst from tension at any moment. We usually remove the entire spleen in these situations and don't typically wait for the masses to be diagnosed as malignant before excising them. Even a benign bloody tumor can prove fatal if it ruptures, so out they must come.

Coco recovered on the VetBus post-op nestled in soft blankets that formed a little dog bed nest. She handled the anesthesia and all of her pain meds very well. Her entire spleen with its mass was submitted to the pathologists for evaluation that would determine her future. Surgically removing the spleen was easy, but awaiting results that could shorten her life by years was agonizing. She slept at home that night with the help of Cadillac pain meds. The next morning, I lifted her off the bed, avoiding her long, zipper-like abdominal incision. I prayed that everything was okay on the inside and could see that her incision looked great on the outside. I placed her onto the ground gingerly to let her walk outside and was pleased to see her moving quite well. Food would be another matter. Opioids often obliterate the appetite, so I didn't have high hopes of her eating much breakfast. However, her special sick-dog diet consisting of warmed up tofu and rice was so appealing that she didn't just nibble on it, but even placed her front paw into the food bowl to secure it while she plow-chowed her entire breakfast. I marveled at her bounce-back less than 24 hours post-splenectomy.

She rested mostly during her two weeks of post-op recovery between special meals, garden sunbathing, and brief walks outside. Meanwhile, I paced mentally awaiting her lab results, checking online several times each day. Finally, they arrived. Before looking at them, I had a moment of peace not knowing, considering I had already lost Bosco that year and couldn't possibly fathom losing another dog. The pathologist's report came back as a benign splenic tumor. What a relief! She was safe. One added bonus of this unfortunate incident was that she could never get a splenic tumor now that her spleen had been removed.

Coco was soon back to her regular routine of racing me to the garage when I filled up her food bowl for each meal, which I have named Coco's canine feeding foxtrot. On the way back to the kitchen she would gallop ahead of me, with the occasional side glance back at me to ensure that I was keeping up with her as she pranced and danced around the bowl and my feet until her meal was topped with water and tofu, and then served.

In between her surgery and lounging life at home, Coco decided to keep things interesting by giving us another health scare. While my mom was visiting, she took Coco out for her usual stroll. I was working from home, attending to paperwork, when Mom rushed back inside, trembling as she held Coco in her arms. Even though she's quite fit for her age, carrying a 19-pound dog who's shaped like a small cannon for several minutes is quite the physical feat for an 88-year-old woman. Coco's eyelids were only half open and she looked like she'd been run over—yet again! Mom explained that while Coco was intently sniffing flowering bushes along the sidewalk, she held up one of her paws as if she had stepped on something sharp and wouldn't put her foot down. Mom immediately picked her up and mustered the strength to carry her home. I couldn't find anything in her foot or leg, so I suspected an insect sting, most likely a bee or a wasp. I ran for my injections to treat her and quickly gave her an antihistamine and a steroid shot. Before they had a chance to kick in, she became lethargic and started sliding down and slumping onto her dog bed. Caught off-guard, I realized I didn't have all of my supplies for an IV catheter to give her IV fluids. In a pinch, I administered the fluids I did have subcutaneously (under the skin) instead of intravenously. She soon responded to the fluids, antihistamines, steroid, and pain meds by perking up and looking around like nothing had happened. Since that episode, there's always an IV catheter ready for action if needed at my house.

I had the opportunity to use those emergency supplies a couple of years later. While walking Coco on a leisurely Sunday afternoon, she did her usual sniff, stride, and sniff routine. In the middle of a grassy field about a quarter mile from my house, she yelped and held her leg up as if she had stepped on something sharp. I checked her foot, but couldn't see anything, especially not without glasses. Still, she was very irritated and immediately licked her foot in discomfort. As I approached her to look at her foot again, she took a few steps away from me and then slumped, splaying her legs out to her sides as she slid to the ground. Her eyelids were almost closed. I felt a faint heartbeat, but almost non-existent pulses and noticed she had stopped breathing for a moment. While compressing her chest with one hand, I covered her nostrils and blew into her mouth, fearing I wouldn't be able to breathe enough life into her again. I continued until I saw her breathe again on her own and felt her pulses. She needed more treatment, but first I had to get her home. It would be just as fast to get her home as it would be to get her to the closest veterinary hospital, so without a car I carried her home at a slow trot, while compressing her chest intermittently with one hand to keep her blood circulating. As soon as I got her home, I treated her as if she were in the ER: epinephrine, IV catheter, IV fluids, steroid injection, antihistamines, and pain meds. As I waited for the treatments to take effect, I examined her leg and foot aided by a pair of glasses and—voilà—I found a tiny black stinger in the area where she had been licking. Now, in addition to poop bags and house keys, I've added a pre-loaded syringe of epinephrine to my dog walking accoutrements to prevent anaphylaxis from any future bee stings.

The only other injections Coco has needed since the bee sting episodes have been treatments to help her arthritis in her elbows and shoulders. Just as Bosco experienced elbow arthritis, so has Coco, confirmed by X-rays and repeated consults with a surgeon. When the surgeon suggested Platelet Rich Plasma (PRP) injections as her next therapy, I investigated the therapy even further than I had when Bosco had his treatments a few years ago. I took a course to learn more about the science behind it and purchased the specialized centrifuge and the injection kits so that I could administer Coco's and other patients' PRP injections myself. We draw a patient's own blood, spin it in the specialized centrifuge to separate out the platelets into a highly concentrated form, and then inject the PRP into the patient's affected joints to facilitate joint healing. Coco will never have a mechanically normal gait due to her unbending back leg, but with a few PRP injections and regular physical therapy, her comfort level has improved significantly. After enduring pain, suffering, and neglect at the hands of humans, it's only fitting that her human help ease any pain or discomfort she may have now. If you've ever loved a dog and wondered about your rescued dog's life before you rescued them, you just want to make them better and never have them hurt or fear again.

It's somewhat curious that after everything Coco has endured, she has an innate desire to nurture or heal both animals and people. She sat on top of Bosco the first time he had a nose bleed before we had even diagnosed his nasal tumor. On the VetBus, she sits beside dogs and cats, of her own volition, before and after their procedures. While my mom recovered from her total hip replacement, Coco would often join her on the couch to snuggle and lay her little head on my mom's healing leg.

Looking back at how Coco's life has evolved since I first met her, it's safe to say she's living a better life where she'll always be cared for and loved. The reservations I initially had about a small dog fitting into the pack quickly vanished as her big dog personality disguised in a little dog's body was given a chance to shine. Not only has she kept up with my working life on the road and the many cats and dogs she encounters, but she also delights in and has given comfort to both veterinary patients and some of their worried owners during stressful times. She ultimately became Bosco's quiet sidekick, which was a great gift for a dog who loved other dogs. The previous reservations I had about her size were outweighed by advantages, such as being able to include her in a trip to Monterey by carrying her onboard the flight in a carrier, or being able to bathe her in the kitchen sink.

Although I thought I was saving her life and providing her with a better home, Coco has made my life so much better. Her positive impact on my life starts first thing when we wake up as she stretches and performs in-bed sleepy-dog yoga against my side, while requesting a head and belly rub, until the moment she nestles against my side again at night. She's my constant companion, whose little sunshine personality is infectious when my spirits plummet, reminding me to enjoy life's simple pleasures. As I mechanically contemplate the list of errands to complete around town, Coco races to my parked car in the garage, as if we are Lewis and Clark forging ahead to explore new frontiers. Always up for an adventure, even at 13 years of age, Coco still brings me laughter, joy, and smiles every day. What a gift this rescued little soul continues to be!

Ode to Coco-Puff

Coco's comfort is my joy

Gleefully devouring every toy.

The pitter-patter-pitter of her twinkle toes

Running with delight, led by her crumb-sniffing nose.

Greeting strangers whom she meets as she requests head rubs

We'd see a wiggly, jiggly, wagging tail if she had more than just a nub.

Her nineteen pounds of spirit fill up the whole house

Even when she's fast asleep, quiet as a mouse.

Aquatic antics are the highlight of every week

Paddling fervently to pursue anything with a squeak.

To be greeted by her playful, gurgly howl when we meet

Is rivaled only by waking to the feel of her strong heartbeat.

Vera Heidolph, DVM

One life at a time

I have come to admire and love many more breeds of dogs and cats throughout my career because it seems the more breeds and species of animals I meet, the more I like. Regrettably, the endearing personalities, captivating eye color, fabulous fluffy coat, or agility capability that attract people to certain breeds don't guarantee that they will be free of diseases or genetic conditions that can diminish the quality or the length of their life. In fact, some dogs and cats with the most wonderful personalities and beautiful looks have lousy genetics that can result in heartache for them and their people. Although the most common reason I hear from prospective pet guardians who want to **buy** their new family member from a breeder or pet store is "I want to know what I'm getting," after 24 years in the field of veterinary medicine, I'm going to burst the bubble by revealing that you're almost guaranteed to be getting several medical and/or surgical conditions with any purebred dog or cat. Every month and every year of a dog's or cat's relatively short life is so precious, so why would we want to support that program, shortening their potential lifespan and our time together?

My purebred Boxer, Dijon, who came from a breeder, could have died at only nine years of age if I hadn't diagnosed and treated her breed-related heart disease. My purebred Rottweiler, Dallas, who was clearly a genetic lemon, required nine non-elective surgeries throughout her life, all because of bad breeding. My rescued purebred Boston Terrier required surgeries just to help her breathe normally. There are simply no guarantees of medical or orthopedic soundness with purebred pooches purchased from breeders. I am often asked which breed is best. I have to say that **Rescued** is my favorite breed! This is not to say that I don't love all of the breeds I have met. It is because the most fatal, yet completely preventable disease that kills millions of cats and dogs every year in the United States alone is pet over-population. The most tragic side effect of choosing a purpose-bred pet instead of a rescue is that by breeding more dogs and cats, we are directly *ADDING* to the pet over-population dilemma. Veterinarians want to save lives. So many animal lovers want to save animals, too. If you've ever loved a dog and are curious about how you could help another dog or cat, this chapter offers a perfect example of how to save animals - one life at a time.

Sweet Pea is the poster child for saving a shelter dog's soul. Whether she was found tied to a tree on that hot July day or tied to the railing of an apartment staircase does not matter. Varying stories exist. She was abandoned, severely neglected, and spiritually dejected. Chronic, untreated skin infections left her bald over half of her trembling body with massive, painful open sores. Both of her eardrums were completely ruptured from years of chronic, untreated ear infections. Her ears were filled to the brim with smelly, irritating wax and dirt. Bright, pink, inflamed, and infected gums surrounded her worn teeth. And yet, beneath all of that pain, infection, and neglect was an innocent soul in desperate need of love and medical attention. The hair she did have was short, black, and white with a black patch around her left eye and a black dot on the top of her head. Her blocky head hung low in fear or pain. Layers of wrinkly skin hung off her hind legs like a Sharpei, yet her face and the rest of her body looked like an American Bulldog. At first, her swollen and blistered feet were too painful for her to even walk, so she was carried or driven in a cart or laundry basket from her dog run at the shelter to the treatment area. She winced in pain with each touch, however gentle. Thank goodness for veterinarians, technicians, and assistants who were so kind and gentle with her as they treated her broken, bloody, and bald skin. She cringed as water touched her sensitive skin with each bath, but never tried to bite. The veterinarians hypothesized that it was most likely the first time Sweet Pea had EVER had a bath in nine years.

Whether they are labeled as holistic or not, veterinarians who care for abused or neglected animals like Sweet Pea are often treating a wounded soul as much as their physical scars, scrapes, and infections. Although many other veterinarians or no-kill shelters might have considered Sweet Pea's condition too severe, costly, or time-consuming to treat, the team at San Diego Humane Society saw the soul who needed saving and valiantly set about doing so. At times, I've seen good-natured healthy dogs, cats, and horses being muscled by technicians, trainers, or veterinarians so that their personalities become mistrusting and aggressive. The San Diego Humane Society team did the exact opposite. Antibiotic pills, creams, and medicated baths helped heal her open skin wounds and lessen Sweet Pea's discomfort so she could gradually walk again, but *how* the team cared for her lifted her despondent spirits.

By the time she could be comfortably handled and bathed in a home environment, this nine-year-old dog had already spent a few months in the shelter. The staff named her Sweet Pea for the sweetness of her spirit, which everyone noticed right away. The San Diego Humane Society team also knew it would take a special individual who wasn't looking for the traditional "Best in Show" for beauty or perfection and would embrace a "medical" adoption. My friend and neighbor, Teresa, had been visiting shelters and rescue organizations for more than two years in search of the right dog. Her criteria were a medium-sized senior dog, who was good with other dogs and people. As she saw the San Diego Humane Society video, "She's the Sweetest of Sweet Peas" on YouTube, Teresa was drawn to her story and to the sunshine she exuded. This once abandoned dog was being appreciated for her playfulness when it came time to chase a ball. She could walk and run and even wag her hairless, rat-like tail. Her floppy, pink tongue hung out of her wide mouth like a swinging wet sock. Once trembling and terrified, she was now trusting as she let people pet her and play with her.

When Teresa first met Sweet Pea, she was unsure of how she might be because of her imposing appearance. She was initially shy but had built up some confidence with the shelter staff to trust a new person. As they visited in the yard, Sweet Pea ran after the ball between sitting by Teresa and allowing her to pet her back. One of the many benefits of rescuing an older dog was that Teresa wouldn't have to run her for hours, like a puppy, to get the beans out. Sweet Pea showed her lively side but settled down when it was time to relax. By the end of Teresa's first meeting with Sweet Pea, she felt a connection.

I accompanied Teresa during her second visit to the shelter to bring my own dog for a test drive and to see how Sweet Pea looked from a medical perspective. My initial conclusion was that she had come a long way from her video. Her hair was starting to grow back in places. She seemed a bit down and out as I glanced at her resting on her bed in her own room at the shelter. How can any dog understand why they have been discarded and dumped like unwanted rubbish? How heartbreaking it must be for them to wonder when they will see their family again, however suboptimal their previous home life might have been. I put on my happy face, reluctant to let Sweet Pea sense any sadness I had for her situation. We walked outside to the dog yard, where we could see Sweet Pea off leash and in action with a ball or a rope toy. Her body posture changed to a more relaxed stance and was open to greeting new people. Once she seemed comfortable with everyone, we introduced her to my Boston Terrier, Coco, whom I deem bulletproof with people, dogs, and cats. The shelter had assessed Sweet Pea as being relatively uninterested in other dogs, which was most likely the result of minimal socialization in her previous life. They sniffed each other briefly, then searched for the nearest toy or ball in the yard and entertained themselves chomping on squeaking toys and balls. As much as I wanted to run up to this imperfect, bald bundle of a dog to hug her and tell her everything was going to be alright and she was coming home for good, I restrained myself. She would have to come to me on her own terms so I wouldn't overwhelm her with my own excitement. Fortunately, her curiosity was greater than any residual fears. She approached with some initial hesitation, but as she neared and felt safer, she embarked on canine recon 101: first, short sniffs, followed by more prolonged and excited sniffs. How I wish I knew what that that recon sniffathon revealed to her! I passed her test of trust and soon had her enjoying a head rub and leaning in for more attention. I had a good feeling about her. Beneath the healing but neglected exterior was a sweet soul experiencing love, attention, and care for what appeared to be the first time in her life. Although it was Teresa who had been searching for her sensational senior citizen for more than two years, it was I who was suddenly impatient and antsy to get Sweet Pea home. I asked Teresa even before we left the shelter if I could be Sweet Pea's godmother. I was confident that her ongoing medical issues could be addressed and we could make Sweet Pea comfortable and healthier.

On the drive home the next day, Teresa realized Sweet Pea had probably never been in a car before. The San Diego Humane Society crew helped load her into the car, but she promptly jumped into the front seat, which wouldn't be safe for the ride home. She was secured before take-off, but that didn't prevent her from expressing her displeasure with this new-fangled four-wheeled contraption and all of the objects rapidly moving by her as they drove along the highway. She howled, fussed, and fretted. There may have been a "poops-ident" (an accidental pooping in the wrong place at the wrong time). Back on terra firma at her new home, Sweet Pea explored Teresa's house and settled in, worn out from the excitement of the adoption event and the harrowing trip around the world, which was really only 25 miles from the shelter to her new home.

Teresa used her imagination and patience over the next few months to convince Sweet Pea that the world was not going to end each time she went for a car ride. With my dog Coco as her sentinel and comfort-canine, she entered a car more willingly. We started with Coco, Sweet Pea, and Teresa all in the back seat while I drove, in order to comfort and hold Sweet Pea and to prevent her from launching into the front seat. A seatbelt alone at that point would not have been enough reassurance. Gradually, with each subsequent vehicular adventure, Sweet Pea sat in the back seat with just Coco while her mom was in the front, ready in case she tried to make a break. We increased her short rides around the block to a few miles bit by bit. The goal was to convince Sweet Pea that "good things happen when you go for a car ride," because the first couple of rides had not been so pleasant. Sometimes, only heavy sedatives can ease a dog's phobias, but the goal was to move away from sedatives to a more innate desire to jump into a car. Lifting a scared stiff 70-pound dog is also not an easy feat and can be taxing on the back.

Between a squeaky toy and Coco in the back seat, Sweet Pea became a willing participant for automotive adventures. Once she made it to the ball park, she relished chasing tennis balls. At home, Sweet Pea could chew on balls and squeaky toys for hours, or more precisely minutes, if the toy succumbed to her near toothless but powerful chomping. Although she started off with enough energy to go for walks, chase balls, and be an active participant in day-to-day activities, we could not anticipate how she would change once she had a few more surgeries. She needed a dental to clean the teeth that could be saved and to extract those that were rotten or painful or both. Prior to her dental, Teresa heard a thumping sound at home and thought something was falling down her carpeted stairway. Instead, she discovered Sweet Pea belly surfing down the stairs, while propelling herself forward with her front paws. We are in California, so we have dogs who like to surf on surfboards in the ocean, but I had never seen or heard of a dog surfing down the stairs. I was perplexed at her display of athleticism until I saw her belly. Her mammary glands hung low, swinging to and fro as she wriggled on her back. Because the skin was so stretched out and pendulous, there was a nasty, red skin fold dermatitis that had developed between the left and right mammary glands creating bright red and open weeping sores down her belly. There were also some lumps that had appeared suddenly in her mammary glands, so we needed to remove those promptly. We extracted a few teeth and removed skin masses and sagging or suspicious mammary glands. Removing some of the masses on her back was like working on elephant skin. Years of skin infections had made it so thick that only staples could hold the incisions together. As we digested the worrisome news that one of her mammary tumors was cancerous, she began acting like a younger version of herself. She no longer surfed down the stairs to alleviate the itchiness and discomfort from her over-bred mammary glands. She was much more interested in eating now that we had removed her infected and painful teeth. She displayed more energy when chasing her ball in the park and bounced up and down like a puppy at her mom's arrival or when greeting me each time I visited her house.

Over the course of the next year, Sweet Pea had more mass removals, most of which were benign, but one was a metastatic lymph node from her mammary cancer that we had removed previously, even though it had clean margins. If it seems like a broken record when I beg clients, family, and friends to spay and neuter their cats and dogs at an early age, it is because doing so is one of the easiest ways to prevent cancers like mammary cancer. If Sweet Pea's original owners had spayed her at a young age, she almost certainly would never have had mammary cancer and would not have had drastically droopy mammary glands or the accompanying painful skin fold dermatitis between her mammary glands. Just one surgery would have prevented the need for half a dozen more surgeries and the cancer that ensued. None of Sweet Pea's medical problems was her fault, but they could have resulted in her death if she had ended up at a shelter that couldn't or wouldn't take the time, effort, and resources to treat her.

Teresa acclimated Sweet Pea regularly to new people and places, thereby transforming her from reticent to receptive. Once Sweet Pea overcame a fear of a person or an object, she was over it and didn't hang onto it. I felt honored to be someone she trusted very quickly and considered her official second home. When I worked from home, I sometimes brought Sweet Pea to my house to hang out with Coco and me or to feed her if Teresa was working late. As a result of my house being her second home, Sweet Pea tugged on her leash with the single-minded goal of running to my front door as soon as she exited Teresa's house, just two doors away. If let off leash, she just raced to my house, even if I was the one who let her off leash. Teresa describes it as doggie Disney, although my place is not very different from hers. Sweet Pea loved to see Coco, who ducked her head to avoid being wagged into submission by Sweet Pea's happy, waving tail. She raced through my backyard as if she didn't have a backyard. One of her favorite outdoor tricks was running at full speed up to my chaise longue and jumping onto it, even if her speed and weight created a flying dog bed that often slid off the other side of the chair with Sweet

Pea still on the cushion. When I sat down, she liked to barrel into my legs, upending them and tossing them into the air with her head, like an orca tossing a seal out of the water. When I left Coco and Sweet Pea alone at my house to run errands, it often looked like a kids' pajama party when I returned. Pillows and blankets on every couch had been dug up, turned over, and tossed onto the ground, presumably as Sweet Pea head-butted everything in a nest-building effort. On the rare occasion when I returned home without both dogs waking up, I would catch them sound asleep on the couch nestled between any remaining pillows or blankets, demonstrating their own canine interior decorating flair. What a joy to see two dogs, both of whom had painful pasts, peacefully and comfortably enjoying a dog snooze!

When I worked from home, both dogs positioned themselves in my office, often forming a yin yang symbol in black and white as they lay close to each other on their dog beds and blankets. On one occasion, Sweet Pea must have wanted to climb the canine corporate ladder by becoming more involved in my monotonous paperwork, rather than just lounging about lazily. Suddenly, she jumped up energetically and wedged her sizable 70-pound body between my legs and my desk chair and into the cubby beneath my desk. As I peered down and saw her happy and excited face panting up at me, I knew what her new title in the corporation would be: Under Secretary! I just had to capture the moment with a picture to memorialize her new position. With her pink tongue dangling through a grin and twinkling eyes gazing at me, she appeared ready for our next adventure, embodying the ideal attitude of a team player. Although I normally dislike paperwork, it's always better with an Under Secretary and her sidekick, Coco.

As tragic as Sweet Pea's previous life must have been, there is beauty and purpose to her metamorphosis and her story. Some of her imperfections helped strangers she met warm up to her more quickly, even though she appeared a bit physically imposing at first because of her blocky head and tough dog look. Whenever possible, Teresa introduced her to passersby while sharing her story. The initial reservations were usually overcome by the time she approached to sniff new acquaintances. My 90-year old mother was a skeptic at first, as she nervously sized up Sweet Pea, considering my mom only weighs 25 pounds more and is a bit fragile on her feet with a new knee and a new hip. During their first encounter, Sweet Pea barked enthusiastically, but my mom thought the barking meant Sweet Pea wanted to eat her for lunch. As we eased into introductions, it was immediately evident that Sweet Pea had no malicious intentions, but rather had already vetted my mom and because she was in my house, Sweet Pea just wanted to play. The next time I caught a glimpse of them together, my mom was sitting on a large circular chair that can spin around 360 degrees. Mom's legs had been lifted up by Sweet Pea sliding underneath them. As she leaned into the chair, it spun around while she held my mom's legs up, acting like the American Bulldozer that she is. She was frequently a clown in her own circus. My mom took a huge shine to Sweet Pea once her brief apprehension was overcome by Sweet Pea's sweet and playful demeanor. She threw balls and squeaky toys for Sweet Pea, who delighted in their activities for hours. Teresa's photograph of Sweet Pea and my mom sitting together smiling in the garden sums up their mutual affection perfectly.

Sweet Pea befriended young and old, large and small, and seemed more energized with each rotten tooth that was extracted or each tumor that was removed. Her playfulness and energy level rose dramatically as her skin infections were treated and healed, and she could play and function comfortably again. Because she exemplified the transformation that a rescued dog can make from broken to beloved, and embodied a young spirit even as a geriatric dog, I encouraged Teresa to enroll her in the *American Rescue Dog Show* hosted by Hallmark. Watching the show on TV the previous year was so uplifting because it promotes rescuing and adopting dogs. Many wonderful dogs and their stories were showcased, shedding some light on the plight of homeless dogs to viewers who were unaware, while lifting up the spirits of those already in the know. After completing an application and submitting numerous enamoring photos and videos of Sweet Pea, she was accepted into the show and prepared to make her foray into fame. To think that a year earlier it would have been impossible for Sweet Pea to go for a car ride of any distance, much less all the way to Los Angeles to the rescue dog show was a testament to Teresa's successful socializing and easing her fears of normal dog activities.

Sweet Pea was entered into the Senior category, although she might have also qualified for some of the other categories, such as Snoring or Couch Potato. The event attracted so many rescued dogs, all with a story of how their lives were transformed. Their rescuers had often gone to extreme lengths to save them, some from the Korean dog meat markets, others from an abusive situation that also put the rescuer at risk. Dozens of dog breeds were represented, which is an important factor for prospective adoptees to consider. Twenty-five percent of shelter dogs are purebreds. There are also dozens of breed-specific rescues if someone has a special love for one breed. Beagles who had been rescued from being euthanized at research laboratories were represented. Pugs of all ages and capabilities were also in full force, as well as Great Danes, Corgis, and Westies. The Special Needs category tugged on everyone's heartstrings because of the difficulties the dogs had overcome, ranging from deafness and blindness to losing one or even two limbs due to abuse. While it was a competition with ribbons and prizes, every single participant in the show had won a new life and a second chance at love.

When it was Sweet Pea's turn to enter the show ring with her mom and the other dogs, her eyes widened at the new sights and sounds, but she trotted ahead eagerly. She had met the judge backstage to warm up to a new person, especially a tall man, which might cause hesitation. All of the judges and trainers at the show were mindful to approach and handle the dogs with care, knowing many had been in a tough place before they were adopted. Teresa had friends and family in the audience, who held up pre-printed fathead pictures of Sweet Pea's lovable face as she entered the ring. Each dog met the judge while their guardian explained why they had adopted a senior dog and what was so special about their dog. As I heard the stories and saw the "competition," I knew it would be stiff. There was a blind old Poodle mix, who trotted about glibly, eager to meet the judge and her fellow competitors. A Great Dane whose previous family had dumped him at a shelter at a starving 80 pounds was now back up to a slim 160 pounds, prancing around his new dad and acting like a puppy. There was also a senior dog who made hospital visits as a therapy dog. Some dogs were so comfortable with cameras that they walked right up to them looking for treats or treasure. Sweet Pea was a bit camera-shy for close-up shots, preferring to hide behind her mom's legs at that point.

Although she didn't win in her category, Sweet Pea's participation in the show was still a victory for her. We celebrated her TV debut together with friends by watching the televised version a month later at home. The camera captured the essence of her sweet face and disposition beautifully, while her waggish nature came across in one of the videos showing her running and playing. We cheered her on each time she appeared on the screen and toasted her and her guardian. Those of us who knew Sweet Pea knew that her celebrity status wouldn't go to her head. She was happy and feeling the loved she had missed for so many years.

We basked in the bliss and euphoria that the *American Rescue Dog Show* had created and enjoyed our canine-centered community, unaware of impending chaos that would imminently change the world and our lives. The COVID-19 epidemic was crossing oceans and international boundaries, rendering it a pandemic. California locked down the state at midnight on March 19, 2020. The good news was that Sweet Pea and Coco, like many other dogs at home with their families, would be our constant companions during a protracted period of seclusion and uncertainty. The bad news was that like many businesses affected by the pandemic, I practically closed the doors of my mobile veterinary practice for two months to comply with state and American Veterinary Medical Association (AVMA) guidelines. The first surgery I scheduled when we could resume operations on May 4th was a mass removal on Sweet Pea's leg, which had doubled in size over two months. It felt like a gut punch to read the pathologist's report on the mass: "subcutaneous hemangiosarcoma."

Hemangiosarcomas (HSAs) are malignant tumors that affect the walls of blood vessels. The report referenced a recent study with a mean survival time of six months, which sounded more like five short minutes. How could I break the news to Teresa that her sweet little girl whose life she had painstakingly pieced back together had such an aggressive tumor with a poor prognosis? It would be a tear-filled conversation, during which I could only say how sorry I was. An abdominal ultrasound showed a small (2.5 cm) mass on her spleen, but that was not what troubled the oncologist. The CT showed that she had much larger masses than in her back leg within her triceps muscles in both front legs and also in her pectoralis muscles in her chest. Radiation therapy was no longer an option. Chemo was discussed, but at this advanced stage, we opted against it. We supplemented with Yunnan baio, the same Chinese herb I had used to help slow down Bosco's bleeding, and also with I'm-Yunity, another herb, which is thought to have some benefits for these types of tumors. She started physical therapy to help her overcome an unrelated lameness she developed a few days after her surgery.

Every minute and every day became more precious than the next, and we needed to get her comfortable and mobile ASAP. Fortunately, she took to swimming immediately, moving with ease and delight in the water with only a life vest for added buoyancy and a squeaky toy as a motivator. After a couple of weeks of physical therapy, her lameness resolved completely so she could enjoy walks with Teresa again and even prance around or take a running leap onto a dog bed, spinning around on it like a merry-go-round. While I focused on the medical management and comfort of Sweet Pea's condition, her mom accelerated her TLC treatments and declarations of love. The gift of the pandemic was that Teresa had to work from home, so now Sweet Pea could spend all day and every day with her mom, luxuriating in love. When Sweet Pea thought Teresa's Zoom meetings had gone on long enough, she sometimes rammed her head into her leg or gummed her arm with her almost toothless mouth to let her know it was playtime. She was finally getting a lifetime's love and attention condensed into a short period of time and was relishing it.

One morning before driving her to swim therapy, we noticed Sweet Pea's abdomen had expanded, just as the tumors on her forearms and chest had been doing gradually. I checked her for pain and pinkness of her gums and she still seemed pain-free and pale pink as always, even though I suspected some sort of bleeding episode. Swimming had become her new favorite pastime, so we decided we would let her have another swim, albeit a gentler version with more breaks between laps. I repeated a blood test that afternoon when we returned home to determine if she was actively bleeding and how much. The test showed that she was becoming more anemic, but still seemed comfortable and snarfed down her sweet potato, tofu, and veggie ground round dinner I cooked for her before her mom tucked her into bed for the night.

Sweet Pea woke Teresa up in the middle of the night acting restlessly, so first she took her outside for a potty break. Because she suddenly seemed extremely uncomfortable and was panting and groaning, Teresa called me for help. Sweet Pea had never complained like that before. Her belly had almost doubled in size overnight, most likely from internal hemorrhage. Her gums were almost white, confirming our fears of uncontrollable hemorrhage. After all of the things Teresa had done for her in their time together, there was only one thing to do now. Through a torrent of tears, we tried to comfort Sweet Pea—Teresa holding her in her arms, telling her how much she loved her while I gave her a sedative, and then we had to say goodbye with one last injection.

In that moment and the sorrow-filled days that followed, I thought of the people who had neglected and abandoned Sweet Pea, knowing how much we would have given just to have one more glorious day with her. I am eternally grateful that Teresa opened her heart and her home to save Sweet Pea and to share her light with the world. Sweet Pea had been the center of our COVID-19 community, lifting our spirits, making us smile and laugh, and reminding us of life's small pleasures every day. Her spirit was infectious and joyous. Losing her is like having the lights turned off and the fun switch turned all the way down. From the moment Teresa adopted her, Sweet Pea's life pivoted 180 degrees from loneliness, abandonment, and neglect to love, care, and purpose. To see her blossom into a happy and healthy dog and to see the positive impact she had on every person and every animal she met is a testament to Teresa saving a very important soul, indeed.

Vera Heidolph, DVM

Sweet Pea

Oh sorrow, deepest river

running though my soul.

My heart with love you expanded

but now your absence leaves a hole.

My confidante, companion

and trustworthy friend.

Tho you championed through many fixes

this last affront we could not mend.

Would that I could

have known you right from your start.

To give you the lifetime of love you deserved

with all of my heart.

Everyone who met you

felt your joy, your spark.

How deafening the silence

without your snoring, snorts, or protective bark.

May you rest in peace

my precious Sweet Pea.

Maybe I rescued you, but maybe you rescued me.

Stories like Sweet Pea's restore my faith in humanity because of the people who rescued her from her previous life. What a difference a steady dose of love and proper medical attention made in just this one dog's life! Imagine if every dog, cat, horse, cow, sheep, chicken, pig, donkey, elephant, or *any* species had those same benefits! It may seem like there are *so* many animals that need to be rescued, adopted, or saved that it becomes overwhelming for just one person. Why bother saving one when you can't help each and *every* one? I imagine some people who have adopted a child might have wished they could have helped more as well. But for that *one* individual whose life has been saved, they can experience love and a family, making it all *so* worth it. One at a time, collectively, spreading the word that rescuing and adopting animals saves a life, while breeding *costs* shelter animals their lives, is a critical fact to circulate.

Why am I willing to make myself unpopular at social gatherings or even with clients, friends, and family by promoting spaying, neutering, and adopting? When I switched gears from investment banking to veterinary medicine, it was not so that I could administer the most vaccines or "produce" the greatest revenue for a veterinary hospital. I wanted to save animals' lives. The disease that kills millions of healthy cats and dogs just in the United States each year is homelessness. If dogs or cats were an endangered species whose existence depended on reproduction, it might make sense that they be bred to prevent extinction. But breeding, even with the best of intentions, only exacerbates the fatal over-population dilemma, so I cannot in good conscience recommend it. Even though adopting, spaying, and neutering are on the rise, we are still killing millions of healthy animals due to unregulated and indiscriminate breeding.

Some breeders "get rid of," aka kill puppies and kittens for trivial external imperfections like suboptimal spot placements on Dalmatians. As veterinarians, we have the unpleasant chore of explaining and trying to fix all of the internal problems that breeders have chosen to ignore in their quest for outer beauty and cute characteristics. Ninety-eight percent of all brachycephalic (smushy-faced dogs like Pugs, Boston Terriers, French Bulldogs, English Bulldogs, and Pekinese) dogs, for example, need to have their airways surgically altered to enable near-normal breathing again. It should be noted that many of those highly desired smushy-faced breeds cannot even reproduce naturally! English Bulldogs and many of their relatives have such disproportionately large heads relative to their bodies that they cannot pass through their mother's birth canal during the birthing process. They get stuck. Those puppies will die without surgical intervention to perform a C-section and cut the puppies out of their mother's uterine horns every time she is bred and has another litter of puppies. The mothers are being bred repeatedly, anesthetized for each litter, only to surgically remove the puppies without any breeding modification that might improve their ability to breathe or breed normally! This short list of life-shortening abnormalities is just the beginning of genetically inherited problems caused by aesthetically-driven breeding that veterinarians routinely try to fix with one type of dog. Perhaps if smushy-faced dogs were sold with a "breathing" option, for an additional $3,000 to $5,000 for surgical repairs of their genetically impaired respiratory tracts, fewer dogs would be sold or breeders might consider breeding for health and not just appearance.

The extreme dark side of breeding is the world of puppy mills. Hundreds of puppy mills around the country have been shut down because their filthy conditions were so deplorable. They are characterized by repeated, indiscriminate breeding of caged and poorly cared for dogs and their puppies. Infections, malnutrition, neglect, and non-existent socialization are par for the course in these facilities. These puppy mills maintain their clandestine activities by housing animals in sheds or barns in stacked, wire cages on all sides, which hurt and injure their feet and allow urine, feces, and vomit to cascade down to the animals below. They rarely see the light of day or feel grass or earth on their feet. These puppies are sold to pet stores or online with fake pictures of bucolic farms and frolicking animals. The fines imposed upon puppy mill criminals, if they are ever caught, are laughable. No pet store divulges that they purchase puppies from puppy mills, but that is their main source. Fortunately, many cities are banning stores from selling purpose-bred puppies and kittens.

When I see the amount of diligent consumer research people conduct before purchasing a phone or a fridge, I wish they would do the same amount of research for their companion animals and resist the urge of an impulse buy when it comes to adding a four-legged lifetime family member. If they did, they wouldn't find their heart strings being tugged upon by a darling puppy or a cute kitten in a pet store or at a breeder's place. Instead, it would benefit animals most if everyone researched shelters and rescues to find the dog or cat who is suitable for them and to whom they can commit forever. In my experience, breeders never tell their prospective buyers that their dogs have heart problems or need surgery to breathe or other critical details. Once an owner has spent $2,000 to $3,000 to buy an adorable puppy, they're in love and cash-poor. I imagine the things a new dog guardian could do for a rescued companion with that large amount of money. As consumers, they are paying hard-earned cash for something with no guarantees and many known medical maladies. Rescuing or adopting companion animals would save money and stop the killing of healthy animals whose only crime is being born. If you've ever loved a dog, then we have something in common. I'm hopeful that we can combine our compassion and creativity and help save more animals, one life at a time.

The lives of three dogs—Sweet Pea, Bosco, and Coco—were saved when their previous owners were willing to discard these darlings as if they had no beating heart or soul. These dogs have enriched our lives, possibly even more than we've enriched theirs. Everyone I've met who has adopted their dog speaks of the canine gratitude that they exude. It doesn't mean that they can't have some attitude now and then, but we all feel that extra love when a dog has been saved. Knowing how close to the brink of death so many of our adopted animals have been fuels the fire to save them all, even if it is just one life at a time. I am hopeful that every dog lover who reads this book will help spread the word, educate and advocate for rescuing, adopting, spaying, and neutering, and play an active role in eliminating euthanasia due to companion animals' over-population. Your reward will be the unconditional love of a canine companion for the rest of their life. If you've ever loved a dog, you may be reading this book with a four-legged companion by your side or you may reminisce about one who was once by your side, but you'll never forget the cozy, blanketing warmth of that canine love. May there be more four-legged companions who benefit from your love and return it to you infinitely.

About the author

Dr. Vera Heidolph is a small animal veterinarian from a small town with big dreams of helping animals. She graduated from Northfield Mount Hermon high school in Northfield, Massachusetts. She received her Bachelor of Arts studying German, French, Spanish, and Japanese from Brock University in St. Catharines, Ontario. She earned her Master of International Management degree from Thunderbird (formerly American Graduate School of International Management) in Glendale, Arizona. After working in investment banking at Salomon Brothers Frankfurt, then Salomon Brothers New York, followed by Deutsche Bank New York, she switched gears and enrolled in pre-vet studies at Rutgers University in New Brunswick, New Jersey. She completed her Doctor of Veterinary Medicine at the Ontario Veterinary College, University of Guelph, followed by a small animal medicine and surgery internship at Red Bank Veterinary Hospital in Red Bank, New Jersey. She lives in San Diego where she has her own mobile veterinary practice—the VetBus. She has volunteered with various animal organizations performing spays and neuters across the United States and in Tijuana, Mexico for decades. She is happiest in the company of dogs.

For more information

If you would like more information on how to help animals, please reach out to these animal organizations, listed alphabetically, for resources or to donate:

- Animals Asia: Website: www.Animalsasia.org; Tel. (424) 282-5305; Mail: Animals Asia Foundation, Limited, 6060 Center Drive, 10th Floor, Los Angeles, CA 90045
- ASPCA (American Society for the Prevention of Cruelty to Animals): Website: www.Aspca.org; Tel. (212) 876-7700; Mail: ASPCA, 424 E. 92nd St., New York, NY 10128-6804
- HSUS (Humane Society of the U.S.): Website: www.humanesociety.org; Tel. (866) 720-2676; Mail: The Humane Society of the United States, 1255 23rd Street NW, Suite 450, Washington, DC 20037
- HSVMA (Humane Society Veterinary Medical Association): Website: www.hsvma.org; Tel. (530) 759-8106; Mail: HSVMA, 700 Professional Drive, Gaithersburg, MD 20879
- MFA (Mercy for Animals): Website: www.mercyforanimls.org; Tel. (866) 632-6446; Mail: 8033 Sunset Blvd., Suite 864, Los Angeles, CA 90046
- PETA (People for the Ethical Treatment of Animals) Website: Peta.org Tel. (757) 622- PETA (7382) Mail: People for the Ethical Treatment of Animals, 501 Front St., Norfolk, VA 23510
- PCRM (Physicians Committee for Responsible Medicine): Website: pcrm.org; Tel. (202) 686-2210; Mail: Physicians Committee for Responsible Medicine, 5100 Wisconsin Ave., NW, Suite 400, Washington, DC 20016-4131
- Rancho Coastal Humane Society: Website: www.rchumanesociety.org; Tel. (760) 753-6413; Mail: Rancho Coastal Humane Society, 389 Requeza St., Encinitas, CA 92024
- San Diego Humane Society: Website: www.sdhumane.org; Tel. (619) 200-7012; Mail: 5480 Gaines St., San Diego, CA 92110
- Sea Shepherd: Website: www.seashepherd.org; Tel. (212) 220-2302, ext. 3; Mail: P.O. Box 8628, Alexandria, VA 22306

Made in the USA
Coppell, TX
07 December 2020

43381245R00160